W9-BUC-162

Undoubtedly Frederick Copleston's A HISTORY OF PHI-
LOSOPHY is a monumental achievement. Below are some
of the comments critics have given to the various volumes in
the series to date:

VOLUME 1
"There can be no doubt that this is the best text of the his-
tory of philosophy now available in English."
The Historical Bulletin

VOLUME 2
". . . unquestionably the finest account of mediaeval philosophy yet published in English."
The (London) Times Literary Supplement

VOLUME 3
". . . it constitutes a remarkable achievement, the most considerable work of scholarship produced by English Scholasticism in our day, a work that has been received with respect
by philosophy scholars everywhere." *Book Reviews*

VOLUME 4
". . . offers a profound and well-organized introduction to
continental rationalism in the seventeenth century."
Cross Currents

VOLUME 5
"Obviously to be the standard history of philosophy for many
years to come." *Blackfriars*

VOLUME 6
"One thing at any rate is beyond doubt. No serious student
of western philosophy can dispense with Fr. Copleston's
History." *Duckett's Register*

VOLUME 7
"Each volume of Fr. Copleston's history provokes astonish-
ment and wonder . . . The present volume is just as learned,
fair-minded, lucid and interesting as its predecessors."
The Month

Volumes of A HISTORY OF PHILOSOPHY now available in Image Books:

A History of Philosophy

VOLUME VIII

Modern Philosophy

Bentham to Russell

PART II

Idealism in America
The Pragmatist Movement
The Revolt against Idealism

by Frederick Copleston, S.J.

IMAGE BOOKS
A Division of Doubleday & Company, Inc.
Garden City, New York

Image Books Edition
by special arrangement with The Newman Press
Image Books Edition published September 1967

DI LICENTIA SUPERIORUM ORDINIS:
J. Corbishley, S.J.
Vice-Praep. Prov. Angliae Soc. Jesu

NIHIL OBSTAT:
T. Gornall, S.J.
Censor Deputatus

IMPRIMATUR:
✠ Joseph Cleary
Episcopus Cresimensis
Vic. Cap.

Birmingamiae die 25a Junii 1965

The *Nihil obstat* and *Imprimatur* are a declaration that a book or pamphlet is considered to be free from doctrinal or moral error. It is not implied that those who have granted the *Nihil obstat* and *Imprimatur* agree with the contents, opinions or statements expressed.

CONTENTS

Brief notes on an ethical discussion at Oxford – American neo-realism – Critical realism in America – The world-view of Samuel Alexander – A reference to A. N. Whitehead.

CONTENTS

Part III

IDEALISM IN AMERICA

Chapter Eleven

INTRODUCTORY

The beginnings of philosophy in America; S. Johnson and J. Edwards – The Enlightenment in America; B. Franklin and T. Jefferson – The influence of the Scottish philosophy – R. W. Emerson and Transcendentalism – W. T. Harris and his programme for speculative philosophy.

1. The remote origins of philosophical reflection in America can be traced back to the Puritans of New England. Obviously, the primary aim of the Puritans was to organize their lives according to the religious and moral principles in which they believed. They were idealistic in the non-philosophical sense of the term. They were also Calvinists who allowed no dissent from what they regarded as the principles of orthodoxy. At the same time we can find among them an element of philosophical reflection, stimulated mainly by the thought of Petrus Ramus or Pierre de la Ramée (1515–72) and by the *Encyclopaedia* of Johann Heinrich Alsted (1588–1638). Petrus Ramus, the celebrated French humanist and logician, became a Calvinist in 1561, expounded a congregationalist theory of the Church, and eventually perished in the massacre of St. Bartholomew's Eve. He thus had special qualifications for being regarded as an intellectual patron by the Congregationalists of New England. Alsted, a follower of Melanchthon and also a disciple of Petrus Ramus, published an encyclopaedia of the arts and sciences in 1630. This work, which had a Platonic colouring, contained a section devoted

to what Alsted called *archeologia*, the system of the principles of knowledge and being. And it became a popular textbook in New England.

The religious affiliations of the first phase of American philosophical thought are shown by the fact that the earliest philosophers were clerics. Samuel Johnson (1696–1772) is an example. At first a Congregationalist minister, he entered the Anglican Church in 1722 and subsequently received Anglican orders. In 1754 he was appointed first president of King's College, New York, which is now Columbia University.

In his autobiography Johnson remarks that when he was studying at Yale the standard of education was low. Indeed, it showed a decline in comparison with the standards of the original settlers who had been brought up in England. True, the names of Descartes, Boyle, Locke and Newton were not unknown, and the introduction of the writings of Locke and Newton were gradually opening up fresh lines of thought. But there was a strong tendency to equate secular learning with some of the works of Ramus and Alsted and to regard the new philosophical currents as a danger to the purity of religious faith. In other words, a 'scholasticism' which had served a useful purpose in the past was being used to check the spread of new ideas.

Johnson himself came under the influence of Berkeley. He made the acquaintance of the philosopher during the latter's sojourn on Rhode Island (1729–31) and it was to Berkeley that he dedicated his *Elementa Philosophica*, which appeared in 1752.[1]

But though deeply impressed by Berkeley's immaterialism, Johnson was not prepared to accept his view that space and time are particular relations between particular ideas, and that infinite space and time are simply abstract ideas. He wished to retain the Newton-Clarke theory of absolute and infinite space and time, on the ground that they are entailed by admission of the existence of a plurality of finite spirits. For example, unless there were absolute space, all finite spirits would coincide with one another. Further, Johnson tried to fit Berkeley's theory of ideas into a Platonic mould, by maintaining that all ideas are ectypes of archetypes existing in the divine mind. In other words, while welcoming Berkeley's immaterialism Johnson endeavoured to adapt it to the Platonic tradition already present in American thought.

A better-known representative of eighteenth-century American thought is Jonathan Edwards (1703–58), a noted Congregationalist theologian. Educated at Yale, in 1717 he made the acquaintance of Locke's *Essay* and in 1730 of Hutcheson's *Inquiry into the Original of Our Ideas of Beauty and Virtue.* Though primarily a Calvinist theologian who for most of his life occupied pastoral posts, he attempted to achieve a synthesis between the Calvinist theology and the new philosophy. Or, to put the matter in another way, he used ideas taken from contemporary philosophy in interpreting the Calvinist theology. In 1757 he became president of the college at Princeton, New Jersey, which is now Princeton University; but he died of smallpox in the following year.

Edwards sees the universe as existing only within the divine mind or spirit. Space, necessary, infinite and eternal, is in fact an attribute of God. Further, it is only spirits which are, properly speaking, substances. There are no quasi-independent material substances which exercise real causal activity. To be sure, Nature exists as appearance; and from the point of view of the scientist, who is concerned with phenomena or appearances, there is uniformity in Nature, a constant order. The scientist as such can speak quite legitimately of natural laws. But from a profounder and philosophical point of view we can admit only one real causal activity, that of God. Not only is the divine conservation of finite things a constantly repeated creation, but it is also true that the uniformity of Nature is, from the philosophical standpoint, an arbitrary constitution, as Edwards puts it, of the divine will. There is really no such thing in Nature as a necessary relation or as efficient causality; all connections depend ultimately as the arbitrary *fiat* of God.

The fact that Edwards rejects, with Berkeley, the existence of material substance but admits the existence of spiritual substances must not, however, be taken to mean that in his view human volition constitutes an exception to the general truth that God is the only real cause. From one point of view, of course, we can say that he gives an empiricist analysis of relations, in particular of the causal relation. But this analysis is combined with the Calvinist idea of the divine omnipotence or causality to produce metaphysical idealism in which God appears as the sole genuine cause. In his work on the *Freedom of the Will* Edwards explicitly rejects the idea of the self-determining human will. In his view it is absurd, and also an expression of Arminianism, to maintain that the human will can choose against the prevailing motive or inclination.[2] Choice is always determined by the prevailing motive, and this in turn is determined by what appears to be the greatest good. Theologically speaking, a man's choice is predetermined by his Creator. But it is a mistake to suppose that this relieves man of all moral responsibility. For a moral judgment about an action depends simply on the nature of the action, not on its cause. A bad action remains a bad action, whatever its cause.

An interesting feature of Edwards' thought is his theory of a sense of God or direct awareness of the divine excellence. In general, he was in sympathy with the revivalist 'Great Awakening' of 1740–1. And he considered that the religious affections, on which he wrote a treatise, manifest an apprehension of the divine excellence which is to be attributed to the heart rather than to the head. At the same time he tried to distinguish between the sense of God and the highly emotive states which are characteristic of revivalist meetings. In doing this he developed a theory of the sense of God in which it is reasonable to see the influence of Hutcheson's aesthetic and moral ideas.

According to Edwards, just as a sense of the sweetness of honey precedes and lies at the basis of our theoretical judgment that honey is sweet, so does a sentiment or sense of, say, the divine holiness lie at the basis of the judgment that God is holy. In general, just as a sense of the beauty of an object or of the moral excellence of a person is presupposed by judgments which give expression to this sense or feeling, so is a sense of the divine excellence presupposed by our 'cerebral' judgments about God. Perhaps the term 'just as' is open to criticism. For the sense of God is for Edwards a consent of our being to the divine being and is of supernatural origin. But the point is that man can be aware of God through a form of experience analogous to sense-experience and to the pleasure which we feel in beholding a beautiful object or an expression of moral excellence.

Perhaps we can see in this theory the influence of Lockian empiricism. I do not mean to imply, of course, that Locke himself based belief in God on feeling and intuition. In regard to this matter his approach was rationalistic; and his mistrust of 'enthusiasm' is notorious. But his general insistence on the primacy of sense-experience may well have been one of the factors which influenced Edwards' mind, though the influence of Hutcheson's idea of the sense of moral beauty or excellence is certainly more obvious.

Edwards did not live long enough to carry out his project of writing a complete theology, developed systematically according to a new method. But he was extremely influential as a theologian; and his attempt to bring together Calvinist theology, idealism, Lockian empiricism and the world-view of Newton constituted the first major expression of American thought.

2. In Europe the eighteenth century was the age of the Enlightenment. And America too had what is customarily called its Enlightenment. In the field of philosophy it does not indeed bear comparison with its counterparts in England and France. But it is none the less of importance in the history of American life.

The first characteristic which we can notice is the attempt to separate the Puritan moral virtues from their theological setting, an attempt which is well exemplified by the reflections of Benjamin Franklin (1706–90). An admirer of William Wollaston, the English deist, he was certainly not the man to walk in the footsteps of Samuel Johnson or Jonathan Edwards. Revelation, as he declared, had for him no weight. And he was convinced that morals should be given a utilitarian in place of a theological basis. Some types of action are beneficial to man and society, while other types of action are detrimental. The former can be regarded as commanded, the latter as forbidden. Virtues such as temperance and diligence are justified by their utility. Their opposites are blameworthy because they are prejudicial to the interests of society and of personal success.

Famous as he is, Franklin can hardly be described as a

profound philosopher, in spite of the fact that he was one of the founders of the American Philosophical Society. And it is a simple matter to caricature his ethical outlook. To be sure, Franklin exalted truthfulness, sincerity and integrity, virtues highly esteemed by the Puritans, as essential for human well-being. But once these virtues are extolled because, on balance, people who are truthful and sincere are more likely to be successful in life than the untruthful and insincere, a certain banal pragmatism takes the place of the religious idealism of the Puritan mind at its best. It is no longer a case of man becoming the image of God, as it was with the more Platonic-minded Puritan theologians. Rather is it a case of 'early to bed and early to rise makes a man healthy and wealthy and wise'. A sensible maxim perhaps, but not particularly uplifting.

However, even if Franklin's reflections tended to assume a somewhat banal character, they represented the same movement to set ethics on its own feet and to separate it from theology which we find in more sophisticated forms in eighteenth-century European philosophy. And the retention of Puritan virtues in a secularized dress was of considerable historical importance in the development of the American outlook.

Another important feature of the Enlightenment in America was the secularization of the idea of society. Calvinism was opposed from the start to control of the Church by the State. And though the general tendency of the Calvinists was to secure, when possible, widespread control over society, in principle at any rate they recognized a distinction between the body of true believers and political society. Moreover, Calvinism in New England took the form of Congregationalism. And though in practice the clergy, once appointed, exercised great power, the congregations were in theory simply voluntary unions of likeminded believers. When stripped, therefore, of its theological and religious associations, this idea of society lent itself to exploitation in the interest of democratic republicanism. And Locke's theory of the social contract or compact was at hand to serve as an instrument.

The process of secularizing the theory of religious society associated with the Congregationalists of New England was, however, only one factor in a complex situation. Another factor was the growth in the New World of pioneer societies which were not primarily associated, if at all, with particular religious bodies and movements. The new frontier societies[3] had to adapt the ideas of law and social organization which they carried with them to the situations in which they found themselves. And their main desire was clearly that of securing, as far as possible, such conditions of order as would prevent anarchy and enable individuals to pursue their several ends in comparative peace. Needless to say, the members of the pioneer societies were not much concerned with political philosophy, or with philosophy of any sort. At the same time they represented a growing society which tacitly implied a Lockian theory of a free union of human beings organizing themselves and submitting themselves to law with a view to preserving a social fabric and order which would permit the peaceful, though competitive, exercise of individual initiative. Further, the growth of these societies, with emphasis on temporal success, favoured the spread of the idea of toleration, which was scarcely a strong point of the Calvinist theologians and ministers.

The idea of political society as a voluntary union of human beings for the purpose of establishing social order as a framework for the peaceful exercise of private initiative was understandably associated with the idea of natural rights which are presupposed by organized society and should be protected by it. The theory of natural rights, sponsored by Locke and by other English and French writers, found expression in *The Rights of Man*[4] by Thomas Paine (1737–1809), a deist who insisted on the sovereignty of reason and on the equal rights of all men. It also found a powerful exponent in Thomas Jefferson (1743–1826) who, as is well known, drafted the Declaration of Independence of 1776. This famous document asserts that it is self-evidently true that all men are created equal, that they are endowed by their Creator with certain inalienable rights, and that among these are the right to life, liberty and the pursuit of happiness. The Declaration further asserts that governments are instituted to secure these rights, and that they derive their powers from the consent of the governed.

It is scarcely necessary to remark that the Declaration of Independence was a national act, not an exercise in political philosophy. And, quite apart from the fact that a good deal of it consists of animadversions on the British monarch and government, the philosophy behind its opening sentences was not fully developed in eighteenth-century America. Thus Jefferson himself simply assumed that the statement that all men are endowed by their Creator with certain inalienable rights is a matter of common sense. That is to say, common reason sees that it must be true, without any need of proof, though, once its truth has been recognized, moral and social conclusions can be drawn from it. At the same time the philosophical portion of the Declaration admirably illustrates the spirit and fruit of the American Enlightenment. And there is, of course, no doubt about its historical importance.

3. Men such as Franklin and Jefferson were obviously not professional philosophers. But in the course of the nineteenth century academic philosophy underwent a very considerable development in the United States. And among the influences contributing to this development was the thought of Thomas Reid and his successors in the Scottish School. In religious quarters the Scottish philosophical tradition was regarded with favour as being at the same time realist in character and a much needed antidote to materialism and positivism. It thus became popular with those Protestant divines who were conscious of the lack of an adequate rational basis for the Christian faith.

One of the principal representatives of this tradition was James McCosh (1811–94), himself a Scottish Presbyterian, who occupied for sixteen years the chair of logic and metaphysics at Queen's College, Belfast, and then in 1868 accepted the presidency of Princeton and made the university a stronghold of the Scottish philosophy. Besides writing a number of other philosophical works, such as *An Examination of John Stuart Mill's Philosophy* (1866) and *Realistic Philosophy* (1887), he published a well-known study, *The Scottish Philosophy*, in 1875.

Among the effects of the popularization in America of the Scottish tradition was the widespread habit of dividing philosophy into mental and moral, the former, namely the science of the human mind or psychology, being looked on as providing the basis for the latter, namely ethics. This division is reflected in the titles of the much-used textbooks published by Noah Porter (1811–92), who in 1847 was nominated to the chair of moral philosophy and metaphysics at Yale, where he was also president for some years. For instance, in 1868 he published *The Human Intellect*, in 1871 *The Elements of Intellectual Science*, an abridgement of the first-named book, and in 1885 *The Elements of Moral Science*. Porter was not, however, simply an adherent of the Scottish School. He had made a serious study not only of British empiricists such as J. S. Mill and Bain but also of Kantian and post-Kantian German thought. And he attempted to effect a synthesis of the Scottish philosophy and German idealism. Thus he maintained that the world is to be regarded as a thought rather than as a thing, and that the existence of the Absolute is a necessary condition of the possibility of human thought and knowledge.

An attempt at combining themes from empiricism, the Scottish philosophy of common sense and German idealism had been made by the French philosopher, Victor Cousin (1792–1867). As rector of the *École normale*, rector of the University of Paris and finally minister of public instruction, Cousin had been in a position to impose his ideas as a kind of philosophical orthodoxy in the centre of French academic life. But an eclectic philosophy, formed from such heterogeneous elements, was obviously open to serious criticism on the ground of incoherence. However, the relevant point here is that his thought exercised a certain influence in America, especially in encouraging a combination of ideas inspired by the Scottish tradition with a transcendentalism inspired by German idealism.

As an example we can mention Caleb Sprague Henry (1804–84), a professor at the University of New York. To all intents and purposes Cousin had based metaphysics on psychology. Psychological observation, properly employed, reveals in man the presence of a spontaneous reason which acts as a bridge between consciousness and being and enables us to pass beyond the limits of subjective idealism, by apprehending, for example, finite substances as objectively existent.

Philosophy, as the work of reflective reason, makes explicit and develops the objective truths apprehended immediately by spontaneous reason. This distinction between spontaneous and reflective reason was accepted by Henry who, as a devout Anglican, proceeded to use it in a theological setting and drew the conclusions that religious or spiritual experience precedes and grounds religious knowledge.[5] By religious or spiritual experience, however, he meant primarily the moral consciousness of good and obligation, a consciousness which manifests the power of God to raise man to a new life. Further, with Henry material civilization becomes the fruit of the 'understanding', whereas Christianity, considered historically as the redemptive work of God, aiming at the creation of an ideal society, is the response to the demands of 'reason' or spirit.

4. At the same time that the Scottish philosophy was penetrating into university circles, the famous American writer Ralph Waldo Emerson (1803–82) was preaching his gospel of transcendentalism. In 1829 he became a Unitarian minister. But the man who found inspiration in Coleridge and Carlyle, who laid emphasis on moral self-development and tended to divest religion of its historical associations, who was more concerned with giving expression to his personal vision of the world than with transmitting a traditional message, was not really suited for the ministry. And in 1832 he abandoned it and gave himself to the task of developing and expounding a new idealist philosophy which, he was confident, was capable of renewing the world in a way in which not only materialism but also traditional religion was incapable of renewing it.

In 1836 Emerson published anonymously a little work entitled *Nature*, which contained the essence of his message. His celebrated *Address*, delivered in 1838 in the divinity school of Harvard, aroused considerable opposition among those who considered it unorthodox. In 1841 and 1844 he published two series of *Essays*, while his *Poems* appeared in 1846. In 1849 he published *Representative Men*, a series of lectures which he had given in 1845–6 on selected famous men from Plato to Napoleon and Goethe. In later years he became a national institution, the Sage of Concord, a fate which sometimes overtakes those who are at first regarded as purveyors of dangerous new ideas.

In a lecture delivered in 1842 in the Masonic Temple at Boston Emerson declares that what are called the 'new views' are really very old thoughts cast into a mould suited to the contemporary world. 'What is popularly called Transcendentalism among us is Idealism; Idealism as it appears in 1842.'[6] The materialist takes his stand on sense-experience and on what he calls facts, whereas 'the idealist takes his departure from his consciousness, and reckons the world an appearance'.[7] Materialism and idealism thus appear to be sharply opposed. Yet once we begin to ask the materialist what the basic facts really are, his solid world tends to break up. And with phenomenalism all is ultimately reduced to the data of consciousness. Hence under criticism materialism tends to pass into idealism, for which 'mind is the only reality . . . [and] Nature, literature, history are only subjective phenomena'.[8]

It does not follow, however, that the external world is simply the creation of the individual mind. Rather is it the product of the one universal spirit or consciousness, 'that Unity, that Over-Soul, within which every man's particular being is contained and made one with all other'.[9] This Over-Soul or eternal One or God is the sole ultimate reality, and Nature is its projection. 'The world proceeds from the same spirit as the body of man. It is a remoter and inferior projection of God, a projection of God in the unconscious. But it differs from a body in one important respect. It is not, like that, now subjected to the human will. Its serene order is inviolable by us. It is, therefore, to us, the present expositor of the divine mind.'[10]

If we ask how Emerson knows all this, it is no good expecting any systematically developed proofs. He does indeed insist that the human reason presupposes and seeks an ultimate unity. But he also insists that 'we know truth when we see it, let sceptic and scoffer say what they choose'.[11] When foolish people hear what they do not wish to hear, they ask how one knows that what one says is true. But 'we know truth when we see it, from opinion, as we know when we are awake that we are awake'.[12] The announcements of the soul, as

Emerson puts it, are 'an influx of the divine mind into our mind':[13] they are a revelation, accompanied by the emotion of the sublime.

We might expect that from this doctrine of the unity of the human soul with the Over-Soul or divine spirit Emerson would draw the conclusion that the individual as such is of little importance, and that moral or spiritual progress consists in submerging one's personality in the One. But this is not at all his point of view. The Over-Soul incarnates itself, as Emerson expresses it, in a particular way in each individual. Hence 'each man has his own vocation. The talent is the call.'[14] And the conclusion is drawn: 'Insist on yourself, never imitate'.[15] Conformism is a vice: self-reliance is a cardinal virtue. 'Whoso would be a man must be a nonconformist.'[16] Emerson provides indeed a theoretical reason for this exaltation of self-reliance. The divine spirit is self-existent, and its embodiments are good in proportion as they share in this attribute. At the same time it is not unreasonable to see in Emerson's moral doctrine the expression of the spirit of a young, vigorous, developing and competitive society.

In Emerson's opinion this self-reliance, if universally practised, would bring about a regeneration of society. The State exists to educate the wise man, the man of character; and 'with the appearance of the wise man, the State expires. The appearance of character makes the State unnecessary.'[17] What is meant is doubtless that if individual character were fully developed, the State as an organ of force would be unnecessary, and that in its place there would be a society based on moral right and love.

It scarcely needs saying that Emerson, like Carlyle, was a seer rather than a systematic philosopher. Indeed, he went so far as to say that 'a foolish consistency is the hobgoblin of little minds, adored by little statesmen and philosophers and divines. With consistency a great soul has simply nothing to do.'[18] True his principal point is that a man should preserve his intellectual integrity and not be afraid to say what he really thinks today simply because it contradicts what he said yesterday. But he remarks, for example, that if in metaphysics we deny personality to God, this should not prevent us from thinking and speaking in a different way 'when the devout motions of the soul come'.[19] And though we can understand what Emerson means, a systematic philosopher who held this point of view would be more likely to follow Hegel in drawing an explicit distinction between the language of speculative philosophy and that of religious consciousness than to content himself with dismissing consistency as a hobgoblin of little minds. In other words, Emerson's philosophy was impressionistic and what is sometimes called 'intuitive'. It conveyed a personal vision of reality, but it was not presented in the customary dress of impersonal argument and precise statement. Some, of course, may consider this to be a point in its favour, but the fact remains that if we are looking for a systematic development of idealism in American thought, we have to look elsewhere.

Emerson was the chief figure in the Transcendentalist Club which was founded at Boston in 1836. Another member, highly esteemed by Emerson, was Amos Bronson Alcott (1799–1888), a deeply spiritual man who, in addition to his attempts to introduce new methods into education, founded a utopian community in Massachusetts, though it did not last long. Given to vague and oracular utterances, he was later pushed by the St. Louis Hegelians into trying to clarify and define his idealism. Among others associated in some way with New England Transcendentalism we may mention Henry David Thoreau (1817–62) and Orestes Augustus Brownson (1803–76). Thoreau, a famous literary figure, was attracted to Emerson when the latter delivered his Phi Beta Kappa Society address on 'The American Scholar' at Harvard in 1857. As for Brownson, his spiritual pilgrimage led him by various stages from Presbyterianism to Catholicism.

5. In 1867 there appeared at St. Louis, Missouri, the first number of *The Journal of Speculative Philosophy*, edited by William Torrey Harris (1835–1909). Harris and his associates contributed powerfully to spreading in America a knowledge of German idealism, and the group are known as the St. Louis Hegelians. Harris was also one of the founders of the Kant-Club (1874). The group had some relations with the Transcendentalists of New England; and Harris helped to start the Concord Summer School of Philosophy in 1880,

with which Alcott collaborated. In 1889 he was appointed
United States Commissioner of Education by President Har-
rison.

In the first number of *The Journal of Speculative Philosophy* Harris spoke of the need for a speculative philosophy
which would fulfil three main tasks. In the first place it
should provide a philosophy of religion suitable for a time
when traditional dogmas and ecclesiastical authority were
losing their hold on men's minds. In the second place it
should develop a social philosophy in accordance with the
new demands of the national consciousness, which was turning away from sheer individualism. In the third place it
should work out the deeper implications of the new ideas in
the sciences, in which field, Harris maintained, the day of
simple empiricism was definitely over. As speculative philosophy meant for Harris the tradition which started with
Plato and attained its fullest expression in the system of
Hegel, he was calling in effect for a development of idealism
under the inspiration of post-Kantian German philosophy
but in accordance with American needs.

There were various attempts to fulfil this sort of programme, ranging from the personal idealism of Howison and
Bowne to the absolute idealism of Josiah Royce. And as
both Howison and Bowne were born before Royce, they
should perhaps be treated first. I propose, however, to devote
the next chapter to Royce and in the following chapter to
discuss briefly the personal idealists and some other philosophers who belonged to the idealist tradition, mentioning the
names of some thinkers who were junior to Royce.

It may be as well, however, to point out at once that it is
difficult to make any very sharp division between personal
and absolute idealism in American thought. In a real sense
Royce too was a personalist idealist. In other words, the form
which absolute idealism took with Bradley, involving the relegation of personality to the sphere of appearances as contrasted with that of reality, was not congenial to the American
mind. And, in general, it was felt that the proper fulfilment
of Harris's programme required that human personality
should not be sacrificed on the altar of the One, though
there were, of course, differences in emphasis, some thinkers

placing the emphasis on the Many, others more on the One. Hence a distinction between personal and absolute idealism is legitimate, provided that we allow for the qualification which has just been made.

We may also remark that the term 'personal idealism' is somewhat ambiguous in the context of American thought. It was used, for example, by William James of his own philosophy. But though the use of the term was doubtless justified, James is best discussed under the heading of pragmatism.

Chapter Twelve

THE PHILOSOPHY OF ROYCE

Remarks on Royce's writings previous to his Gifford Lectures – The meaning of Being and the meaning of ideas – Three inadequate theories of Being – The fourth conception of Being – The finite self and the Absolute; moral freedom – The social aspect of morality – Immortality – Infinite series and the idea of a self-representative system – Some critical comments.

1. Josiah Royce (1855–1916) entered the University of California at the age of sixteen and received his baccalaureate in 1875. A paper which he wrote on the theology of the *Prometheus Bound* of Aeschylus won him a grant of money that enabled him to spend two years in Germany, where he read German philosophers such as Schelling and Schopenhauer, and studied under Lotze at Göttingen. After taking his doctorate in 1878 at Johns Hopkins University he taught for a few years in the University of California and then went to Harvard as a lecturer in philosophy. In 1885 he was nominated as assistant professor, and in 1892 professor. In 1914 he accepted the Alford chair of philosophy at Harvard.

In 1885 Royce published *The Religious Aspect of Philosophy*. In it he argues that the impossibility of proving the universal and absolute validity of the moral ideal embraced by any given individual tends to produce moral scepticism and pessimism. Reflection, however, shows that the very search for a universal and absolute ideal reveals in the seeker a moral will which wills the harmonization of all particular ideals and values. And there then arises in the mind of the individual the consciousness that he ought so to live that his life and the lives of other men may form a unity, converging towards a common ideal goal or end. With this idea Royce associates an exaltation of the social order, in particular of the State.[1]

Turning to the problem of God, Royce rejects the traditional proofs of God's existence and develops an argument for the Absolute from the recognition of error. We are accustomed to think that error arises when our thought fails to conform with its intended object. But we obviously cannot place ourselves in the position of an external spectator, outside the subject-object relationship, capable of seeing whether thought conforms with its object or not. And reflection on this fact may lead to scepticism. Yet it is clear that we are capable of recognizing error. We can not only make erroneous judgments but also know that we have made them. And further reflection shows that truth and falsity have meaning only in relation to a complete system of truth, which must be present to absolute thought. In other words, Royce accepts a coherence theory of truth and passes from it to the assertion of absolute thought. As he was later to express it, an individual's opinions are true or false in relation to a wider insight. And his argument is that we cannot stop until we arrive at the idea of an all-inclusive divine insight which embraces in a comprehensive unity our thinking and its objects and is the ultimate measure of truth and falsity.

In *The Religious Aspect of Philosophy*, therefore, the Absolute is described as thought. 'All reality must be present to the unity of the Infinite Thought.'[2] But Royce does not understand this term in a sense which would exclude descriptions of the Absolute in terms of will or of experience. And in *The Conception of God* (1897) he argues that there is an absolute experience which is related to ours as an organic whole is related to its constituent elements. Though, therefore, Royce frequently uses the term 'God', it is obvious that the divine being is for him the One, the totality.[3] At the same time God or the Absolute is conceived as self-conscious. And the natural conclusion to draw is that finite selves are thoughts of God in his own act of self-knowledge. It is thus perfectly understandable that Royce drew upon himself the criticism of the personal idealists.[4] In point of fact, however, he had no wish to submerge the Many in the One in such a way as to reduce finite self-consciousness to an inexplicable illusion. Hence he had to develop a theory of the relation between the One and the Many which would neither reduce the Many to illusory appearance nor make the term 'One' altogether inappropriate. And this was one of the main themes of Royce's Gifford Lectures, to which we shall turn in the next section.

Royce's idea of God as the absolute and all-inclusive experience naturally compels him, like Bradley, to devote attention to the problem of evil. In *Studies in Good and Evil* (1898) he rejects any attempt to evade the issue by saying that suffering and moral evil are illusions. On the contrary, they are real. We cannot avoid the conclusion, therefore, that God suffers when we suffer. And we must suppose that suffering is necessary for the perfecting of the divine life. As for moral evil, this too is required for the perfection of the universe. For the good will presupposes the evil as something to be overcome. True, from the point of view of the Absolute the world, the object of infinite thought, is a perfect unity in which evil is already overcome and subordinated to the good. But it is none the less a constituent element in the whole.

If God is a name for the universe, and if suffering and evil are real, we must obviously locate them in God. If, however, there is an absolute point of view from which evil is eternally overcome and subordinated to the good, God can hardly be simply a name for the universe. In other words, the problem of the relation between God and the world becomes acute. But Royce's ideas on this subject are best discussed in connection with his main presentation of his philosophy.

2. The two volumes of *The World and the Individual*, representing series of Gifford Lectures, appeared respectively in 1900 and 1901. In them Royce sets out to determine the

nature of Being. If it is asserted that God is, or that the world is, or that the finite self is, we can always ask for the meaning of 'is'. This term, which Royce calls 'the existential predicate',[5] is often assumed to be simple and indefinable. But in philosophy the simple and ultimate is as much a subject for reflection as the complex and derived. Royce is not, however, concerned with the verb 'to be' simply in the sense of exist. He is also concerned with determining 'the special sorts of Reality that we attribute to God, to the World, and to the Human Individual'.[6] In traditional language he is concerned with essence as well as with existence, in his own language with the *what* as well as with the *that*. For if we assert that X is or exists, we assert that there is an X, something possessing a certain nature.

In point of fact the problem of determining the meaning of what Royce calls the existential or ontological predicate immediately becomes for him the problem of determining the nature of reality. And the question arises, how are we to tackle this problem? It might perhaps appear that the best way to approach it would be to look at reality as presented in experience and try to understand it. But, Royce insists, we can understand reality only by means of ideas. And it thus becomes all-important to understand what an idea is and how it stands to reality. 'I am one of those who hold that when you ask the question: What is an Idea? and: How can Ideas stand in any true relation to Reality? you attack the world-knot in the way that promises most for the untying of its meshes.'[7]

After his initial announcement that he is going to deal with the problem of Being, Royce's shift of attention to the nature of ideas and their relation to reality is likely to appear both disappointing and exasperating to his readers. But his method of procedure is easily explicable. We have seen that in *The Religious Aspect of Philosophy* Royce described God as absolute thought. And his approach to the problem of Being by way of a theory of ideas is suggested by the metaphysical position which he has already adopted, namely the primacy of thought. Thus when he asserts 'the primacy of the World as Idea over the World as Fact',[8] he is speaking in terms of the idealist tradition as he sees it, the tradition according to which the world is the self-realization of the absolute Idea.

In the first place Royce draws a distinction between the external and internal meanings of an idea. Let us suppose that I have an idea of Mount Everest. It is natural to think of this idea as referring to and representing an external reality, namely the actual mountain. And this representative function is what Royce understands by the external meaning of an idea. But now let us suppose that I am an artist, and that I have in my mind an idea of the picture which I wish to paint. This idea can be described as 'the partial fulfilment of a purpose'.[9] And this aspect of an idea is what Royce calls its internal meaning.

Common sense would doubtless be prepared to admit that the idea in the mind of an artist can reasonably be described as the partial fulfilment of a purpose.[10] And to this extent it recognizes the existence of internal meaning. But, left to itself, common sense would probably regard the representative function of the idea as primary, even though it is a question of representing what does not yet exist, namely the projected work of art. And if we consider an idea such as that of the number of the inhabitants of London, common sense would certainly emphasize its representative character and ask whether or not it corresponds with external reality.

Royce, however, maintains that it is the internal meaning of an idea which is primary, and that in the long run external meaning turns out to be only 'an aspect of the completely developed internal meaning'.[11] Suppose, for example, that I wish to ascertain the number of people, or of families, resident in a certain area. Obviously, I have a purpose in wishing to ascertain these facts. Perhaps I am in charge of a housing scheme and wish to ascertain the number of individuals and of families in order to be able to estimate the number of houses or flats required for the already resident population in a district which is to be reconstructed. It is clearly important that my idea of the population should be accurate. External meaning is thus of importance. At the same time I try to obtain an accurate idea with a view to the fulfilment of a purpose. And the idea can be regarded as a partial or incomplete fulfilment of this purpose. In this sense the internal meaning of the idea is primary. According to Royce, its external meaning, taken simply by itself, is an abstraction, an abstraction, that is to say, from its context, namely the fulfilment of a purpose. When it is replaced in its context, the internal meaning is seen to take precedence.

What, it may be asked, is the connection between this theory of the meaning of ideas and the solution of the problem of reality? The answer is obviously that Royce intends to represent the world as the embodiment of an absolute system of ideas which are, in themselves, the incomplete fulfilment of a purpose. 'We propose to answer the question: What is to be? by the assertion that: To be means simply to express, to embody the complete internal meaning of a certain absolute system of ideas—a system, moreover, which is genuinely implied in the true internal meaning or purpose of every finite idea, however fragmentary.'[12] Royce admits that this theory is not novel. For example, it is essentially the same as the line of thought which 'led Hegel to call the world the embodied Idea'.[13] But though the theory is not novel, 'I believe it to be of fundamental and of inexhaustible importance'.[14]

In other words, Royce first interprets the function of human ideas in the light of an already existing idealist conviction about the primacy of thought. And he then uses this interpretation as the basis for an explicit metaphysics. At the same time he works dialectically towards the establishment of his own view of the meaning of 'to be' by examining in turn different types of philosophy with a view to exhibiting their inadequacy. And though we cannot enter into the details of this discussion, it is appropriate to indicate its general lines.

3. The first type of philosophy discussed by Royce is what he calls realism. By this he understands the doctrine that 'the mere knowledge of any Being by any one who is not himself the Being known, "makes no difference whatever" to that known Being'.[15] In other words, if all knowledge were to disappear from the world, the only difference that this would make to the world would be that the particular fact of knowledge would no longer exist. Truth and falsity consist in the correspondence or non-correspondence of ideas with

things; and nothing exists simply in virtue of the fact that it is known. Hence we cannot tell by inspecting the relations between ideas whether the objects referred to exist or not. Hence the *what* is sundered from the *that*. And this, Royce remarks, is why the realist has to deny the validity of the ontological argument for God's existence.

Royce's criticism of 'realism' is not always very clear. But his general line of thought is as follows. By realism in this context he evidently means an extreme nominalistic empiricism, according to which the world consists of a plurality of entities that are mutually independent. The disappearance of one would not affect the existence of the rest. Any relations which are superadded to these entities must, therefore, be themselves independent entities. And in this case, Royce argues, the terms of the relations cannot really be related. If we start with entities which are sundered from one another, they remain sundered. Royce then argues that ideas must themselves be entities, and that on realist premises an unbridgeable gulf yawns between them and the objects to which they are thought to refer. In other words, if ideas are entities which are completely independent of other entities, we can never know whether they correspond with objects external to themselves, nor indeed whether there are such objects at all. Hence we can never know whether realism, as an idea or set of ideas, is true or false. And in this sense realism, as a theory of reality, is self-defeating: it undermines its own foundations.[16]

From realism Royce proceeds to a consideration of what he calls 'mysticism'. As the core of realism consists in defining as 'real' any being which is essentially independent of any idea which refers to it from without, the realist, Royce claims, is committed to dualism. For he must postulate the existence of at least one idea and one object which is external to it. Mysticism, however, rejects dualism and asserts the existence of a One in which the distinctions between subject and object, idea and the reality to which it refers, vanish.

Mysticism, as understood in this sense, is as self-defeating as realism. For if there is only one simple and indivisible Being, the finite subject and its ideas must be accounted illusory. And in this case the Absolute cannot be known. For it could be known only by ideas. In fact any assertion that there is a One must be illusory. It is true that our fragmentary ideas need completion in a unified system, and that the whole is the truth. But if a philosopher stresses unity to such an extent that ideas have to be accounted illusion, he cannot at the same time consistently maintain that there is a One or Absolute. For it is plain that the Absolute has meaning for us only in so far as it is conceived by means of ideas.

If therefore we wish to maintain that knowledge of reality is possible at all, we cannot take the path of mysticism. We must allow for plurality. At the same time we cannot return to realism as described above. Hence realism must be modified in such a way that it is no longer self-defeating. And one way of attempting such a modification is to take the path of what Royce calls 'critical rationalism'.

The critical rationalist undertakes to 'define Being in terms of validity, to conceive that whoever says, of any object, *It is*, means only that a certain idea . . . *is valid*, has truth, defines an experience that, at least as a mathematical ideal, and perhaps as an empirical event, is determinately *possible*'.[17] Suppose that I assert that there are human beings on the planet Mars. According to the critical rationalist, I am asserting that in the progress of possible experience a certain idea would be validated or verified. Royce gives as examples of critical rationalism Kant's theory of possible experience and J. S. Mill's definition of matter as a permanent possibility of sensations. We might add logical positivism, provided that we substitute for 'idea' 'empirical proposition'.

In Royce's view critical rationalism has this advantage over realism that by defining Being in terms of possible experience, the validation of an idea (better, the verification of a proposition), it avoids the objections which arise from realism's complete sundering of ideas from the reality to which they are assumed to refer. At the same time critical rationalism has this great drawback that it is incapable of answering the question, '*what is a valid or a determinately possible experience at the moment when it is supposed to be only possible?* What is a valid truth at the moment when nobody verifies its validity?'[18] If I assert that there are men on Mars, this statement doubtless implies, in a definable sense of this term, that the presence of men on Mars is an object of possible experience. But if the statement happens to be true, their existence is not simply possible existence. Hence we can hardly define Being simply in terms of the possible validation or verification of an idea. And though critical rationalism does not make knowledge of reality impossible, as is done by both realism and mysticism, it is unable to provide an adequate account of reality. Hence we must turn to another and more adequate philosophical theory, which will subsume in itself the truths contained in the three theories already mentioned but which will at the same time be immune from the objections which can be brought against them.

4. It has already been indicated that by 'realism' Royce understands nominalism rather than realism as this term is used in the context of the controversy about universals. And if we bear this fact in mind, we shall not be so startled by his assertion that for the realist the only ultimate form of being is the individual. For the nominalist slogan was that only individuals exist. At the same time we must also bear in mind the fact that Hegel, who was no nominalist, used the term 'individual' to mean the concrete universal, and that in the Hegelian philosophy the ultimate form of being is the individual in this sense of the term, the Absolute being the supreme individual, the all-inclusive concrete universal. Hence when Royce asserts that the truth contained in realism is that the only ultimate form of being is the individual, it would be misleading to say simply that he is accepting the nominalist slogan. For he re-interprets the term 'individual' under the inspiration of the idealist tradition. According to his use of the term 'an individual being is a Life of Experience fulfilling Ideas, in an absolutely final form. . . . The essence of the Real is to be Individual, or permit no other of its own kind, and this character it possesses only as the unique fulfilment of purpose.'[19]

Now we have seen that an idea is the incomplete or partial fulfilment of a purpose, the expression of will. And the complete embodiment of the will is the world in its entirety. Hence any idea ultimately 'means'[20] the totality. And it follows that in the totality, the world as a whole, I can recognize myself. To this extent therefore we can find truth in 'mysticism' and agree with the oriental mystic who 'says of the self and the World: *That art Thou*'.[21]

It is evident, however, that as embodied in any particular phase of consciousness the will expresses itself in attention only to a part of the world or to certain facts in the world. The rest relapses into a vague background at the margin of consciousness. It becomes in fact the object of possible experience. In other words, it is necessary to introduce a concept from critical rationalism.

So far we have been thinking of the point of view of the individual finite subject. But though there is an obvious sense in which the world is 'my world' and nobody else's, it is also obvious that if I regard the world as being simply and solely the embodiment of my will, I am committed to solipsism. It is also clear that if I postulate the existence of other lives of experience besides my own but regard each life as completely self-enclosed, I fall back into the thesis of realism, namely that reality consists of completely separate and mutually independent entities. Hence to avoid solipsism without returning to the realist thesis which we have already rejected we must introduce a new dimension or plane, that of intersubjectivity.

It is commonly said, Royce remarks, that we come to know the existence of other persons by analogical reasoning. That is to say, observing certain patterns of external behaviour we attribute to them wills like our own. But if this means that we first have a clear knowledge of ourselves and then infer the existence of other persons, 'it is nearer the truth to say that we first learn about ourselves from and through our fellows, than that we learn about our fellows by using the analogy of ourselves'.[22] We have indeed ever-present evidence of the existence of others. For they are the source of new ideas. They answer our questions; they tell us things; they express opinions other than our own; and so on. Yet it is precisely through social intercourse or at least in the consciousness of the presence of others, that we form our own ideas and become aware of what we really will and aim at. As Royce puts it, our fellows 'help us to find out what our true meaning is'.[23]

If, however, Royce rejects the view that we first possess a

clear consciousness of ourselves and then infer the existence of other persons, still less does he intend to imply that we first have a clear and definite idea of other persons and then infer that we too are persons. He says, indeed, that 'a vague belief in the existence of our fellows seems to antedate, to a considerable extent, the definite formation of any consciousness of ourselves'.[24] But his thesis is that the clear awareness of ourselves and of other persons arises out of a kind of primitive social consciousness, so that it is a question of differentiation rather than of inference. Empirical self-consciousness depends constantly upon a series of contrast-effects. 'The Ego is always known as in contrast to the Alter.'[25] Both emerge from the original social consciousness.

As experience develops, the individual comes more and more to regard the inner lives of others as something private, removed from his direct observation. At the same time he becomes progressively conscious of external objects as instruments of purposes which are common to himself and others as well as of his and their particular purposes or interests. There thus arises the consciousness of a triad, 'my fellow and Myself, with Nature between us'.[26]

The world of Nature is known by us only in part, a great deal remaining for us the realm of possible experience. But we have already noted the difficulty encountered by critical rationalism in explaining the ontological status of objects of possible experience; and in any case science makes it impossible for us to believe that Nature is simply and solely the embodiment of human will and purpose. The hypothesis of evolution, for example, leads us to conceive finite minds as products. In this case, however, the question arises, how can we save the idealist definition of Being in terms of the internal meaning of ideas considered as the partial fulfilment of a purpose?

Royce's answer to this question is easy to foresee. The world is ultimately the expression of an absolute system of ideas which is itself the partial fulfilment of the divine will. God, expressing himself in the world, is the ultimate Individual. Or, to put the matter in another way, the ultimate Individual is the life of absolute experience. Each finite self is a unique expression of the divine purpose; and each embodies or expresses itself in its world. But 'my world' and 'your world' are unique facets of 'the world', the embodiment of the infinite divine will and purpose. And what is for us simply the object of possible experience is for God the object of actual creative experience. 'The whole world of truth and being must exist only as present, in all its variety, its wealth, its relationships, its entire constitution, to the unity of a single consciousness, which includes both our own and all finite conscious meanings in one final eternally present insight.'[27] Royce is thus able to preserve his theory of Being, namely that 'whatever is, is consciously known as the fulfilment of some idea, and is so known either by ourselves at this moment, or by a consciousness inclusive of our own'.[28]

5. We have seen that for Royce the individual is a *life* of experience. And if we are looking for the nature of the self in a meta-empirical sense,[29] we have to conceive it in ethical terms, not in terms of a soul-substance. For it is through the possession of a unique ideal, a unique vocation, a unique life-task which is what my past has 'meant' and which my future is to fulfil that '*I am defined and created a Self*'.[30] Perhaps, therefore, we can say, speaking in a manner that puts us in mind of existentialism, that for Royce the finite individual continually creates himself as this unique self by realizing a unique ideal, by fulfilling a certain unique vocation.[31]

It is in terms of this idea of the self that Royce attempts to meet the objection that absolute idealism deprives the finite self of reality, value and freedom. He has, of course, no intention of denying any of the empirical data relating to the dependence of the psychical on the physical or to the influence on the self of social environment, education and such like factors. But he insists that each finite self has its own unique way of acknowledging and responding by its deeds to this dependence,[32] while from the metaphysical point of view the life of each finite self is a unique contribution to the fulfilment of the general purpose of God. Royce has indeed to admit that when I will, God wills in me, and that my act is part of the divine life. But this admission, he maintains, is quite compatible with the statement that the finite self can act freely. For by the very fact that I am a *unique* expression of the divine will, the will from which my acts proceed is *my* will. 'Your individuality in your act *is* your freedom.'[33] That is to say, my way of expressing the divine will is myself; and if my acts proceed from myself, they are free acts. There is indeed a sense in which it is true to say that the divine Spirit compels us, but 'in the sense that it compels you to be an individual, and to be free'.[34]

Now, Royce maintains that every finite will seeks the Absolute, so much so that 'to seek anything but the Absolute itself is, indeed, even for the most perverse Self, simply impossible'.[35] In other words, every finite self tends by its very nature, whether it is aware of the fact or not, to unite its will ever more closely with the divine will. Obligation bears on us in relation to conduct which would bring us nearer to this end. And a moral rule is a rule which, if followed, would bring us nearer to the end than if we acted in a manner contrary to the rule. It is thus clear enough that in Royce's ethics the concept of the good is paramount, and that obligation bears on us in relation to the means necessary to attain this good, namely the conscious union of our will with the divine will. But it is not so clear how any room can be left for rebellion against the divine will or against a known dictate of the moral law. For if we all inevitably seek the Absolute, it appears to follow that if a person acts in a manner which will not as a matter of fact bring him nearer to the final end which he is always seeking, he does so simply out of ignorance, out of defective knowledge. Hence the question arises, 'can a finite self, knowing the Ought, in any sense freely choose to rebel or to obey?'[36]

Royce answers in the first place that though a man who has clear knowledge of what he ought to do will act in accordance with this knowledge, he can voluntarily concentrate his attention elsewhere, so that here and now he no longer has clear knowledge of what he ought to do. 'To sin is *consciously to forget*, through a narrowing of the field of attention, an Ought that one already recognizes.'[37]

Given Royce's premises, this answer is hardly adequate. We can, of course, easily give a cash-value to his idea of a shift of attention. Suppose, for example, that I am sincerely convinced that it would be wrong for me to act in a certain way which I regard as productive of sensual pleasure. The more I concentrate my attention on the pleasurable aspects of this way of acting, so much the more does my conviction of its wrongness tend to retreat to the margin of consciousness and become ineffective. We all know that this sort of situation occurs frequently enough. And the ordinary comment would be that the agent should be careful not to concentrate his attention on the pleasurable aspects of a way of acting which he sincerely believes to be wrong. If he concentrates his attention in this manner, he is ultimately responsible for what happens. But though this point of view is clearly reasonable, the question immediately arises, how can the agent be properly held responsible for choosing to concentrate his attention in a certain direction if he is in his entirety an expression of the divine will? Have we simply not pushed the difficulty a stage further back?

Royce rather tends to evade the issue by turning to the subject of the overcoming of evil in the totality. But his general line of answer seems to be that as a man's direction of his attention proceeds from his will, the man is himself responsible for it and thus for the outcome. The fact that the man's will is itself the expression of the divine will does not alter the situation. In the circumstances it does not appear that Royce can very well say anything else. For though he certainly wishes to maintain human freedom and responsibility in a real sense, his determination to maintain at the same time the doctrine of the all-comprehensive Absolute inevitably influences his account of freedom. Moral freedom becomes 'simply this freedom to hold by attention, or to forget by inattention, an Ought already present to one's finite consciousness'.[38] If it is asked whether the holding or forgetting is not itself determined by the Absolute, Royce can only answer that it proceeds from a man's own will, and that to act in accordance with one's will *is* to act freely, even if one's finite will is a particular embodiment of the divine will.

6. As Royce lays great emphasis, in a manner which reminds us of Fichte, on the uniqueness of the task which each finite self is called to perform, he can hardly be expected to devote much time to developing a theory of universal moral rules.[39] And it is perhaps not an exaggeration to say that the funda-

mental precept is for him, as for Emerson, 'Be an individual! That is, find and fulfil your unique task.' At the same time it would be quite wrong to depict him as belittling the idea of the community. On the contrary, his ethical theory can be regarded as a contribution to the demand made by Harris in his programme for speculative philosophy, that a social theory should be developed which would fulfil the needs of a national consciousness that was moving away from sheer individualism. For Royce all finite selves are mutually related precisely because they are unique expressions of one infinite will. And all individual vocations or life-tasks are elements in a common task, the fulfilment of the divine purpose. Hence Royce preaches loyalty to the ideal community, the Great Community as he calls it.[40]

In *The Problem of Christianity* (1913) Royce defines loyalty as 'the willing and thoroughgoing devotion of a self to a cause, when the cause is something which unites many selves in one, and which is therefore the interest of a community'.[41] And he sees in the Church, the community of the faithful, especially as represented in the Pauline Epistles, the embodiment of the spirit of loyalty, of devotion to a common ideal and of loyalty to the ideal community which should be loved as a person. It does not follow, however, that Royce intended to identify what he calls the Great Community with an historic Church, any more than with an historic State. The Great Community is more like Kant's kingdom of ends; it is the ideal human community. Yet though it is an ideal to be sought after rather than an actual historic society existing here and now, it none the less lies at the basis of the moral order, precisely because it is the goal or *telos* of moral action. It is true that the individual alone can work out his moral vocation; it cannot be done for him. But because of the very nature of the self genuine individuality can be realized only through loyalty to the Great Community, to an ideal cause which unites all men together.

Largely under the influence of C. S. Peirce, Royce came to emphasize the role of interpretation in human knowledge and life; and he applied this idea in his ethical theory. For example, the individual cannot realize himself and attain true selfhood or personality without a life-goal or life-plan, in relation to which concepts such as right and wrong, higher self and lower self, become concretely meaningful. But a man comes to apprehend his life-plan or ideal goal only through a process of interpreting himself to himself. Further, this self-interpretation is achieved only in a social context, through interaction with other people. Others inevitably help me to interpret myself to myself; and I help others to interpret themselves to themselves. In a sense this process tends to division rather than to union, inasmuch as each individual becomes thereby more aware of himself as possessing a unique life-task. But if we bear in mind the social structure of the self, we are led to form the idea of an unlimited community of interpretation, of humanity, that is to say, as engaged throughout time in the common task of interpreting both the physical world and its own purposes, ideals and values. All growth in scientific knowledge and moral insight involves a process of interpretation.

The supreme object of loyalty as a moral category is, Royce came to think, this ideal community of interpretation. But towards the close of his life he stressed the importance of limited communities both for moral development and for the achievement of social reform. If we consider, for instance, two individuals who are disputing about, say, the possession of some property, we can see that this potentially dangerous situation is transformed by the intervention of a third party, the judge. A triadic relation is substituted for the potentially dangerous dyadic relation; and a small-scale community of interpretation is set up. Thus Royce tries to exhibit the mediating or interpretative and morally educative functions of such institutions as the judicial system, always in the light of the idea of interpretation. He applies this idea even to the institution of insurance and develops, as a safeguard against war, a scheme of insurance on an international scale.[42] Some of his commentators may have seen in such ideas a peculiarly American fusion of idealism with a rather down-to-earth practicality. But it does not follow, of course, that such a fusion is a bad thing. In any case Royce evidently felt that if substantive proposals were to be put forward in ethical theory, something more was required than exhorting men to be loyal to the ideal community of interpretation.

7. From what has been said hitherto it is clear that Royce attaches to the unique personality a value which could not be attributed to it in the philosophy of Bradley. It is not surprising, therefore, that he is far more interested than Bradley in the question of immortality, and that he maintains that the self is preserved in the Absolute.

In discussing this subject Royce dwells, among other aspects of the matter, on the Kantian theme that the moral task of the individual can have no temporal end. 'A consciously last moral task is a contradiction in terms. . . . The service of the eternal is an essentially endless service. There can be no last moral deed.'[43] Obviously, this line of argument could not by itself prove immortality. It is true that if we recognize a moral law at all, we have to regard it as bearing upon us as long as we live. But it does not follow from this premiss alone that the self survives bodily death and is able to continue fulfilling a moral vocation. But for Royce as a metaphysician the universe is of such a kind that the finite self, as a unique expression of the Absolute and as representing an irreplaceable value, must be supposed to continue in existence. The ethical self is always something in the making; and as the divine purpose must be fulfilled, we are justified in believing that after the death of the body the self attains genuine individuality in a higher form. But 'I know not in the least, I pretend not to guess, by what processes the individuality of our human life is further expressed. I wait until this mortal shall put on—Individuality.'[44] Evidently, in Royce's assertion of immortality what really counts is his general metaphysical vision of reality, coupled with his evaluation of personality.

8. At the end of the first volume of Royce's Gifford Lectures there is a Supplementary Essay in which he takes issue with Bradley on the subject of an infinite multitude. Bradley, it will be remembered, maintains that relational thought involves us in infinite series. If, for example, qualities A and B are related by relation R, we must choose between saying that R is reducible without residue to A and B or that it is not so reducible. In the first case we shall be compelled to conclude that A and B are not related at all. In the second case we shall have to postulate further relations to relate

both A and B with R, and so on without end. We are then committed to postulating an actually infinite multitude. But this concept is self-contradictory. Hence we must conclude that relational thought is quite incapable of giving a coherent account of how the Many proceed from and are unified in the One, and that the world as presented in such thought belongs to the sphere of appearance as contrasted with that of reality. Royce, however, undertakes to show that the One can express itself in infinite series which are 'well-ordered' and involve no contradiction, and that thought is thus capable of giving a coherent account of the relation between the One and the Many. It is perhaps disputable whether Bradley's difficulties are really met by first ascribing to him the thesis that an actually infinite multitude is 'a self-contradictory conception'[45] and then arguing that an endless series in mathematics does not involve a contradiction. But though Royce develops his own conception of the relation between the One and the Many in the context of a controversy with Bradley, what he is really interested in is, of course, the explanation of his own ideas.

Royce's attention was directed by C. S. Peirce to the logic of mathematics;[46] and the Supplementary Essay shows the fruit of Royce's reflections on this subject. In an endless mathematical series, such as that of the whole numbers, the endlessness of the series is due to a recurrent operation of thought, a recurrent operation of thought being describable as 'one that, *if once finally expressed*, would involve, in the region where it had received expression, an infinite variety of serially arranged facts, corresponding to the purpose in question'.[47] In general, if we assume a purpose of such a kind that if we try to express it by means of a succession of acts, the ideal data which begin to express it demand as part of their own 'meaning' additional data which are themselves further expressions of the original meaning and at the same time demand still further expressions, we have an endless series produced by a recurrent operation of thought.

A series of this kind can properly be regarded as a totality. To be sure, it is not a totality in the sense that we can count to the end and complete the series. For it is *ex hypothesi* infinite or endless. But if we take, for example, the series of whole numbers, 'the mathematician can view them all as *given* by means of their universal definition, and their consequent clear distinction from all other objects of thought'.[48] In other words, there is no intrinsic repugnance between the idea of a totality and that of an infinite series. And we can conceive the One as expressing itself in an infinite series or, rather, a plurality of co-ordinate infinite series, the plurality of lives of experience. This gives us, of course, a dynamic rather than a static concept of the One. And this is essential to Royce's metaphysics, with its emphasis on divine will and purpose and on the 'internal meaning' of ideas.

An infinite series of this kind is described by Royce as a self-representative system. And he finds examples in 'all continuous and discrete mathematical systems of any infinite type'.[49] But a simple illustration given by Royce himself will serve better to clarify what he means by a self-representative system. Suppose that we decide that on some portion of England a map is to be constructed which will represent the country down to the smallest detail, including every contour and marking, whether natural or artificial. As the map itself will be an artificial feature of England, another map will have to be constructed within the first map and representing it too, if, that is to say, our original purpose is to be carried out. And so on without end. True, this endless representation of England would not be physically possible. But we can conceive an endless series of maps within maps, a series which, though it cannot be completed in time, can be regarded as already given in our original purpose or 'meaning'. The observer who understood the situation and looked at the series of maps, would not see any last map. But he would know why there could be no last map. Hence he would see no contradiction or irrationality in the endlessness of the series. And the series would constitute a self-representative system.

If we apply this idea in metaphysics, the universe appears as an infinite series, an endless whole, which expresses a single purpose or plan. There are, of course, subordinate and co-ordinate series, in particular the series which constitute the lives of finite selves. But they are all comprised within one unified infinite series which has no last member but which is 'given' as a totality in the internal meaning of the divine idea or absolute system of ideas. The One, according to Royce, must express itself in the endless series which constitutes its life of creative experience. In other words, it must express itself in the Many. And as the endless series is the progressive expression or fulfilment of a single purpose, the whole of reality is one self-representative system.

9. It is clear that Royce, with his emphasis on personality, has no intention of abandoning theism altogether and of using the term 'the Absolute' simply as a name for the world considered as an open totality, a series which has no assignable last member. The world is for him the embodiment of the internal meaning of a system of ideas which are themselves the partial fulfilment of a purpose. And the Absolute is a self; it is personal rather than impersonal; it is an eternal and infinite consciousness. Hence it can reasonably be described as God. And Royce depicts the infinite series which constitutes the temporal universe as present all at once, *tota simul*, to the divine consciousness. Indeed, he is quite prepared to commend St. Thomas Aquinas for his account of the divine knowledge; and he himself uses the analogy of our awareness of a symphony as a whole, an awareness which is obviously quite compatible with the knowledge that this part precedes that. So, according to Royce, God is aware of temporal succession, though the whole temporal series is none the less present to the eternal consciousness.

At the same time Royce rejects the dualistic sundering of the world from God which he regards as characteristic of theism, and he blames Aquinas for conceiving 'the temporal existence of the created world as sundered from the eternal life which belongs to God'.[50] The Many exist within the unity of the divine life. 'Simple unity is a mere impossibility. God cannot be One except by being Many. Nor can we various Selves be Many, unless in Him we are One.'[51]

In other words, Royce tries to re-interpret theism in the light of absolute idealism. He tries to preserve the idea of a personal God while combining it with the idea of the all-comprehensive Absolute represented as the Universal of universals.[52] And this is not an easy position to maintain. In fact its ambiguity is well illustrated by Royce's use of the term 'individual'. If we speak of God as the supreme or ultimate Individual, we naturally tend to think of him as a personal being and of the world as the 'external' expression of his creative will. But for Royce the term 'individual' means, as we have seen, a life of experience. And according to this meaning of the term God becomes the life of absolute and infinite experience, in which all finite things are immanent. Whereas the interpretation of the existence of finite things as the expression of purposeful will suggests creation in a theistic sense, the description of God as absolute experience suggests a rather different relation. No doubt Royce tries to bring the two concepts together through the conception of creative experience; but there seems to be in his philosophy a somewhat unstable marriage between theism and absolute idealism.

It is, of course, notoriously difficult to express the relation between the finite and the infinite without tending either to a monism in which the Many are relegated to the sphere of appearance or are submerged in the One or to a dualism which renders the use of the term 'infinite' quite inappropriate. And it is certainly not possible to avoid both positions without a clear theory of the analogy of being. But Royce's statements on the subject of being are somewhat perplexing.

On the one hand we are told that being is the expression or embodiment of the internal meaning of an idea, and so of purpose or will. But though the subordination of being to thought may be characteristic of metaphysical idealism, the question obviously arises whether thought itself is not a form of being. And the same question can be asked in regard to will. On the other hand we are told that the ultimately real, and so presumably the ultimate form of being, is the individual. And as God is the Individual of individuals, it appears to follow that he must be the supreme and absolute being. Yet we are also told to regard 'individuality, and consequently Being, as above all an expression of Will'.[53] To regard individuality as an expression of will is not so difficult, if, that is to say, we interpret individuality as a life of expression. But to regard being as an expression of will is not so easy. For the question again arises, is will not being? Of course, it would be possible to restrict the use of the term 'being' to material being. But then we could hardly regard individuality, in Royce's sense of the term, as being.

In spite, however, of the ambiguity and lack of precision in his writing, Royce's philosophy impresses by its sincerity. It is evidently the expression of a deeply held faith, a faith in the reality of God, in the value of the human personality and in the unity of mankind in and through God, a unity which can be adequately realized only through individual contributions to a common moral task. Royce was indeed something of a preacher. But the philosophy which he preached certainly meant for him a great deal more than an intellectual exercise or game.

It should be added that in the opinion of some commentators[54] Royce came to abandon his theory of the Absolute Will and to substitute for it the idea of an unlimited community of interpretation, an unlimited community, that is to say, of finite individuals. And from the purely ethical point of view such a change would be understandable. For it would dispose of the objection, of which Royce himself was aware, that it is difficult, if indeed possible at all, to reconcile the theory of the Absolute Will with the view of human beings as genuine moral agents. At the same time the substitution of a community of finite individuals for the Absolute would be a pretty radical change. And it is by no means easy to see how such a community could take over, as it were, the cosmological function of the Absolute. Even if, therefore, the idea of the Absolute retreats into the background in Royce's latest writings, one hesitates to accept the view that he positively rejected the idea, unless, of course, one is driven to do so by strong empirical evidence. There is indeed some evidence. In his last years Royce himself referred to a change in his idealism. Hence we cannot say that the claim that he substituted the unlimited community of interpretation for his earlier concept of the Absolute is unfounded. Royce does not seem, however, to have been explicit as one could wish about the precise nature and extent of the change to which he refers.

Chapter Thirteen

PERSONAL IDEALISM AND
OTHER TENDENCIES

Howison's criticism of Royce in favour of his own ethical pluralism – The evolutionary idealism of Le Conte – The personal idealism of Bowne – The objective idealism of Creighton – Sylvester Morris and dynamic idealism – Notes on the prolongation of idealism into the twentieth century – An attempt at transcending the opposition between idealism and realism.

1. George Holmes Howison (1834–1916), a member of the Philosophical Society of St. Louis and of W. T. Harris's Kant-Club, was at first a professor of mathematics. But in 1872 he accepted the chair of logic and philosophy in the Massachusetts Institute of Technology at Boston, a post which he occupied until 1878 when he went to Germany for two years. In Germany he came under the influence of the right-wing Hegelian Ludwig Michelet (1801–93), and, like Michelet himself, he interpreted Hegel's absolute Idea or cosmic Reason as a personal being, God. In 1884 Howison became a professor in the University of California. His work *The Limits of Evolution and Other Essays*, appeared in 1901.

It has already been mentioned that Howison participated in the discussion which formed the basis for *The Conception of God* (1897), a work to which reference was made in the chapter on Royce. In his introduction to the book Howison draws attention to the existence of a certain measure of basic agreement among the participants in the discussion, particularly in regard to the personality of God and about the close relation between the concepts of God, freedom and immortality. But though he recognizes certain family likenesses between different types of idealism, this does not prevent him from developing a sharp criticism of Royce's philosophy.

In the first place, if being is defined in terms of its relation to the internal meaning of an idea, how, Howison asks, are we to decide whether the idea in question is my idea or that of an infinite all-inclusive self? The factor which leads Royce and those who share his general outlook to reject solipsism in favour of absolute idealism is an instinctive response to the demands of common sense rather than any logical and compelling argument. In the second place, though Royce certainly intends to preserve individual freedom and responsibility, he can do so only at the cost of consistency. For absolute idealism logically involves the merging of finite selves in the Absolute.

Howison's own philosophy has been described as ethical pluralism. Existence takes the form of spirits and of the contents and order of their experience, the spatio-temporal world owing its being to the co-existence of spirits. Each spirit is a free and active efficient cause, having the origin of its activity within itself. At the same time each spirit is a member of a community of spirits, the City of God, the members being united in terms of final causality, that is, by their attraction to a common ideal, the full realization of the City of God. The human consciousness is not simply self-enclosed, but, when developed, it sees itself as a member of what Howison describes as Conscience or Complete Reason. And the movement towards a common ideal or end is what is called evolution.

This may sound remarkably like Royce's view, except perhaps for Howison's insistence that the spring of the activity of each spirit is to be sought within itself. But Howison tries to avoid what he regards as the logical and disastrous consequences of Royce's philosophy by emphasizing final causality. God is represented as the personified ideal of every spirit. By this Howison does not mean that God has no existence except as a human ideal. He means that the mode of divine action on the human spirit is that of final causality, rather than that of efficient causality. God draws the finite self as an ideal; but the self's response to God is its own activity rather than the action of God or the Absolute. In other words, God acts by illuminating the reason and attracting the will to the ideal of the unity of free spirits in himself rather than by determining the human will through efficient causality or the exercise of power.

2. Another participant in the discussion referred to above was Joseph Le Conte (1823–1901), professor in the University of California. Trained as a geologist, Le Conte interested himself in the philosophical aspects of the theory of evolution and expounded what can be described as evolutionary idealism.[1] As the ultimate source of evolution he saw a divine Energy which expresses itself immediately in the physical and chemical forces of Nature. But the efflux of this divine Energy becomes progressively individuated concomitantly with the advancing organization of matter. Le Conte's philosophy is thus pluralistic. For he maintains that in the process of evolution we find the emergence of successively higher forms of self-active individuals, until we reach the highest form of individual being yet attained, namely the human being. In man the efflux or spark of the divine life is able to recognize and to enter into conscious communion with its ultimate source. In fact we can look forward to a progressive elevation of man to the level of 'regenerated' man, enjoying a higher degree of spiritual and moral development.

Howison's approach to philosophy tended to be through the critical philosophy of Kant, when rethought in the light of metaphysical idealism. Le Conte's approach was rather by way of an attempt to show how the theory of evolution liberates science from all materialistic implications and points the way to a religious and ethical idealism. He exercised some influence on the mind of Royce.

3. Besides Howison, whose philosophy has been labelled as ethical idealism, one of the most influential representatives of personal idealism in America was Borden Parker Bowne (1847–1910). As a student at New York Bowne wrote a criticism of Spencer. During subsequent studies in Germany he came under the influence of Lotze, especially in regard to the latter's theory of the self.[2] In 1876 Bowne became Professor of Philosophy in the University of Boston. His writings include *Studies in Theism* (1879), *Metaphysics* (1882), *Philosophy of Theism* (1887), *Principles of Ethics* (1892), *The Theory of Thought and Knowledge* (1897), *The Immanence of God* (1905), and *Personalism* (1908). These

titles show clearly enough the religious orientation of his thought.

Bowne at first described his philosophy as transcendental empiricism, in view of the conspicuous role played in his thought by a doctrine of categories inspired by Kant. These are not simply empirically derived, fortuitous results of adaptation to environment in the process of evolution. At the same time they are the expression of the nature of the self and of its self-experience. And this shows that the self is an active unity and not a mere logical postulate, as Kant thought. Indeed, the self or person, characterized by intelligence and will, is the only real efficient cause. For efficient causality is essentially volitional. In Nature we find indeed uniformities, but no causality in the proper sense.

This idea of Nature forms the basis for a philosophy of God. Science describes how things happen. And it can be said to explain events, if we mean by this that it exhibits them as examples or cases of empirically discovered generalizations which are called 'laws'. 'But in the causal sense science explains nothing. Here the alternative is supernatural explanation or none.'[3] True, in science itself the idea of God is no more required than in shoemaking. For science is simply classificatory and descriptive. But once we turn to metaphysics, we see the order of Nature as the effect of the constant activity of a supreme rational will. In other words, as far as its causation is concerned, any event in Nature is as supernatural as a miracle would be. 'For in both alike God would be equally implicated.'[4]

We can now take a broad view of reality. If, as Bowne believes, to be real is to act, and if activity in the full sense can be attributed only to persons, it follows that it is only persons who are, so to speak, fully real. We thus have the picture of a system of persons standing to one another in various active relations through the instrumentality of the external world. And this system of persons must, according to Bowne, be the creation of a supreme Person, God. On the one hand a being which was less than personal could not be the sufficient cause of finite persons. On the other hand, if we can apply the category of causality to a world in which the infra-personal exercises no real efficient causality, this can only be because the world is the creation of a personal being who is immanently active in it. Ultimate reality thus appears as personal in character, as a system of persons with a supreme Person at their head.

Personalism, as Bowne came to call his philosophy, is 'the only metaphysics that does not dissolve away into self-cancelling abstractions'.[5] Auguste Comte, according to Bowne, was justified not only in confining science to the study of uniformities of co-existence and sequence among phenomena and in excluding from it all properly causal inquiry but also in rejecting metaphysics in so far as this is a study of abstract ideas and categories which are supposed to provide causal explanations. But personalism is immune from the objections which can be raised against metaphysics as Comte understood the term. For it does not seek the causal explanations which, on Comte's own showing, science cannot provide, in abstract categories. It sees in these categories simply the abstract forms of self-conscious life, and the ultimate causal explanation is found in a supreme rational will. True, personalist metaphysics may seem to involve a return to what Comte regarded as the first stage of human thought, namely the theological stage, in which explanations were sought in divine wills or in a divine will. But in personalism this stage is raised to a higher level, inasmuch as capricious wills are replaced by an infinite rational will.[6]

4. Objective idealism, as it is commonly called, had as its principal representative James Edwin Creighton (1861–1924), who in 1892 succeeded J. G. Schurman[7] as head of the Sage School at Cornell University. In 1902 he became the first president of the American Philosophical Association. His principal articles were collected and published posthumously in 1925 with the title *Studies in Speculative Philosophy*.[8]

Creighton distinguishes two types of idealism. The first, which he calls mentalism, is simply the antithesis of materialism. While the materialist interprets the psychical as a function of the physical, the mentalist reduces material things to psychical phenomena, to states of consciousness or to ideas. And as the material world cannot without absurdity be reduced to any given finite individual's states of consciousness, the mentalist is inevitably driven to postulate an absolute mind. The clearest example of this type of idealism is the philosophy of Berkeley. But there are variants, such as panpsychism.

The other main type of idealism is objective or speculative idealism, which does not attempt to reduce the physical to the psychical but regards Nature, the self and other selves as three distinct but co-ordinate and complementary moments or factors within experience. In other words, experience presents us with the ego, other selves and Nature as distinct and irreducible factors which are at the same time comprised within the unity of experience. And objective idealism attempts to work out the implications of this basic structure of experience.

For example, though Nature is irreducible to mind, the two are mutually related. Nature, therefore, cannot be simply heterogeneous to mind; it must be intelligible. And this means that though philosophy cannot do the work of the empirical sciences it is not committed merely to accepting the scientific account of Nature, without adding anything. Science puts Nature in the centre of the picture: philosophy exhibits it as a co-ordinate of experience, in its relation to spirit. This does not mean that the philosopher is competent to contradict, or even to call in question scientific discoveries. It means that it is his business to show the significance of the world as represented by the sciences in reference to the totality of experience. In other words, there is room for a philosophy of Nature.

Again, objective idealism is careful to avoid placing the ego in the centre of the picture by taking it as an ultimate point of departure and then trying to prove, for example, the existence of other selves. The objective idealist, while recognizing the distinction between individuals, recognizes also that there are no isolated individual selves apart from society. And he will study, for instance, the significance of morality, political institutions and religion as activities or products, as the case may be, of a society of selves within the human environment, namely Nature.

In conformity with these ideas, which have an obvious affinity with Hegelianism, the Cornell School of idealism emphasized the social aspect of thought. Instead of being divided up into as many systems as there are philosophers, philosophy should be, like science, a work of co-operation. For it is the reflection of spirit, existing in and through a society of selves, rather than of the individual thinker considered precisely as such.

5. Objective idealism, represented chiefly by Creighton, was associated with Cornell University. Another form of idealism, so-called dynamic idealism, was associated with the University of Michigan, where it was expounded by George Sylvester Morris (1840–89).[9] After having studied at Dartmouth College and the Union Theological Seminary at New York, Morris passed some years in Germany, where he came under the influence of Trendelenburg[10] at Berlin. In 1870 he began to teach modern languages and literature at Michigan, and from 1878 he also lectured on ethics and the history of philosophy at Johns Hopkins University. Subsequently he became dean of the philosophical faculty at Michigan. His writings include *British Thought and Thinkers* (1880), *Philosophy and Christianity* (1883), and *Hegel's Philosophy of the State and of History: An Exposition* (1887). He also translated into English Ueberweg's *History of Philosophy* (1871–3), in the second volume of which he inserted an article on Trendelenburg.

Under the influence of Trendelenburg Morris placed in the forefront of his philosophy the Aristotelian idea of movement, that is, of the actualization of a potentiality, of the active expression of an entelechy. Life is obviously movement, energy; but thought too is a spontaneous activity, akin to other forms of natural energy. And it follows from this that the history of thought is not properly described as a dialectical development of abstract ideas or categories. Rather is it the expression of the activity of the spirit or mind. And philosophy is the science[11] of the mind as an active entelechy. That is to say, it is the science of experience in act or of lived experience.

To say that philosophy is the science of the activity of the spirit or mind, of experience in act, is not, however, to say that it has no connection with being. For the analysis of experience shows that subject and object, knowledge and being, are correlative terms. That which exists or has being is that which is known or knowable. It is that which falls within the potential field of active experience. And this is why we have to reject the Kantian Theory of the unknowable thing-in-itself, together with the phenomenalism which produces this theory.[12]

In his later years Morris moved closer to Hegel, whom he regarded as an 'objective empiricist', concerned with the integration of human experience by the reason. His most famous pupil was John Dewey, though Dewey came to abandon idealism for the instrumentalism associated with his name.

6. Idealism in America obviously owed much to the influence of European thought. But equally obviously, it proved congenial to many minds and received a native stamp, which is shown above all perhaps in the emphasis so often placed on personality. It is not surprising, therefore, that American idealism was by no means simply a nineteenth-century phenomenon, due to the discovery of German thought and to influence from British idealism. It has shown a vigorous life in the present century.

Among the representatives of personal idealism in the first half of the twentieth century we can mention the names of Ralph Tyler Flewelling (1871–), for many years a Professor of Philosophy in the University of South California and founder of *The Personalist* in 1920,[13] Albert Cornelius Knudson (1873–1953)[14] and Edgar Sheffield Brightman (1884–1953), Bowne Professor of Philosophy in the University of Boston.[15] The titles of their publications provide abundant evidence of the continuation of that religious orientation of personalism which we have already had occasion to notice. But apart from the fact that it is so often religiously minded people who are attracted in the first instance to personal idealism, there is, as has been mentioned above, an intrinsic reason for the religious orientation of this line of thought. The basic tenet of personalism has been stated as the principle that reality has no meaning except in relation to persons; that the real is only in, of or for persons. In other words, reality consists of persons and their creations. It follows, therefore, that unless the personal idealist equates ultimate reality with the system of finite selves, as McTaggart did, he must be a theist. There is room, of course, for some-what different conceptions of God. Brightman, for example, maintained that God is finite.[16] But a concern not only with philosophical theism but also with religion as a form of ex-perience is a universal feature of American personal idealism.

This is not to say, however, that the personal idealists have been concerned only with the defence of a religious outlook. For they have also devoted their attention to the subject of values, connecting them closely with the idea of the self-realization or development of personality. And this in turn has reacted on the theory of education, emphasis being laid on moral development and the cultivation of personal values. Finally, in political theory this type of idealism, with its in-sistence on freedom and on respect for the person as such, has been sharply opposed to totalitarianism and a strong ad-vocate of democracy.

Evolutionary idealism has been represented in the first half of the present century by John Elof Boodin (1869–1950).[17] The main idea of this type of idealism is familiar enough, namely that in the evolutionary process we can see the emer-gence of successively higher levels of development through the creative activity of an immanent principle, the nature of which should be interpreted in the light of its higher rather than of its lower products.[18] In other words, evolutionary idealism substitutes for a purely mechanistic conception of evolution, based on laws relating to the redistribution of en-ergy, a teleological conception according to which mechanical processes take place within a general creative movement tending towards an ideal goal.[19] Thus Boodin distinguishes between different interacting levels or fields in the evolution-ary process or processes, in each of which there are interacting individual systems of energy. These levels or fields range from the primary physico-chemical level up to the ethical-social level. And the all-inclusive field is the divine creative spirit, 'the spiritual field in which everything lives and moves and has its being'.[20]

Evolutionary idealism does not indeed deny the value of human personality. For Boodin the human spirit participates in the divine creativity by the realization of values. At the same time, inasmuch as the evolutionary idealist fixes his attention chiefly on the total cosmic process rather than on the finite self,[21] he is more inclined than the personal idealist to a pantheistic conception of God. And this tendency is verified in the case of Boodin.

Absolute idealism has been continued in the present century by the well-known philosopher William Ernest Hocking (b. 1873), a pupil of Royce and William James at Harvard and later Alford Professor of Philosophy in that University.[22] At the level of common sense, Hocking argues, physical objects and other minds appear as entities which are purely external to myself. And it is at this level that the question arises how we come to know that there are other minds or other selves. But reflection shows us that there is an underlying social consciousness which is as real as self-consciousness. In fact they are interdependent. After all, the very attempt to prove that there are other minds presupposes an awareness of them. And further reflection, Hocking maintains, together with intuitive insight, reveals to us the presence of the enveloping divine reality which renders human consciousness possible. That is to say, our participation in social consciousness involves an implicit awareness of God and is in some sense an experience of the divine, of absolute mind. Hence the ontological argument can be stated in this way: 'I have an idea of God, therefore I have an experience of God'.[23]

We have noted that Hocking was a pupil of Royce. And like his former professor he insists that God is personal, a self. For 'there is nothing higher than selfhood and nothing more profound'.[24] At the same time he insists that we cannot abandon the concept of the Absolute. And this means that we must conceive God as in some sense including within himself the world of finite selves and the world of Nature. Indeed, just as the human self, taken apart from its life of experience, is empty, so is the concept of God an empty concept if he is considered apart from his life of absolute experience. 'The domain of religion in fact is a divine self, a Spirit which is as Subject to all finite things, persons and arts as Object, and presumably to much else that these categories do not include.'[25] The world is thus necessary to God, though at the same time we can conceive it as created. For

Nature is in fact an expression of the divine mind, as well as the means by which finite selves communicate with one another and pursue common ideals. In addition to the scientific view of Nature, which treats Nature as a self-contained whole, we need the concept of it as a divine communication to the finite self. As for the divine essence in itself, it transcends the grasp of discursive thought, though mystical experience yields a valid insight.

With Hocking, therefore, as with Royce, we find a form of personalistic absolute idealism. He tries to find a middle position between a theism which would reduce God to the level of being a self among selves, a person among persons, and an absolute idealism which would leave no room for the concept of God as personal. And this desire to find a middle position is shown in Hocking's treatment of religion. On the one hand he dislikes the tendency, shown by some philosophers, to offer as the alleged essence of religion a concept which abstracts from all historical religion. On the other hand he rejects the notion of one particular historical faith becoming the world-faith by displacing all others. And though he attributes to Christianity a unique contribution to the recognition of the ultimate personal structure of reality, he looks to a process of dialogue between the great historical religions to produce, by a convergent movement, the world-faith of the future.

We have already had occasion more than once to note the concern of American idealists with religious problems. It is hardly an exaggeration to say that with some of the personal idealists, such as Bowne, philosophy was practically used as an apologetic in defence of the Christian religion. In the case of personalistic absolute idealism,[26] however, as with Hocking, it is more a question of developing a religious view of the world and of suggesting a religious vision for the future than of defending a particular historical religion. And this is clearly more in line with W. T. Harris's programme for speculative philosophy. For Harris assumed that traditional doctrines and ecclesiastical organization were in process of losing their grip on men's minds, that a new religious outlook was needed, and that it was part of the business of speculative philosophy or metaphysical idealism to meet this need.

At the same time idealism does not necessarily involve ei-

ther the defence of an already existing religion or positive
preparation for a new one. It is, of course, natural to expect
of the metaphysical idealist some interest in religion or at
least an explicit recognition of its importance in human life.
For he aims, in general, at a synthesis of human experience,
and in particular, at doing justice to those forms of experience
which the materialist and positivist tend either to belittle
or to exclude from the scope of philosophy. But it would be
a mistake to think that idealism is necessarily so connected
either with Christian faith or with the mystical outlook of a
philosopher such as Hocking that it is inseparable from pro-
foundly held religious convictions. A preoccupation with religious problems was not a characteristic of the objective idealism of Creighton; nor is it a characteristic of the thought
of Brand Blanshard (b. 1892), Sterling Professor of Philosophy at Yale, the twentieth-century American idealist who is
best known in Great Britain.[27]

In his notable two-volume work, *The Nature of Thought*
(1939–40), Blanshard devotes himself to critical analyses of
interpretations of thought and knowledge which he considers
false or inadequate and to a defence of reason conceived
primarily as the discovery of necessary connections. He rejects the restriction of necessity to purely formal propositions
and its reduction to convention, and he represents the movement of thought as being towards the logical ideal of an all-
inclusive system of interdependent truths. In other words, he
maintains a version of the coherence theory of truth. Similarly, in *Reason and Analysis* (1962) Blanshard devotes himself on the negative side to a sustained criticism of the
analytic philosophy of the last forty years, including logical
positivism, logical atomism and the so-called linguistic movement, and on the positive side to an exposition and defence
of the function of reason as he conceives it. True, he has
given two series of Gifford Lectures. But in *Reason and Goodness* (1961), which represents the first series, the emphasis
is laid on vindicating the function of reason in ethics, as
against, for example, the emotive theory of ethics, certainly
not on edification, either moral or religious.[28]

These remarks are not intended either as commendation
or as criticism of Blanshard's freedom from the preoccupa-

tion with religious problems and from the tone of uplift which have been conspicuous features of many of the publications of American idealists. The point is rather that the example of Blanshard shows that idealism is able to make out a good case for itself and to deal shrewd blows at its enemies without exhibiting the features which in the eyes of some of its critics rule it out of court from the start, as though by its very nature it served extra-philosophical interests. After all, Hegel himself deprecated any confusion between philosophy and uplift and rejected appeals to mystical insights.

7. In Marxist terminology idealism is commonly opposed to materialism, as involving respectively the assertion of the ultimate priority of mind or spirit to matter and the assertion of the ultimate priority of matter to mind or spirit. And if idealism is understood in this way, no synthesis of the opposites is possible. For the essential dispute is not about the reality of either mind or matter. It is about the question of ultimate priority. And both cannot be ultimately prior at the same time.

Generally, however, idealism is contrasted with realism. It is by no means always clear how these terms are being understood. And in any case their meanings can vary with different contexts. But an attempt has been made by an American philosopher, Wilbur Marshall Urban (b. 1873),[29] to show that idealism and realism are ultimately based on certain judgments of value about the conditions of genuine knowledge, and that these judgments can be dialectically harmonized. He does not mean, of course, that opposed philosophical systems can be conflated. He means that the basic judgments on which idealist and realist philosophies ultimately rest can be so interpreted that it is possible to transcend the opposition between idealism and realism.

The realist, Urban maintains, believes that there cannot be genuine knowledge unless things are in some sense independent of mind. In other words, he asserts the priority of being to knowledge. The idealist, however, believes that there can be no genuine knowledge unless things are in some sense dependent on mind. For their intelligibility is bound up with this dependence. At first sight, therefore, realism and idealism are incompatible, the first asserting the priority of being to thought and knowledge, the second asserting the priority of thought to being. But if we consider the basic judgments of value, we can see the possibility of overcoming the opposition between them. For example, the realist claim that knowledge cannot be described as genuine knowledge of reality unless things are in some sense independent of mind can be satisfied provided that we are willing to admit that things are not dependent simply on the human mind, while the idealist claim that knowledge cannot be described as genuine knowledge of reality unless things are in some sense mind-dependent can be satisfied if it is assumed that the reality on which on all finite things ultimately depend is spirit or mind.

It seems to the present writer that there is a great deal of truth in this point of view. Absolute idealism, by rejecting the claim of subjective idealism that the human mind can know only its own states of consciousness, goes a long way towards meeting the realist's claim that genuine knowledge of reality is not possible unless the object of knowledge is in some real sense independent of the subject. And a realism that is prepared to describe ultimate reality as spirit or mind goes a long way towards meeting the idealist claim that nothing is intelligible unless it is either spirit or the self-expression of spirit. At the same time the dialectical harmonization of opposed views, which Urban has in mind, seems to demand certain stipulations. We have to stipulate, for example, that the idealist should cease talking like Royce, who uses the word 'being' for the expression of will and purpose, for the embodiment of the internal meaning of an idea, and should recognize that will is itself a form of being. In fact, to reach agreement with the realist he must, it appears, recognize the priority of existence; *prius est esse quam esse tale*. If, however, he admits this, he has to all intents and purposes been converted to realism. We also have to stipulate, of course, that realism should not be understood as equivalent to materialism. But then many realists would insist that realism in no way entails materialism.

The ideal of transcending the traditional oppositions in philosophy is understandable, and doubtless laudable. But there is this point to consider. If we interpret realism in terms of basic judgments of value about the conditions of genuine knowledge, we have implicitly adopted a certain approach to philosophy. We are approaching philosophy by way of the theme of knowledge, by way of the subject-object relationship. And many philosophers who are customarily labelled realists doubtless do this. We speak, for example, of realist theories of knowledge. But some realists would claim that they take as their point of departure being, particularly in the sense of existence, and that their approach is recognizably different from that of the idealist, and that it is the different approaches to philosophy which determine the different views of knowledge.

PART IV

THE PRAGMATIST MOVEMENT

Chapter Fourteen

THE PHILOSOPHY OF C. S. PEIRCE

The life of Peirce – The objectivity of truth – Rejection of the method of universal doubt – Logic, ideas and the pragmatist analysis of meaning – Pragmatism and realism – The pragmatist analysis of meaning and positivism – Ethics, pure and practical – Peirce's metaphysics and world-view – Some comments on Peirce's thought.

1. Although it is possible to find pragmatist ideas in the writings of some other thinkers,[1] the originator of the pragmatist movement in America was to all intents and purposes Charles Sanders Peirce (1839–1914). To be sure, the term 'pragmatism' is associated chiefly with the name of William James. For James's style as lecturer and writer and his obvious concern with general problems of interest to reflective minds quickly brought him before the public eye and kept him there, whereas during his lifetime Peirce was little known or appreciated as a philosopher. But both James and Dewey recognized their indebtedness to Peirce. And after his death Peirce's reputation has steadily increased, even if, by the nature of his thought, he remains very much a philosopher's philosopher.

Peirce was the son of a Harvard mathematician and astronomer, Benjamin Peirce (1809–80), and his own formal education culminated in the chemistry degree which he received at Harvard in 1863. From 1861 until 1891 he was on the staff of the United States Coast and Geodetic Survey, though from 1869 he was also associated for some years with the Harvard Observatory. And the one book which he published, *Photometric Researches* (1878), embodied the results of a series of astronomical observations which he had made.

In the academic years of 1864-5 and 1869-70 Peirce lectured at Harvard on the early history of modern science, and in 1870-1 on logic.[2] From 1879 until 1884 he was a lecturer on logic at Johns Hopkins University; but for various reasons his appointment was not renewed.[3] And he never again held any regular academic post, in spite of William James's efforts on his behalf.

In 1887 Peirce settled with his second wife in Pennsylvania and tried to make ends meet by writing reviews and articles for dictionaries. He wrote indeed a great deal, but apart from a few articles his work remained unpublished until the posthumous publication of his *Collected Papers*, six volumes appearing in 1931-5 and two further volumes in 1958.

Peirce did not approve of the way in which William James was developing the theory of pragmatism, and in 1905 he changed the name of his own theory from pragmatism to pragmaticism, remarking that the term was ugly enough to render it secure from kidnappers. At the same time he appreciated the friendship of James, who did what he could to put remunerative work in the way of the neglected and poverty-stricken philosopher. Peirce died of cancer in 1914.

2. It is probably correct to say that in the minds of most people for whom the word 'pragmatism' has any definite meaning, it is associated primarily with a certain view of the nature of truth, namely with the doctrine that a theory is to be accounted true in so far as it 'works', in so far, for example, as it is socially useful or fruitful. It is therefore just as well to understand from the outset that the essence of Peirce's pragmatism or pragmaticism lies in a theory of meaning rather than in a theory of truth. This theory of meaning will be examined presently. Meanwhile we can consider briefly what Peirce has to say about truth. And it will be seen that whether or not the identification of truth with 'what works' represents the real view of William James, it certainly does not represent that of Peirce.

Peirce distinguishes different kinds of truth. There is, for

example, what he calls transcendental truth, which belongs to
things as things.[4] And if we say that science is looking for
truth in this sense, we mean that it is inquiring into the real
characters of things, the characters which they have whether
we know that they have them or not. But here we are concerned with what Peirce calls complex truth, which is the
truth of propositions. This again can be subdivided. There
is, for example, ethical truth or veracity, which lies in the
conformity of a proposition with the speaker's or writer's belief. And there is logical truth, the conformity of a proposition with reality in a sense which must now be defined.

'When we speak of truth and falsity, we refer to the possibility of the proposition being refuted.'[5] That is to say, if
we could legitimately deduce from a proposition a conclusion
which would conflict with an immediate perceptual judgment,
the proposition would be false. In other words, a proposition
would be false if experience would refute it. If experience
would not refute a proposition, the proposition is true.

This may suggest that for Peirce truth and verification are
the same thing. But reflection will show that he is perfectly
justified in rejecting this identification. For he is saying, not
that a proposition is true if it is empirically verified, but that
it is true if it would not be empirically falsified, supposing
that such a testing were possible. In point of fact it may not
be possible. But we can still say that a proposition is false
if, to put it crudely, it *would* conflict with reality as revealed
in experience if a confrontation were possible, and that otherwise it is true. Peirce can therefore say without inconsistency
that 'every proposition is either *true* or *false*'.[6]

Now, there are some propositions which could not conceivably be refuted. Such, for example, are the propositions
of pure mathematics. Hence on the interpretation of truth
mentioned above the truth of a proposition in pure mathematics lies in 'the impossibility of ever finding a case in which
it fails'.[7] Peirce sometimes writes in a rather disconcerting
way about mathematics. He says, for instance, that the pure
mathematician deals exclusively with hypotheses which are
the products of his own imagination, and that no proposition
becomes a statement of pure mathematics 'until it is devoid
of all definite meaning'.[8] But 'meaning' has to be under-

stood here in the sense of reference. A proposition of pure mathematics does not say anything about actual things:[9] the pure mathematician, as Peirce puts it, does not care whether or not there are real things corresponding to his signs. And this absence of 'meaning' is, of course, the reason why the propositions of pure mathematics cannot possibly be refuted and so are necessarily true.

There are other propositions, however, of which we do not know with absolute certainty whether they are true or false. These are what Leibniz calls truths of fact, in distinction from truths of reason. And they include, for example, scientific hypotheses and metaphysical theories about reality. In the case of a proposition which cannot possibly be refuted we know that it is true.[10] But a scientific hypothesis can *be* true without our knowing that it is. And in point of fact we cannot know with certainty that it is true. For while empirical refutation shows that an hypothesis is false, what we call verification does not prove that an hypothesis is true, though it certainly provides a ground for accepting it provisionally. If from hypothesis x it is legitimately deduced that in certain circumstances event y should occur, and if in these circumstances y does not occur, we can conclude that x is false. But the occurrence of y does not prove with certainty that x is true. For it may be the case, for example, that the conclusion that in the same set of circumstances event y should occur, can be deduced from hypothesis z, which on other grounds is preferable to x. Scientific hypotheses can enjoy varying degrees of probability, but they are all subject to possible revision. In fact all formulations of what passes for human knowledge are uncertain, fallible.[11]

It should not be necessary to add that Peirce's principle of fallibilism does not entail a denial of objective truth. Scientific inquiry is inspired by a disinterested search for objective truth. Nobody would ask a theoretical question unless he believed that there was such a thing as truth. And 'truth consists in a conformity of something *independent of his thinking it to be so,* or of any man's opinion on that subject'.[12] But if we combine the idea of the disinterested search for objective truth, known as such, with the principle of fallibilism, according to which dogmatism is the enemy of the pursuit of truth, we must conceive absolute and final truth as the ideal goal of inquiry. This ideal stands eternally above our struggles to attain it, and we can only approximate to it.

Truth, therefore, can be defined from different points of view. From one point of view truth can be taken to mean 'the Universe of all Truth'.[13] 'All propositions refer to one and the same determinately singular subject . . . namely, to The Truth, which is the universe of all universes, and is assumed on all hands to be real.'[14] From an epistemological point of view, however, truth can be defined as 'that concordance of an abstract statement with the ideal limit towards which endless investigation would tend to bring scientific belief'.[15]

If such passages recall to our minds the idealist notion of truth as the whole, the total system of truth, rather than anything which would normally be associated with the term 'pragmatism', there is nothing to be surprised at in this. For Peirce openly acknowledged points of similarity between his own philosophy and that of Hegel.

3. In regard to the pursuit of truth Peirce rejects the Cartesian thesis that we should begin by doubting everything until we can find an indubitable and presuppositionless point of departure. In the first place we cannot doubt simply at will. Real or genuine doubt arises when some experience, external or internal, clashes or appears to clash with one of our beliefs. And when this occurs, we undertake further inquiry with a view to overcoming the state of doubt, either by reestablishing our former belief on a firmer basis or by substituting for it a better-grounded belief. Doubt is thus a stimulus to inquiry, and in this sense it has a positive value. But to doubt the truth of a proposition, we must have a reason for doubting the truth of *this* proposition or of a proposition on which it depends. Any attempt to apply the method of universal doubt simply leads to pretended or fictitious doubt. And this is not genuine doubt at all.

Peirce is obviously thinking in the first place of scientific inquiry. But he applies his ideas in a quite general way. We all start with certain beliefs, with what Hume called natural beliefs. And the philosopher will indeed try to make explicit our uncriticized natural beliefs and subject them to critical scrutiny. But even he cannot doubt them at will: he requires a reason for doubting the truth of this or that particular belief. And if he has or thinks that he has such a reason, he will also find that his very doubt presupposes some other belief or beliefs. In other words, we cannot have, nor do we need, an absolutely presuppositionless point of departure. Cartesian universal doubt is not genuine doubt at all. 'For genuine doubt does not talk of beginning with doubting.'[16] The follower of Descartes would presumably reply that he is primarily concerned with 'methodic' rather than with 'real' or 'genuine' doubt. But Peirce's point is that methodic doubt, in so far as it is distinguishable from genuine doubt, is not really doubt at all. Either we have a reason for doubting or we do not. In the first case the doubt is genuine. In the second case we have only pretended or fictitious doubt.

If we bear in mind this point of view, we can understand Peirce's claim that 'the scientific spirit requires a man to be at all times ready to dump his whole cartload of beliefs, the moment experience is against them'.[17] He is obviously speaking of theoretical beliefs, which are characterized above all by expectation. If a man holds belief x, he believes, for example, that in certain circumstances event y should occur. And if it does not occur, he will, of course, doubt the truth of the belief. Antecedently to a clash between experience and belief, anyone who possesses the scientific spirit will be prepared to abandon any belief about the world if such a clash should occur. For, as we have already seen, he regards all such beliefs as subject to possible revision. But it by no means follows from this that he will begin or should begin with universal doubt.

4. Pragmatism, as Peirce conceives it, is 'not a *Weltanschauung* but is a method of reflection having for its purpose to render ideas clear'.[18] It belongs, therefore, to methodology, to what Peirce calls 'methodeutic'. And as he emphasizes the logical foundations and connections of pragmatism, it is appropriate to say something first about his account of logic.

Peirce divides logic into three main parts, the first of which is speculative grammar. This is concerned with the formal conditions of the meaningfulness of signs. A sign, called by Peirce a 'representamen', stands for an object to someone in whom it arouses a more developed sign, the 'interpretant'. A sign stands, of course, for an object in respect of certain 'characters', and this respect is called the 'ground'. But we can say that the relation of significance or the semiotic function of signs is for Peirce a triadic relation between representamen, object and interpretant.[19]

The second main division of logic, critical logic, is concerned with the formal conditions of the truth of symbols. Under this heading Peirce treats of the syllogism or argument, which can be divided into deductive, inductive and 'abductive' argument. Inductive argument, which is statistical in character, assumes that what is true of a number of members of a class is true of all members of the class. And it is in connection with induction that Peirce considers the theory of probability. Abductive argument is predictive in character. That is to say, it formulates an hypothesis from observed facts and deduces what should be the case if the hypothesis is true. And we can then test the prediction. When looked at from one point of view, Royce tells us, pragmatism can be described as the logic of abduction. The force of this remark will become clear presently.

The third main division of logic, speculative rhetoric, deals with what Peirce calls the formal conditions of the force of symbols or 'the general conditions of the reference of Symbols and other Signs to the Interpretants which they aim to determine'.[20] In communication a sign arouses another sign, the interpretant, in an interpreter. Peirce insists that the interpreter is not necessarily a human being. And as he wishes to avoid psychology as much as possible, he lays emphasis on the interpretant rather than on the interpreter. In any case it simplifies matters if we think of a sign arousing a sign in a person. We can then see that speculative rhetoric will be concerned in large measure with the theory of meaning. For meaning is 'the intended interpretant of a symbol'.[21] Whether we are speaking of a term, a proposition or an argument, its meaning is the entire intended interpretant. And as pragmatism is for Peirce a method or rule for determining meaning, it obviously belongs to or is closely connected with speculative rhetoric, which is also called 'methodeutic'.

More precisely, pragmatism is a method or rule for making

ideas clear, for determining the meaning of ideas. But there are different types of ideas.[22] First, there is the idea of a percept or sense-datum considered in itself, without relation to anything else. Such would be the idea of blueness or of redness. In Peirce's terminology this is the idea of a 'firstness'. Secondly, there is the idea of acting which involves two objects, namely the agent and the patient or that which is acted upon. This is the idea of a 'secondness'.[23] Thirdly, there is the idea of a sign relation, of a sign signifying to an interpreter that a certain property belongs to a certain object or, rather, to a certain kind of object. This is an idea of a 'thirdness'. And such ideas, which can be thought of as universal ideas, are called by Peirce intellectual concepts or conceptions.[24] In practice pragmatism is a method or rule for determining their meaning.

Peirce formulates the principle of pragmatism in several ways. One of the best known is as follows. *'In order to ascertain the meaning of an intellectual conception one should consider what practical consequences might conceivably result by necessity from the truth of that conception; and the sum of these consequences will constitute the entire meaning of the conception.'*[25] For example, suppose that someone tells me that a certain kind of object is hard, and suppose that I do not know what the word 'hard' means. It can be explained to me that to say that an object is hard means, among other things, that if one exerts moderate pressure on it, it does not give in the way that butter does; that if someone sits on it, he does not sink through; and so on. And the sum total of 'practical consequences' which necessarily follow if it is true to say that an object is hard, gives the entire meaning of the concept. If I do not believe this, I have only to exclude all such 'practical consequences' from the meaning of the term. I shall then see that it becomes impossible to distinguish between the meanings of 'hard' and 'soft'.

Now, if we understand Peirce as saying that the meaning of an intellectual concept is reducible to the ideas of certain sense-data, we shall have to conclude that he is contradicting his assertion that intellectual concepts are not reducible to ideas of 'firstness'. And if we understand him as saying that the meaning of an intellectual concept is reducible to the ideas of certain actions, we shall have to conclude that he is contradicting his assertion that such concepts are not reducible to ideas of 'secondness'. But he is saying neither the one nor the other. His view is that the meaning of an intellectual concept can be explicated in terms of the ideas of necessary relations between ideas of secondness and ideas of firstness, between, that is to say, ideas of volition or action and ideas of perception. As he explains, when he talks about 'consequences', he is referring to the relation (*consequentia*) between a consequent and an antecedent, not simply about the consequent (*consequens*).

From this analysis it obviously follows that the meaning of an intellectual concept has a relation to conduct. For the conditional propositions in which the meaning is explicated are concerned with conduct. But, equally obviously, Peirce is not suggesting that in order to understand or to explain the meaning of an intellectual concept we have actually to do something, to perform certain actions mentioned in the explication of the meaning. I can explain to an interpreter the meaning of 'hard' by causing to arise in his mind the idea that if he were to perform a certain action in regard to the object which is described as hard, he *would* have a certain experience. It is not required that he should actually perform the action before he can understand what 'hard' means. It is not even necessary that the action should be practicable, provided that it is conceivable. In other words, the meaning of an intellectual concept is explicable in terms of conditional propositions; but, for the meaning to be understood, it is not necessary that the conditions should be actually fulfilled. It is only necessary that they should be conceived.

It is to be noted that this theory of meaning does not contradict Peirce's view, which has been mentioned above, that we must distinguish between truth and verification. If, for example, I say that a given object has weight, and if I explain that this means that in the absence of an opposing force it will fall, the fulfilment of the conditional proposition is said to verify my statement. But to verify means to show that a proposition is true, that is, that it is true antecedently to any verification, true independently of any action performed by me or by anyone else.

5. Although it involves touching on ontology, it is convenient at this point to draw attention to Peirce's conviction that the pragmatist theory of meaning demands the rejection of nominalism and the acceptance of realism. An intellectual concept is a universal concept; and its meaning is explicated in conditional propositions. These conditional propositions are in principle verifiable. And the possibility of verification shows that some at least of the propositions which explicate the meaning of intellectual concepts express something in reality which is so independently of its being expressed in a judgment. For example, a statement such as 'iron is hard' is a prediction: if x, then y. And regularly successful or verified prediction shows that there must be something real now, of a general nature, which accounts for a future actuality. This something real now is for Peirce a real possibility. He compares it to the essence or common nature in the philosophy of Duns Scotus;[26] but for him it has a relational structure, expressed in the conditional proposition which explicates the meaning of a universal concept. Hence he calls it a 'law'. Universal concepts, therefore, have an objective foundation or counterpart in reality, namely 'laws'.

We have been speaking of ideas of thirdness. But Peirce's realism can also be seen in his account of ideas of firstness. The idea of white, for example, has its objective counterpart in reality, namely, not simply white things but whiteness, an essence. Whiteness as such does not indeed exist as an actuality. Only white things exist in this way. But for Peirce whiteness is a real possibility. From the epistemological point of view it is the real possibility of an idea, an idea of a firstness.[27]

In general, human knowledge and science demand as a necessary condition the existence of a realm of real possibilities, 'essences', of a general nature. Hence we cannot accept the nominalist thesis that generality belongs only to words in their function as standing for a plurality of individual entities.[28]

6. When we read the formulation of the pragmatist principle which is quoted in the fourth section of this chapter,[29] we are naturally put in mind of the neopositivist criterion of meaning. But in order to be able to discuss the relation be-

tween Peirce's theory of meaning and positivism, we have first
to make some distinctions with a view to clarifying the issue.

In the first place, when Peirce himself talks about positivism, he is speaking, needless to say, of classical positivism as
represented, for example, by Auguste Comte and Karl Pearson. And while he allows that positivism in this sense has
been of service to science, he also explicitly attacks some features which he finds in it or at any rate attributes to it. For
instance, he attributes to Comte the view that a genuine
hypothesis must be practically verifiable by direct observation; and he proceeds to reject this view, on the ground that
for an hypothesis to be meaningful it is required only that
we should be able to *conceive* its practical consequences, not
that it should be practically verifiable. Again, Peirce refuses
to allow that nothing except what is directly observable
should be postulated in an hypothesis. For in an hypothesis
we infer the future, a 'will be' or 'would be', and a 'would be'
is certainly not directly observable.[30] Further, it is a mistake
to regard hypotheses as being simply fictional devices for
stimulating observation. An hypothesis can have, for example,
an initial probability, as being the result of legitimate inference. In general, therefore, Peirce regards the positivists as
too preoccupied with the process of practical verification and
as being far too quick to say that this or that is inconceivable.

We cannot, however, infer without more ado from Peirce's
criticism of Comte and Pearson that his theory of meaning
has nothing in common with neopositivism (or logical positivism as it is generally called in England). For though the
neopositivists were originally given to identifying the meaning of an empirical hypothesis with its mode of verification,
they did not intend to imply that its meaning can be identified with the actual process of verification. They identified
the meaning with the *idea* of the mode of verification, considered, in Peirce's terminology, as the practical consequences
of the hypothesis. Further, they did not insist that an hypothesis should be directly verifiable, in order to be meaningful. It is not the intention of the present writer to express
agreement with the neopositivist criterion of meaning. In
point of fact he does not agree with it. But this is irrelevant.
The relevant point is that the theory of meaning expounded

by the neopositivists escapes at any rate some of the criticisms which Peirce levelled, whether fairly or unfairly, against positivism as he knew it.

It must also be emphasized that the question is not whether Peirce was or was not a positivist. For it is perfectly clear that he was not. As will be seen presently, he sketched a metaphysics which under some aspects at least bore a resemblance to Hegelian absolute idealism. The question is rather whether the neopositivists are justified in looking on Peirce as a predecessor, not only in the sense that his 'pragmaticist' analysis of meaning has a clear affinity to their own but also in the sense that genuine consistency with his theory of meaning would have ruled out the sort of metaphysics which he in fact developed. In other words, once given his theory of meaning, ought Peirce to have been a positivist? That is to say, ought he to have anticipated neopositivism to a much greater extent than was in fact the case?

In his well-known paper on *How to make our ideas clear* Peirce asserts that 'the essence of belief is the establishment of a habit; and different beliefs are distinguished by the different modes of action to which they give rise'.[31] If there is no difference at all between the lines of conduct or action to which two *prima facie* different beliefs give rise, they are not two beliefs but one.

It is easy to think of a simple example. If one man says that he believes that there are other persons besides himself while another man says that he believes the opposite, and if we find them acting in precisely the same way by talking with others, questioning them, listening to them, writing them letters and so on, we naturally conclude that, whatever he may say, the second man really has exactly the same belief as the first man, namely that there are other persons besides himself.

Peirce applies this idea to the alleged difference in belief between Catholics and Protestants in regard to the Eucharist,[32] maintaining that as there is no difference in action or conduct between the two parties, there cannot be any real difference in belief. At first sight at any rate this thesis appears to be in flat contradiction with the facts. For example, practising Catholics genuflect before the Blessed Sacrament, pray before the Tabernacle in which the Blessed Sacrament is reserved, and so on, while the Protestants whom Peirce has in mind do not, for the very good reason that they do not believe in the 'real presence'. But closer inspection of what Peirce says on the subject shows that he is really arguing that Catholics and Protestants have the same expectations in regard to the sensible effects of the Sacrament. For, irrespective of their theological beliefs, both parties expect, for example, that consumption of the consecrated bread will have the same physical effects as consumption of unconsecrated bread. And this is, of course, quite true. The Catholic who believes in transubstantiation does not deny that after the consecration the 'species' of bread will have the same sensible effects as unconsecrated bread.

The relevance of Peirce's argument to the subject of his relation to positivism may not be immediately apparent. But in point of fact his line of argument is extremely relevant. For he explicitly says that he wishes to point out 'how impossible it is that we should have an idea in our minds which relates to anything but conceived sensible effects of things. Our idea of anything *is* our idea of its sensible effects; and if we fancy that we have any other we deceive ourselves, and mistake a mere sensation accompanying the thought for a part of the thought itself.'[33] In the immediate context this means that to agree that an object has all the sensible effects of bread and to claim at the same time that it is really the Body of Christ is to indulge in 'senseless jargon'.[34] In a wider context it seems to follow clearly from Peirce's thesis that all metaphysical talk about spiritual realities which cannot be construed as talk about 'sensible effects' is nonsense, or that it has no more than emotive significance.

Needless to say, we are not concerned here with theological controversy between Catholics and Protestants. The point of referring to the passage in which Peirce mentions the matter is simply that in it he explicitly states that our idea of anything *is* the idea of its sensible effects. If such a statement does not give good ground for the contention that certain aspects of Peirce's thought constitute an anticipation of neopositivism, it is difficult to think of statements which would do so. But this does not alter the fact that there are other aspects of his thought which differentiate it sharply enough from positivism. Nor, as far as I know, has anyone attempted to deny the fact.

7. Turning to ethics, we can note that it is described by Peirce in various ways, as, for example, the science of right and wrong, the science of ideals, the philosophy of aims. But he also tells us that 'we are too apt to define ethics to ourselves as the science of right and wrong'.[35] To be sure, ethics is concerned with right and wrong; but the fundamental question is, 'What am I to aim at, what am I after?'[36] In other words, the fundamental problem of ethics is that of determining the end of ethical conduct, conduct meaning here deliberate or self-controlled action. The concept of the good is thus basic in Peirce's ethics.

For Peirce, therefore, ethics consists of two main divisions. Pure ethics inquires into the nature of the ideal, the *summum bonum* or ultimate aim of conduct. 'Life can have but one end. It is Ethics which defines that end.'[37] Practical ethics is concerned with the conformity of action to the ideal, to the end. The former, pure ethics, can be called a prenormative science, while practical ethics is strictly normative in character. Both are required. On the one hand a system of practical ethics gives us a programme for future deliberate or controlled conduct. But all deliberate conduct has an aim; it is for the sake of an end. And as the ultimate end or aim is determined in pure ethics, this is presupposed by practical ethics. On the other hand pragmatism requires that the concept of the end should be explicated in terms of conceived practical consequences, in conditional propositions relating to deliberate or controlled conduct. It does not follow, however, that in ethics a pragmatist will be an advocate of action for the sake of action. For, as we have seen, deliberate or rational action, and it is with this that ethics is concerned, is directed to the realization of an end, an ideal.

'Pure ethics,' Peirce tells us, 'has been, and always must be, a theatre of discussion, for the reason that its study consists in the gradual development of a distinct recognition of a satisfactory aim.'[38] This satisfactory aim or end of conduct must be an infinite end, that is, one which can be pursued indefinitely. And this is to be found in what we may call the

rationalization of the universe. For the rational or reasonable is the only end which is fully satisfactory in itself. And
this means in effect that the *summum bonum* or supreme
good is really the evolutionary process itself considered as
the progressive rationalization of reality, as the process
whereby that which exists comes more and more to embody
rationality. The ultimate end is thus a cosmic end. But 'in
its higher stages evolution takes place more and more largely
through self-control'.[39] And this is where specifically human
action comes in. It is self-control which makes possible 'an
ought-to-be of conduct'.[40]

Peirce thus has the vision of the cosmic process as moving
towards the realization of reason or rationality, and of man as
co-operating in the process. Further, as the ultimate end is a
general end, a cosmic aim, so to speak, it follows that it must
be a social end, common to all men. Conscience, created and
modified by experience, is in a sense pre-ethical: it belongs
to what Peirce calls a community-consciousness, existing at a
level of the soul at which there are hardly distinct individuals.
And in point of fact a great part of one's moral vocation is
settled by one's place and function in the community to
which one belongs. But our vision should rise above the
limited social organism to 'a conceived identification of one's
interests with those of an unlimited community'.[41] And universal love is the all-important moral ideal.

Inasmuch as Peirce's pragmatism is primarily a theory of
meaning and a method of making our concepts clear, it is
primarily a matter of logic. But it has, of course, an application in ethics. For ethical concepts are to be interpreted in
terms of conceived modes of conduct, though, as we have
seen, reflection or deliberate or controlled conduct leads inevitably to reflection on the end of conduct. If we interpret
ethical concepts and propositions in terms of good and bad
consequences, we cannot avoid asking the question, what is
the good? In other words, pragmatism is not a doctrine simply of practice, of action for action's sake. Theory and practice, Peirce insists, go together. For the matter of that, pragmatism in its application to science is not a doctrine of action
for action's sake. We have already noted how Peirce rejected
what he regarded as the positivist worship of actual verifica-

tion. True, the pragmatist analysis of scientific hypotheses can be said to look forward to conduct or action; but in itself the analysis is a theoretical inquiry. Similarly, ethics looks forward to moral conduct; it is a normative science. But it is none the less a science, a theoretical inquiry, though it would, of course, be barren if no conduct resulted.

Sometimes Peirce speaks as though ethics were fundamental and logic an application of it. For thinking or reasoning is itself a form of conduct, and it is 'impossible to be thoroughly and rationally logical except upon an ethical basis'.[42] Indeed, logic, as concerned with what we ought to think, 'must be an application of the doctrine of what we deliberately choose to do, which is ethics'.[43] At the same time Peirce does not really mean that logic can be derived from ethics, any more than ethics can be derived from logic. They are for him distinct normative sciences. But inasmuch as pragmatism teaches that 'what we think is to be interpreted in terms of what we are prepared to do',[44] there must be connections between logic and ethics.

One connection worth noting is this. We have seen that according to Peirce absolute certainty concerning the truth of an hypothesis cannot be attained at any given moment by any given individual. At the same time there can be an 'infinite' or unending approximation to it through the unlimited or continuing community of observers, by means of repeated verification which raises probability towards the ideal limit of certainty. So in the moral sphere the experiment of conduct, so to speak, tends to increase, through the unlimited community of mankind, clear recognition of the nature of the supreme end of life and of its 'meaning', its implications in regard to concrete action. And we can envisage, at any rate as an ideal limit, universal agreement.

Indeed, Peirce does not hesitate to say that 'in regard to morals we can see ground for hope that debate will ultimately cause one party or other to modify their sentiments up to complete accord'.[45] This obviously presupposes that the basis of morality is objective, that the supreme good or ultimate end is something to be discovered and about which agreement is possible in principle. And this point of view obviously differentiates Peirce's ethics from the emotive theory, especially in its older and cruder form, which is associated with the early phase of modern neopositivism. So does his idea of analyzing moral propositions on lines analogous to his analysis of scientific propositions,[46] not to speak of his general vision of evolution as moving towards the embodiment of reason in the unlimited community, a vision which has much more affinity with absolute idealism than with positivism.

8. Sometimes Peirce speaks of metaphysics in a thoroughly positivist manner. For example, in a paper on pragmatism he states that pragmatism will serve to show that 'almost every proposition of ontological metaphysics is either meaningless gibberish—one word being defined by other words, and they by still others, without any real conception ever being reached —or else is downright absurd'.[47] When this rubbish has been swept away, philosophy will be reduced to problems capable of investigation by the observational methods of the genuine sciences. Pragmatism is thus 'a species of prope-positivism'.[48]

At the same time Peirce goes on to say that pragmatism does not simply jeer at metaphysics but 'extracts from it a precious essence, which will serve to give life and light to cosmology and physics'.[49] In any case he has no intention of rejecting metaphysics, provided that he himself is practising it. And while it is only right to mention the fact that Peirce sometimes derides metaphysics, this does not alter the fact that he has his own brand of it.

Peirce gives a number of different definitions or descriptions of metaphysics, when, that is to say, the term 'metaphysics' is not being used as a term of abuse. We are told, for example, that 'metaphysics consists in the results of the absolute acceptance of logical principles not merely as regulatively valid, but as truths of being'.[50] It is in accordance with this view that Peirce connects the fundamental ontological categories with the logical categories of firstness, secondness and thirdness. And he asserts that as metaphysics results from the acceptance of logical principles as principles of being, the universe must be regarded as having a unifying explanation. At other times Peirce emphasizes the observational basis of metaphysics. 'Metaphysics, even bad metaphysics, really rests on observations, whether consciously or not.'[51]

And it is in accordance with this view that Peirce derives the fundamental ontological categories from phenomenology or 'phaneroscopy', by inquiring into the irreducible formal elements in any and every experience. We are also told that 'metaphysics is the science of Reality',[52] reality including for Peirce not only the actually existent but also the sphere of real possibility.

To a certain extent at least these various ways of describing metaphysics can be harmonized. For example, to say that metaphysics is the science of reality is not incompatible with saying that it is based on experience or observation. It may even be possible to harmonize the view that metaphysics rests on observations with the view that it results from the acceptance of logical principles, providing at any rate that we do not interpret this second view as meaning that metaphysics can be deduced from logic without any recourse to experience. At the same time it does not seem to be possible to construct from Peirce's various utterances an absolutely consistent and unambiguous account of metaphysics. For one thing, he does not appear to have made up his mind definitely about the precise relation between ontology and logic. For present purposes, therefore, we had better confine ourselves to indicating briefly some of Peirce's metaphysical ideas. We cannot undertake here to create that consistent system which the philosopher himself did not achieve.

We can start with Peirce's three fundamental categories. The first, that of 'firstness', is 'the idea of that which is such as it is regardless of anything else'.[53] And Peirce calls it the category of quality, in the sense of 'suchness'. From the phenomenological point of view we can conceive a feeling, as of sadness, or a sensed quality, as of blueness, without reference to subject or object but simply as a unique something, 'a purely monadic state of feeling'.[54] To convert the psychological concept into a metaphysical one, Peirce tells us, we have to think of a monad as 'a pure nature, or quality, in itself without parts or features, and without embodiment'.[55] But the term 'monad', with its Leibnizian associations, can be misleading. For Peirce goes on to say that the meanings of the names of the so-called secondary qualities are as good examples of monads as can be given. It is understandable therefore that he speaks of the category of firstness as that of quality. In any case firstness is a pervasive feature of the universe, representing the element of uniqueness, freshness and originality which is everywhere present, in every phenomenon, every fact, every event. To obtain some idea of what is meant, Peirce suggests that we should imagine to ourselves the universe as it appeared to Adam when he looked on it for the first time, and before he had drawn distinctions and become reflectively aware of his own experience.

The second fundamental category, that of 'secondness', is dyadic, corresponding to the idea of secondness in logic. That is to say, secondness is 'the conception of being relative to, the conception of reaction with, something else'.[56] From one point of view secondness can be called 'fact', while from another point of view it is existence or actuality. For 'existence is that mode of being which lies in opposition to another'.[57] And this category too pervades the universe. Facts are facts, as we say; and this is why we sometimes speak of 'brute' facts. Actuality or existence involves everywhere effort and resistance. It is in this sense dyadic.

The third fundamental category, that of 'thirdness', is said to be the category of mediation, its logical prototype being the mediating function of a sign between object and interpretant. Ontologically, thirdness mediates between firstness, in the sense of quality, and secondness, in the sense of fact or of action and reaction. It thus introduces continuity and regularity, and it takes the form of laws of various types or grades. For instance, there can be laws of quality, determining 'systems of qualities, of which Sir Isaac Newton's law of colour-mixture, with Dr. Thomas Young's supplement thereto, is the most perfect known example'.[58] There can also be laws of fact. Thus if a spark falls into a barrel of gunpowder (treated as a first), it causes an explosion (treated as a second); and it does so according to an intelligible law, which thus has a mediating function.[59] Then again there are laws of regularity which enable us to predict that future facts of secondness will always take on a certain determinate character or quality. In its various forms, however, the category of thirdness, like those of firstness and secondness, pervades the universe; and we can say that everything stands in some relation to every other thing.[60]

Now, quality can be said, in Mill's language, to be a permanent possibility of sensation. It is, however, a real possibility, independent of subjective experience. And we can thus say that the first quality gives us the first mode of being, namely real possibility, though the concept of possibility is admittedly wider than that of quality. Similarly, the second category, being from one point of view that of actuality or existence, gives us the second mode of being, namely actuality as distinct from possibility. Again, by involving the concept of law the third category gives us the third mode of being, which Peirce calls 'destiny', as governing future facts. But it must be understood that in Peirce's use of the term the concept of 'destiny' is wider than the concept of law, if we mean by law the idea of it which is associated with determinism. For to be free from determining law is as much 'destiny' as to be subject to it.

We have, therefore, three fundamental ontological categories and three corresponding metaphysical modes of being. Peirce also distinguishes three modes or categories of existence or actuality. The first is what he calls 'chance', a term used 'to express with accuracy the characteristics of freedom or spontaneity'.[61] The second mode of existence is law, laws being of various types but all being the result of evolution. The third mode of existence is habit, or, rather, the tendency to habit-making. The word 'habit', however, must be understood in a wide sense. For, according to Peirce, all things possess a tendency to take habits,[62] whether they are human beings, animals, plants or chemical substances. And the laws which state uniformities or regularities are the results of long periods of such habit-taking.

We can now briefly consider the actual world or universe in the light of these modes or categories of actuality or existence.[63] 'Three elements are active in the world: first, chance; second, law; and third, habit-taking.'[64] We are invited to think of the universe as being originally in a state of pure indetermination, a state in which there were no distinct things, no habits, no laws, a state in which absolute chance reigned. From one point of view this absolute indetermination was 'nullity',[65] the negation of all determination, while from another point of view, considered, that is to say, as the real possibility of all determination, it was 'being'.[66] At the same time chance is spontaneity, freedom, creativity. It thus annuls itself as unlimited possibility or potentiality by taking the form of possibilities of this or that sort, that is to say, of some definite qualities or suchnesses, falling under the ontological category of firstness. And as the universe evolves and 'monads' act and react in 'secondnesses', habits are formed and there are produced those regularities or laws which fall into the category of thirdness. The ideal limit of the process is the complete reign of law, the opposite of the reign of absolute chance.

The first stage is evidently, in a real sense, an abstraction. For if chance is spontaneity and creativity, we can hardly speak, as Peirce explicitly recognizes, of an assignable time or period during which there was absolutely no determination. Similarly, the complete reign of law, in which all chance or spontaneity is absent, is also in a sense an abstraction, an ideal limit. For according to Peirce's principle of 'tychism',[67] chance is always present in the universe. Hence we can say that the universe is a process of creative and continuous determination, moving from the ideal limit of absolute indetermination to the ideal limit of absolute determination, or, better, from the ideal limit of bare possibility to the ideal limit of the complete actualization of possibility. Another way of putting the matter is to say that evolution is a process of advance from absolute chance considered as 'a chaos of unpersonalized feeling'[68] to the reign of pure reason embodied in a perfectly rational system. We have already seen, in connection with his ethical doctrine, how Peirce regards the universe as moving towards an ever fuller embodiment of rationality.

It does not follow from Peirce's doctrine of absolute chance as the primitive state of the universe that chance is the sole explanation of evolution. On the contrary, 'evolution is nothing more nor less than the working out of a definite end',[69] a final cause. And this idea enables Peirce to adopt and adapt the old idea of the cosmic significance of love, an idea which goes back at any rate to the Greek philosopher Empedocles.

A final end works by attraction, and the response is love. To the idea of 'tychism', therefore, we have to add that of 'agapism' as a cosmological category. And to these two we must add a third, namely 'synechism', which is 'the doctrine that all that exists is continuous'.[70]

Synechism, we may note, rules out any ultimate dualism between matter and mind. Indeed, 'what we call matter is not completely dead, but is merely mind hidebound with habits'[71] which make it act with a specially high degree of mechanical regularity. And Peirce remarks that 'tychism' must give rise to a 'Schelling-fashioned idealism which holds matter to be mere specialized and partially deadened mind'.[72] So convinced is he of this, that he does not hesitate to say that 'the one intelligible theory of the universe is that of objective idealism, that matter is effete mind, inveterate habits becoming physical laws'.[73]

Now, if it is asked whether Peirce believed in God, the answer is affirmative. But if it is asked what part is played in his philosophy by the concept of God, the answer is more complex. His general principle is that philosophy and religion should not be mixed up. Not that this prevents him from writing about God. But when he talks about 'musement' as an activity of the mind which leads directly to God, he is not thinking of what would normally be called a systematic metaphysical argument. If, for example, I contemplate the starry heavens, as Kant did, and allow instinct and the heart to speak, I cannot help believing in God. Appeal to one's own 'instinct' is more effective than any argument.[74] Peirce does indeed make it clear that in his opinion contemplation of the 'three universes' of tychism, agapism and synechism 'gives birth to the hypothesis and ultimately to the belief that they, or at any rate two of the three, have a Creator independent of them'.[75] But he calls this the 'neglected argument', also the 'humble argument', and he brings it under the heading of 'musement'. The direction of Peirce's thought is, however, perfectly plain. A theory of evolution which enthroned mechanical law above the principle of creative growth or development would be hostile to religion; but 'a genuine evolutionary philosophy . . . is so far from being antagonistic to the idea of a personal creator that it is really inseparable from that idea'.[76] While, therefore, in his systematic metaphysics Peirce concentrates on the doctrine of categories, his general world-view is certainly theistic.

9. From the point of view of the history of pragmatism Peirce's chief contribution is, of course, his analysis of meaning, his rule for making concepts clear. And if this is considered in a general way, it has an obvious value. For it can serve as a useful goad or stimulus, making us give concrete content to our concepts, instead of letting words do duty for clear ideas. In other words, it stimulates to conceptual analysis. It seems to me pretty obvious, for example, that if there were no assignable difference between what Peirce calls the 'practical consequences' or 'practical effects' of the words 'hard' and 'soft', there would in fact be no difference in meaning. True, as a general criterion of meaning Peirce's principle of pragmaticism lies open to the same sort of objections which have been brought against the neopositivist criterion of meaning. There is great difficulty in interpreting all factual statements as predictions or sets of predictions. But this does not alter the fact that the principle of pragmaticism brings out aspects of the semantic situation which have to be taken into account in developing a theory of meaning. In other words, Peirce made a valuable contribution to logic. And if he allowed what he saw clearly to obscure other aspects of the situation, there is nothing exceptional in this.

We have seen, however, that when applying the principle of pragmaticism in a particular context Peirce states roundly that our idea of anything *is* our idea of its sensible effects. If this statement is taken seriously in its universal form, it appears to undermine Peirce's own metaphysical world-view. He does indeed make an attempt to apply his principle to the concept of God without dissolving the concept.[77] And he suggests[78] that if the pragmaticist is asked what he means by 'god', he can reply that just as long acquaintance with the works of Aristotle makes us familiar with the philosopher's mind, so does study of the physico-psychical universe give us an acquaintance with what may be called in some analogous sense the divine 'mind'. But if his statement elsewhere about 'sensible effects' is taken seriously, it seems to follow either that we have no clear concept of God or that the idea of God is simply the idea of his sensible effects. And in point of fact Peirce himself suggests in one place[79] that the question whether there really is such a being as God is the question whether physical science is something objective or simply a fictional construction of the scientists' minds.

It may be objected that the last sentence involves taking a remark out of its general context, and that in any case too much emphasis has been placed on the statement that our idea of anything is the idea of its sensible effects. After all, when he made the statement Peirce was talking about the sensible effects of bread. Further, he gives various formulations of the principle of pragmatism, and in view of the way in which he often uses the principle we ought not to over-emphasize a statement made in a particular context.

This is doubtless true. But Peirce made the statement in question. And the point which we are trying to make here is that he did not construct a system in which all the elements of his thought were harmonized and rendered consistent. Peirce approached philosophy through mathematics and science, and his theory of meaning was doubtless largely suggested by reflection on scientific statements considered as fallible hypotheses, as verifiable or falsifiable predictions. But his interests were wide and his mind was original and fertile; and he developed a metaphysical world-view in which pragmatism was not forgotten but which demanded reconsideration of the nature and scope of the pragmatist principle. To claim that it is impossible to synthesize Peirce's logic and his metaphysics would be to claim too much, at least if synthesis is understood as permitting revision and modification of the elements to be synthesized. But two things at any rate are clear; first that Peirce did not himself work out such a synthesis, and, secondly, that no synthesis is possible if the pragmatic principle is understood in such a way that it leads straight to neopositivism.

To say, however, that Peirce did not achieve a fully coherent synthesis of the various elements in his thought is not to deny that he was in a real sense a systematic thinker. Indeed, from one point of view it is hardly an exaggeration to claim that he was possessed by a passion for system. We have only to think, for example, of the way in which he used the ideas of firstness, secondness and thirdness, employing them to link together logic, epistemology, ontology and cosmology. It is undeniable that out of his various papers there arise the general outlines of an imposing system.

We have said that Peirce approached philosophy by way of mathematics and science. And we would naturally expect his metaphysics to be a prolongation or extension of his reflections on the scientific view of the world. So it is to some extent. At the same time the general results have a marked affinity with metaphysical idealism. But Peirce was well aware of this; and he considered that if one constructs a world-view based on the scientific conception of the world, one is inevitably pushed in the direction of metaphysical idealism, an idealism which is able to accommodate the 'Scholastic realism' on which Peirce always insisted. In other words, he did not start with idealist premises. He started with realism and was determined to maintain it. But he recognized that though his approach was different from that of the idealists, his conclusions had a recognizable resemblance to theirs. We find much the same situation in the case of Whitehead in the present century.

We have already noted Peirce's commendation of Schelling's view of matter, and his explicit statement that objective idealism is the one intelligible theory of the universe. Here we can note his partial affinity with Hegel. Sometimes indeed Peirce speaks against Hegel, maintaining, for example, that he was too inclined to forget that there is a world of action and reaction, and that Hegel deprived 'firstness' and 'secondness' of all actuality. But when speaking of his own doctrine of categories, logical and metaphysical, Peirce notes the 'Hegelian sound'[80] of what he has to say and remarks that his statements are indeed akin to those of Hegel. 'I sometimes agree with the great idealist and sometimes diverge from his footsteps.'[81] While prepared to say on occasion that he entirely rejects the system of Hegel, Peirce is also prepared to say on occasion that he has resuscitated Hegelianism in a new form, and even to claim that, so far as a philosophical concept can be identified with the idea of God, God is the absolute Idea of Hegel, the Idea which manifests itself in the world and tends towards its complete self-revelation in the ideal limit or term of the evolutionary process.[82] It is not altogether surprising, therefore, if Peirce speaks of Hegel as 'in some respects the greatest philosopher that ever lived',[83] even if he also criticizes Hegel for a lamentable deficiency in 'critical severity and sense of fact'.[84]

We have mentioned the name of Whitehead. There does not seem to be any evidence that Whitehead was influenced by Pierce, or even that he had studied Peirce's writings. But this renders the resemblance between their thought all the more notable. It is, of course, a limited resemblance, but it is none the less real. For example, Whitehead's doctrine of eternal objects and actual entities was anticipated to some extent by Peirce's distinction between 'generals' and facts. Again, Whitehead's doctrine of novelty in the universe, in the cosmic process, recalls Peirce's doctrine of spontaneity and originality. Further, it is perhaps not altogether fanciful to see in Peirce's thought an anticipation of Whitehead's famous distinction between the primordial and consequent natures of God. For Peirce tells us that God as Creator is the 'Absolute First',[85] while as terminus of the universe, as God completely revealed, he is the 'Absolute Second'.[86] Perhaps one is put in mind more of Hegel than of Whitehead; but then the philosophy of Whitehead himself, anti-idealist though it was by original intention, bears some resemblance in its final form to absolute idealism.

To return finally to Peirce in himself. He was an original philosopher and powerful thinker. Indeed, the claim that he is the greatest of all purely American philosophers is by no means unreasonable. He had a strong tendency to careful analysis and was far from being one of those philosophers whose chief concern appears to be that of providing uplift and edification. At the same time he had a speculative mind which sought for a general or overall interpretation of reality. And this combination is, we may well think, precisely what is required. At the same time the example of Peirce is a living illustration of the difficulty of effecting such a combination. For we find in his thought unresolved ambiguities. For instance, Peirce is a resolute realist. Reality is independent of human experience and thought. Indeed, the real is to be defined precisely in terms of this independence. And it is this account of the real which permits Peirce to attribute independent reality to the world of possibles and to depict God as the only absolute reality. At the same time his pragmatism or pragmaticism seems to demand what Royce called the 'critical rationalist' interpretation of reality, namely in terms of conceivable human experience. That which gives rise to actual experience is actually real. That which is conceived as giving rise to possible experience is potentially actual, a real possibility. On this interpretation of reality we could not claim that God is an actually existing being without claiming that he is the object of actual experience. Alternatively, we would have to analyze the concept of God in such a way as to reduce it to the idea of those effects which we do experience. So we are back once more with the latent tension in Peirce's philosophy as a whole between his metaphysics and a logical analysis of the meaning of concepts which appears to point in quite a different direction from that of his speculative metaphysics.

Chapter Fifteen

THE PRAGMATISM OF JAMES AND SCHILLER

The life and writings of William James – James's conception of radical empiricism and pure experience – Pragmatism as theory of meaning and as theory of truth – The relations between radical empiricism, pragmatism and humanism in the philosophy of James – Pragmatism and belief in God – Pragmatism in America and England – The humanism of C. F. S. Schiller.

1. William James (1842–1910) was born at New York and received his school education partly in America and partly abroad, acquiring in the process a fluency in the French and German languages. In 1864 he entered the Harvard Medical

School, receiving the degree of doctor of medicine in 1869. After a period of bad health and mental depression he became an instructor in anatomy and physiology at Harvard. But he was also interested in psychology, and in 1875 he began giving courses in the subject. In 1890 he published his *Principles of Psychology* in two volumes.

Apart from an early attempt to become a painter, James's higher education was thus mainly scientific and medical. But like his father, Henry James, senior,[1] he was a man of deep religious feeling, and he found himself involved in a mental conflict between the scientific view of the world, interpreted as a mechanistic view which excluded human freedom, and a religious view which would include belief not only in God but also in the freedom of man. As far as the legitimacy of belief in freedom was concerned, James found help in the writing of the French philosopher Charles Renouvier (1815–1903). And it was largely the desire to overcome the opposition between the outlook to which science seemed to him to point and the outlook suggested by his religious and humanistic inclinations which drove James to philosophy. In 1879 he started to lecture on the subject at Harvard, and in the following year he became an assistant professor of philosophy. In 1885 he was nominated professor of philosophy.

In 1897 James published *The Will to Believe and Other Essays in Popular Philosophy*.[2] His famous *Varieties of Religious Experience*,[3] appeared in 1902. This was followed by *Pragmatism* in 1907, *A Pluralistic Universe*[4] in 1909 and, in the same year, *The Meaning of Truth*. James's posthumously published writings include *Some Problems of Philosophy* (1911), *Memories and Studies* (1911), *Essays in Radical Empiricism* (1912), and *Collected Essays and Reviews* (1920). His *Letters*, edited by his son, Henry James, appeared in 1926.

2. In the preface to *The Will to Believe* James describes his philosophical attitude as that of radical empiricism. He explains that by empiricism he understands a position which is 'contented to regard its most assured conclusions concerning matters of fact as hypotheses liable to modification in the course of future experience'.[5] As for the word 'radical', this indicates that the doctrine of monism itself is treated

as an hypothesis. At first hearing this sounds very odd. But in this context James understands by monism the view that the multiplicity of things forms an intelligible unity. He does not mean by monism the theory that the world is one single entity or one single fact. On the contrary, he excludes this theory in favour of pluralism. What he is saying is that radical empiricism postulates a unity which is not immediately given, but that this postulate, which stimulates us to discover unifying connections, is treated as itself an hypothesis which has to be verified, and not as an unquestionable dogma.[6]

In *Some Problems of Philosophy*, in the context of a discussion of types of metaphysics, empiricism is contrasted with rationalism. 'Rationalists are the men of principles, empiricists the men of facts.'[7] The rationalist philosopher, as James sees him, moves from the whole to its parts, from the universal to the particular, and he endeavours to deduce facts from principles. Further, he tends to claim final truth on behalf of his system of deduced conclusions. The empiricist, however, starts with particular facts; he moves from parts to wholes; and he prefers, if he can, to explain principles as inductions from facts. Further, the claim to final truth is foreign to his mind.

Obviously, there is nothing new here. Familiar lines of contrast between rationalism and empiricism are presented by James in a more or less popular manner. But in the preface to *The Meaning of Truth* we can find a more clearly defined account of radical empiricism. It is there said to consist 'first of a postulate, next of a statement of fact, and finally of a generalized conclusion'.[8] The postulate is that only those matters which are definable in terms drawn from experience should be considered debatable by philosophers. Hence if there is any being which transcends all possible experience, it also transcends philosophical discussion. The statement of fact is that relations, conjunctive and disjunctive, are as much objects of experience as the things related. And the generalized conclusion from this statement of fact is that the knowable universe possesses a continuous structure, in the sense that it does not consist simply of entities which can be related only through categories imposed from without.

James is insistent on the reality of relations. 'Radical empiricism takes conjunctive relations at their face value, holding them to be as real as the terms united by them.'[9] And among conjunctive relations is the causal relation. Hence what James calls radical empiricism differs from the empiricism of Hume, according to whom 'the mind never perceives any real connection among distinctive existences'.[10] It is also opposed to Bradley's theory of relations. 'Mr. Bradley's understanding shows the most extraordinary power of perceiving separations and the most extraordinary impotence in comprehending conjunctions.'[11]

The meaning of the word 'experience' is notoriously imprecise. But according to James ordinary experience, in which we are aware of distinct things of various kinds and of relations of different types, grows out of pure experience, described as 'the immediate flux of life which furnishes the material to our later reflection with its conceptual categories'.[12] True, only new-born infants and people in a state of semi-coma can be said to enjoy in its purity a state of pure experience, which is 'but another name for feeling or sensation'.[13] But pure experience, the immediacy of feeling or sensation, is the embryo out of which articulated experience develops; and elements or portions of it remain even in our ordinary experience.

From this doctrine of pure experience we can draw two conclusions. First, in this basic flux of experience the distinctions of reflective thought, such as those between consciousness and content, subject and object, mind and matter, have not yet emerged in the forms in which we make them. In this sense pure experience is 'monistic'. And James can speak of it as the 'one primal stuff or material in the world, a stuff of which everything is composed'.[14] This is the doctrine of 'neutral monism', which James associates with radical empiricism. Pure experience cannot be called, for example, either physical or psychical: it logically precedes the distinction and is thus 'neutral'.

Secondly, however, the fact that radical empiricism is pluralistic rather than monistic in the ontological sense and asserts the reality of many things and of the relations between them, means that pure experience must be regarded as containing in itself potentially the distinctions of developed experience. It is shot through, as James expresses the matter, not only with nouns and adjectives but also with prepositions and conjunctions. The causal relation, for example, is present in the flux of sensation, inasmuch as all sensation is teleological in character.

Now, if pure monism is understood in a purely psychological sense, as simply stating, that is to say, that the primitive and basic form of experience is a state of 'feeling' in which distinctions, such as that between subject and object, are not as yet present, it is doubtless compatible with a realistic pluralism. But if it is understood in an ontological sense, as meaning that the flux of undifferentiated experience is the ontological 'stuff' out of which all emerges, it is difficult to see how it does not lead straight to some form of monistic idealism. However, James assumes that the doctrine of pure experience, which is obviously psychological in origin, is compatible with the pluralistic view of the universe that he associates with radical empiricism.

In so far as radical empiricism involves pluralism and belief in the reality of relations, it can be said to be a worldview. But if it is understood simply in terms of the three elements mentioned above, namely a postulate, a statement of fact, and a generalized conclusion, it is an embryonic rather than a full-grown world-view. The problem of God, for example, is left untouched. James does indeed maintain that there are specifically religious experiences which suggest the existence of a superhuman consciousness that is limited and not all-inclusive in a sense which would conflict with pluralism. And he remarks that if empiricism were to become 'associated with religion, as hitherto, through some strange misunderstanding, it has been associated with irreligion, I believe that a new era of religion as well as of philosophy will be ready to begin'.[15] But James's theism will be more conveniently treated after we have outlined the basic tenets of pragmatism and the relation between pragmatism and radical empiricism.

3. In origin and primarily pragmatism is, James tells us, 'a

method only'.[16] For it is in the first place 'a method of settling metaphysical disputes that might otherwise be inter-
minable'.[17] That is to say, if A proposes theory x while B
proposes theory y, the pragmatist will examine the practical
consequences of each theory. And if he can find no difference
between the respective practical consequences of the two
theories, he will conclude that they are to all intents and
purposes one and the same theory, the difference being purely
verbal. In this case further dispute between A and B will
be seen to be pointless.

What we have here is obviously a method for determining
the meanings of concepts and theories. In an address delivered in 1881 James remarked that if two apparently different definitions of something turn out to have identical
consequences, they are really one and the same definition.[18]
And this is the theory of meaning which finds expression in
Pragmatism. 'To attain perfect clearness in our thoughts of
an object, we need only consider what conceivable effects of
a practical kind the object may involve—what sensations we
are to expect from it, and what reactions we must prepare.
Our conception of these effects, whether immediate or remote, is then for us the whole of our conception of the object, so far as that conception has positive significance at
all.'[19]

As so described, the pragmatism of James evidently follows the main lines of the pragmatist method as conceived
by Peirce. James was, indeed, influenced by some other
thinkers as well, such as the scientists Louis Agassiz and
Wilhelm Ostwald; but he made no secret of his indebtedness to Peirce. He refers to him in a footnote relating to the
address of 1881.[20] He again admits his debt to Peirce in a
public lecture given in 1898.[21] And after the passage quoted
in the last paragraph he adds that 'this is the principle of
Peirce, the principle of pragmatism',[22] and remarks that
Peirce's doctrine remained unnoticed until he, James,
brought it forward in the lecture of 1898 and applied it to
religion.

There are, it is true, certain differences between the positions of Peirce and James. For example, when Peirce spoke
about the practical consequences of a concept he empha-

sized the general idea of a habit of action, the idea of the
general manner in which the concept could conceivably
modify purposive action. James, however, tends to emphasize particular practical effects. As we have seen in the passage which is quoted above from *Pragmatism*, he there
emphasizes particular sensations and reactions. Hence Peirce
accused him of having been led away from the universal to
the particular under the influence of an ultra-sensationalistic
psychology, of being, as Dewey put it, more of a nominalist.
In Peirce's terminology, James is concerned with antecedents and consequents more than with consequences, a consequence being the conceived relation between an antecedent
and a consequent.

At the same time, if James's pragmatism were simply a
method for making concepts clear, for determining their
meanings, we could say that he adopts Peirce's principle, even
if he gives it, as Dewey expresses it, a 'nominalistic' twist.
In point of fact, however, pragmatism is not for James simply
a method of determining the meanings of concepts. It is
also a theory of truth. Indeed, James explicitly states that
'the pivotal part of my book named *Pragmatism* is its account of the relation called "truth" which may obtain between our idea (opinion, belief, statement, or what not) and
its object'.[23] And it was largely James's development of
pragmatism into a theory of truth which led Peirce to re-
name his own theory 'pragmaticism'.

It is important to understand that James's theory of truth
does not presuppose a denial of the correspondence theory.
Truth is for him a property of certain of our beliefs, not of
things. 'Realities are not *true*, they *are*; and beliefs are true
of them.'[24] In modern language, logical truth and falsity
are predicated of propositions, not of things or of facts.
Strictly speaking at any rate, it is the proposition enunciating
a fact which is true, not the fact itself. Julius Caesar's existence at a certain period of history cannot properly be
called true; but the statement that he existed is true, while
the statement that he did not exist is false. At the same
time the statement that Julius Caesar existed is not true
in virtue of the meanings of the symbols or words employed

in the statement. Hence we can say that it is true in virtue of a relation of correspondence with reality or fact.

In James's opinion, however, to say that a true belief (he also speaks of true ideas) is one which corresponds or agrees with reality raises rather than solves a problem. For what precisely is meant by correspondence in this context? Copying? An image of a sensible object might be called a copy of the object. But it is not so easy to see how a true idea of, say, justice can reasonably be described as a copy.

James's analysis of 'correspondence' is on these lines. Truth is a relation between one part of experience and another. The *terminus a quo* of the relation is an idea, which belongs to the subjective aspect of experience, while the *terminus ad quem* is an objective reality. What, then, is the relation between the terms? Here we have to employ the pragmatist interpretation of an idea as a plan or rule of action. If our following out this plan leads us to the *terminus ad quem*, the idea is true. More accurately, 'such mediating events *make* the idea true'.[25] In other words, the truth of an idea is the process of its verification or validation. If, for example, I am lost in a wood and then come upon a path which I think of as possibly or probably leading to an inhabited house where I can obtain directions or help, my idea is a plan of action. And if my following out this plan verifies or validates the idea, this process of verification constitutes the truth of the idea: it is the 'correspondence' to which the correspondence theory of truth really refers.

Now, it is noticeable that on the same page on which James tells us that an idea 'becomes true, is made true by events',[26] he also tells us that 'true ideas are those that we can assimilate, validate, corroborate and verify'. In other words, he cannot help admitting that there are truths which can or could be verified, but which have not yet been verified. Indeed, he is prepared to state that unverified truths 'form the overwhelmingly large number of the truths we live by',[27] and that truth lives 'for the most part on a credit system'.[28]

If, however, truths are *made* true by verification or validation, it follows that unverified truths are potentially true, truths *in posse*. And this enables James to deal a blow at the philosophical rationalists or intellectualists who exalt

static, timeless truths which are true prior to any verification. 'Intellectualist truth is only pragmatist truth *in
posse*.'[29] And the total fabric of truth would collapse if it
did not rest on some actually verified truths, that is, on
some actual truths, just as a financial system would collapse
if it possessed no solid basis in cash.

In discussing James's theory of truth it is obviously important not to caricature it. James was inclined to write in a
popular style and to use some rather down-to-earth phrases
which gave rise to misunderstanding. For example, his expression of the view that an idea or belief is true if it 'works'
was apt to suggest the conclusion that even a falsehood could
be called 'true' if it were useful or expedient to believe it.
But when James speaks about a theory 'working', he means
that it 'must mediate between all previous truths and certain new experiences. It must derange common sense and
previous belief as little as possible, and it must lead to some
sensible terminus or other that can be verified exactly. To
"work" means both these things.'[30]

Misunderstanding was also caused by the way in which
James spoke of satisfaction as a basic element in truth. For
his way of speaking suggested that in his view of belief could
be accounted true if it caused a subjective feeling of satisfaction, and that he was thus opening the door to every kind
of wishful thinking. But this was not at any rate his intention. 'Truth in science is what gives us the maximum possible sum of satisfaction, taste included, but consistency both
with previous truth and with novel fact is always the most
imperious claimant.'[31] The successful 'working' of an hypothesis, in the sense explained above, involves the satisfaction of an interest. But the hypothesis is not accepted
simply because one wishes it to be true. If, however, there
is no evidence which compels us to choose one rather than
the other of two hypotheses which purport to explain the
same set of phenomena, it is a matter of scientific 'taste' to
choose the more economical or the more elegant hypothesis.

It is indeed true that in his famous essay on *The Will to
Believe* James explicitly declares that 'our passional nature
not only lawfully may, but must, decide our option between propositions, whenever it is a genuine option that can-

not by its nature be decided on intellectual grounds'.[32] But he makes it clear that by a genuine option he means one 'of the forced, living, and momentous kind'.[33] That is to say, when it is a question of a living and important issue, one which influences conduct, when we cannot avoid choosing one of two beliefs, and when the issue cannot be decided on intellectual grounds, we are entitled to choose on 'passional' grounds, to exercise the will to believe, provided that we recognize our option for what it is. It is then a question of the right to believe in certain circumstances. And whether one agrees with James's thesis or not, one should not represent him as claiming that we are entitled to believe any proposition which affords us consolation or satisfaction, even if the balance of evidence goes to show that the proposition is false.[34] It is true, for instance, that according to James we are entitled, other things being equal, to embrace a view of reality which satisfies the moral side of our nature better than another view. And it is by no means everyone who would agree with him. But this is no reason for disregarding the qualification 'other things being equal', where 'other things' include, of course, already known truths and the conclusions deducible from them.

Though, however, we should be careful not to caricature the pragmatist theory of truth, it by no means follows that it is immune from serious criticism. One obvious line of criticism, attributed by James to the 'rationalists', is that in so far as it identifies truth with verification the pragmatist theory confuses the truth of a proposition with the process of showing that it is true. This was one of Peirce's objections to turning pragmatism from a method of determining meaning into a theory of truth.

James's reply is to challenge his critic, the rationalist as he calls him, to explain 'what the *word* true *means*, as applied to a statement, without invoking the *concept of the statement's workings*'.[35] In James's opinion the rationalist cannot explain what he means by correspondence with reality without referring to the practical consequences of the proposition in question, to what would verify or validate it, if it were true. The rationalist thus implicitly commits him-

self to the pragmatist theory of truth, though he proposes
to attack it in the name of a different theory.

In a discussion of this topic confusion is only too apt to
arise. Suppose that I say that the statement that Julius Caesar
crossed the Rubicon is true in virtue of its correspondence
with reality, with historical fact. And suppose that I am
asked to explain what I mean by this relation of correspondence with reality. I can hardly do so without mentioning the
state of affairs or, rather, the action or series of actions which
are referred to in the statement. And it is perfectly true that
the occurrence of this series of actions at an assignable date
in history is ultimately what validates or 'verifies' the statement. In this sense I cannot explain what I mean by correspondence without referring to what would validate or
verify the statement. At the same time the term 'verification'
would normally be understood to refer to the measures
which we might conceivably take to show that a statement is
true, when we already know what the statement means. That
is to say, verification would normally be understood as referring to conceivable means of showing that the state of
affairs which must obtain or must have obtained if the statement is true actually does or did obtain. And if verification
is understood in this sense, it seems perfectly correct to say
with the 'rationalist' that it is a case of *showing* a statement
to be true rather than of *making* it true.

We might, however, first define 'true' in such a way that it
would follow logically that only an actually verified statement
is true. A statement which could be verified but has not yet
been verified would then be potentially true, a truth *in posse*.
But it is evident that James does not regard the pragmatist
theory of truth as being simply and solely the result of arbitrary definition. Hence it is not unreasonable to claim that
the theory is acceptable or unacceptable according as it is
reduced or not reduced to a thesis which, once understood,
appears obvious. That is to say, if it is reduced to the thesis
that an empirical statement is true or false according as the
state of affairs asserted or denied is (was or will be) the case
or not, the theory is acceptable, though what is stated is
'trivial'. If, however, the theory identifies the truth of a statement with the process which would show that the state of

affairs asserted or denied is the case or not, it is very difficult to see how it does not stand wide open to the objections of the 'rationalists'.

It is not suggested that these remarks constitute an adequate answer to James's question about the nature of correspondence. From the point of view of a professional logician to say, for example, that a proposition is a copy or picture of reality simply will not do. Even apart from the fact that it will not fit the propositions of pure mathematics and formal logic,[36] it is far too imprecise a description of the relation between a true empirical proposition and the state of affairs asserted or denied. And it is to James's credit that he saw this. But it is worth noting that he also seems to have felt that his theory of truth ran the risk of being reduced to a triviality. For he says that one can expect the theory to be first attacked, then to be admitted as true but obvious and insignificant, and finally to be regarded as 'so important that its adversaries claim that they themselves discovered it'.[37] If, however, the theory contains something more than what is 'obvious', it is this something more which we may well be inclined to consider the questionable element in James's pragmatism.

4. How does pragmatism stand to radical empiricism? According to James, there is no logical connection between them. Radical empiricism 'stands on its own feet. One may entirely reject it and still be a pragmatist.'[38] And yet he also tells us that 'the establishment of the pragmatist theory of truth is a step of first rate importance in making radical empiricism prevail'.[39]

Up to a certain point James is doubtless justified in saying that radical empiricism and pragmatism are independent of one another. For instance, it is perfectly possible to hold that relations are as real as their terms and that the world has a continuous structure without accepting the pragmatist conceptions of meaning and truth. At the same time the postulate of radical empiricism is, as we have seen, that only those matters should be considered as subjects of philosophical debate which are definable in terms derived from experience. And the pragmatist is said to hold of the truth-relation that 'everything in it is experienceable. . . . The "workableness" which ideas must have, in order to be true, means particular workings, physical or intellectual, actual or possible, which they may set up from next to next inside of concrete experience.'[40] In other words, pragmatism will regard as possessing a claim to truth only those ideas which can be interpreted in terms of experienceable 'workings'. And acceptance of this view would obviously tend to make radical empiricism prevail, if by radical empiricism we mean the above-mentioned postulate.

We can put the matter in this way. Pragmatism, James remarks, has 'no doctrines save its method'.[41] Radical empiricism, however, which James develops into a metaphysics or world-view, has its doctrines. These doctrines, considered in themselves, can be held on other grounds than those provided by radical empiricism. This is true, for example, of belief in God. But in James's view the use of the pragmatist theory of truth or method of determining truth and falsity would contribute greatly to making the doctrines of radical empiricism prevail. He may have been over-optimistic in thinking this; but it is what he thought.

Now, James also makes use of the word 'humanism' to describe his philosophy. In a narrower sense of the term he uses it to refer to the pragmatist theory of truth when considered as emphasizing the 'human' element in belief and knowledge. For example, 'humanism says that satisfactoriness is what distinguishes the true from the false'.[42] It sees that truth is reached 'by ever substituting more satisfactory for less satisfactory opinions'.[43] We have already noted that James tries to avoid pure subjectivism by insisting that a belief cannot be accounted satisfactory and so true, if it is incompatible with previously verified beliefs or if the available evidence tells against it. But in his view no belief can be final, in the sense of being incapable of revision. And this is precisely what the 'humanist' sees. He sees, for example, that our categories of thought have been developed in the course of experience, and that even if we cannot help employing them, they might conceivably change in the future course of evolution.

To borrow a Nietzschean phrase, the humanist understands that our beliefs are human, all-too-human. And it is in this sense that we should understand James's definition of humanism as the doctrine that '*though one part of our experience may lean upon another part to make it what it is in any one of several aspects in which it may be considered, experience as a whole is self-containing and leans on nothing*'.[44] What he means is that while there are standards which grow up *within* experience, there is no absolute standard of truth *outside* all experience, to which all our truths must conform. The humanist regards truth as relative to changing experience, and so as relative to man; and he regards absolute truth as 'that ideal vanishing-point towards which we imagine that all our temporary truths will some day converge'.[45] And, to do him justice, James is prepared to apply this outlook to humanism itself.[46]

The term 'humanism', however, is also used by James in a wider sense. Thus he tells us that the issue between pragmatism and rationalism, and so between humanism and rationalism, is not simply a logical or epistemological issue: '*it concerns the structure of the universe itself*'.[47] The pragmatist sees the universe as unfinished, changing, growing and plastic. The rationalist, however, maintains that there is one 'really real' universe, which is complete and changeless. James is thinking partly of 'Vivekanda's mystical One'.[48] But he is also thinking, of course, of Bradley's monism, according to which change is not fully real and degrees of truth are measured in relation to a unique absolute experience which transcends our apprehension.[49]

Now, James himself remarks that the definition of humanism which is quoted above in the last paragraph but one seems at first sight to exclude theism and pantheism. But he insists that this is not really the case. 'I myself read humanism theistically and pluralistically.'[50] Humanism thus becomes a pluralistic and theistic metaphysics or world-view, coinciding with developed radical empiricism. But James's theism can be considered separately in the next section.

5. When discussing the application of pragmatism as a method to substantial philosophical problems, James remarks that Berkeley's criticism of the idea of material substance was thoroughly pragmatist in character. For Berkeley gives the 'cash-value',[51] as James puts it, of the term 'ma-

terial substance' in ideas or sensations. Similarly, when examining the concept of the soul Hume and his successors 'redescend into the stream of experience with it, and cash it into so much small-change value in the way of "ideas" and their peculiar connections with each other'.[52]

James himself applies the pragmatist method to a problem of intimate personal concern, namely to the issue between theism and materialism. In the first place we can consider theism and materialism retrospectively, as James puts it. That is to say, we can suppose that the theist and the materialist see the world itself and its history in the same way, and that the theist then adds the hypothesis of a God who set the world going, while the materialist excludes this hypothesis as unnecessary and invokes 'matter' instead. How are we to choose between these two positions? On pragmatist principles at any rate we cannot choose. For 'if no future detail of experience or conduct is to be deduced from our hypothesis, the debate between materialism and theism becomes quite idle and insignificant'.[53]

When, however, theism and materialism are considered 'prospectively', in relation to what they promise, to the expectations which they respectively lead us to entertain, the situation is quite different. For materialism leads us to expect a state of the universe in which human ideals, human achievements, consciousness and the products of thought will be as if they had never been,[54] whereas theism 'guarantees an ideal order that shall be permanently preserved'.[55] Somehow or other God will not allow the moral order to suffer shipwreck and destruction.

Looked at from this point of view, therefore, theism and materialism are very different. And on pragmatist principles we are entitled, other things being equal, to embrace that belief which corresponds best with the demands of our moral nature. But James does not mean to imply that there is no evidence at all in favour of theism, other than a desire that it should be true. 'I myself believe that the evidence for God lies primarily in inner personal experiences.'[56] In A Pluralistic Universe he resumes what he has already maintained in The Varieties of Religious Experience by arguing that 'the believer is continuous, to his own consciousness at any rate, with a wider self from which saving experiences flow in'.[57] Again, 'the drift of all the evidence we have seems to me to sweep us very strongly towards the belief in some form of superhuman life with which we may, unknown to ourselves, be co-conscious'.[58] At the same time the evil and suffering in the world suggest the conclusion that this superhuman consciousness is finite, in the sense that God is limited 'either in power, or in knowledge, or in both at once'.[59]

This idea of a finite God is used by James in his substitution of 'meliorism' for optimism on the one hand and pessimism on the other. According to the meliorist the world is not necessarily becoming better, nor is it necessarily becoming worse: it *can* become better, if, that is to say, man freely co-operates with the finite God in making it better.[60] In other words, the future is not inevitably determined, either for better or for worse, not even by God. There is room in the universe for novelty, and human effort has a positive contribution to make in the establishment of a moral order.

James thus used pragmatism to support a religious worldview. But we have seen that when stating the pragmatist theory of meaning he declared that our whole conception of an object is reducible to our ideas of the 'conceivable effects of a practical kind the object may involve',[61] explicitly mentioning the sensations we may expect and the reactions we should prepare. And we may well doubt whether this is a promising foundation for a theistic world-view. But as was noted in the section on his life, the reconciliation of a scientific with a religious outlook constituted for him a personal problem. And taking a theory of truth which was built on to a theory of meaning that originated in an analysis of empirical hypotheses, he used it to support the only world-view which really satisfied him. In the process, of course, he extended the concept of experience far beyond sense-experience. Thus he maintained that religious empiricism is much more truly 'empirical' than irreligious empiricism, inasmuch as the former takes seriously the varieties of religious experience whereas the latter does not. In a sense his problem was the same as that of Kant, to reconcile the scientific outlook with man's moral and religious consciousness. His instrument of unification or harmonization was pragmatism.

The result was presented as the development of radical empiricism. And the attitude adopted was described as humanism.

6. The pragmatist movement was above all an American phenomenon. True, one can find manifestations of the pragmatist attitude even in German philosophy. In the seventh volume of this *History* mention was made of the emphasis laid by F. A. Lange[62] on the value for life of metaphysical theories and religious doctrines at the expense of their cognitive value, and the way in which Hans Vaihinger[63] developed what we may call a pragmatist view of truth which had obvious affinities with Nietzsche's fiction-theory.[64] Attention was also drawn to the influence exercised on William James by G. T. Fechner,[65] especially through his distinction between the 'day' and 'night' views of the universe and his claim that, other things being equal, we are entitled to give preference to the view which most contributes to human happiness and cultural development. As for French thought, mention was made in the first section of this chapter of the help derived by James from the writings of Charles Renouvier. And Renouvier, it may be noted, maintained that belief and even certitude are not exclusively intellectual affairs, but that affirmation involves also feeling and will. Though, however, we can certainly find affinities with pragmatism not only in German but also in French thought,[66] the pragmatist movement remains primarily associated with the names of three American philosophers, Peirce, James and Dewey.

This does not mean that England was without its pragmatist movement. But English pragmatism was neither so influential nor so impressive as its American counterpart. It would not be possible to give a reasonable account of American philosophy without including pragmatism. Peirce was an outstanding thinker on any count and nobody would question the influence exercised by James and Dewey on intellectual life in the United States. They brought philosophy to the fore, so to speak, to public notice; and Dewey especially applied it in the educational and social fields. But no great sin of omission would be committed if in an account of the development of modern British philosophy no mention were made of pragmatism, even though it caused a temporary flutter in the philosophical dovecotes. However, in an account of nineteenth-century British thought in which allusion has been made to a considerable number of minor philosophers some mention of pragmatism seems to be desirable.

In 1898 the Oxford Philosophical Society was founded, and an outcome of its discussions was the publication in 1902 of *Personal Idealism*, edited by Henry Sturt. In his preface to this collection of essays by eight members of the Society Sturt explained that the contributors were concerned with developing the theme of personality and with defending personality against naturalism on the one hand and absolute idealism on the other. The naturalist maintains that the human person is a transitory product of physical processes, while the absolute idealist holds that personality is an unreal appearance of the Absolute.[67] In fine, 'Naturalism and Absolutism, antagonistic as they seem to be, combine in assuring us that personality is an illusion'.[68] Oxford idealism, Sturt went on to say, had always been opposed to naturalism; and to this extent absolute and personal idealism maintained a common front. But for this very reason the personal idealists felt that absolute idealism was a more insidious adversary than naturalism. The absolute idealists adopted the impracticable course of trying to criticize human experience from the point of view of absolute experience. And it failed to give any adequate recognition to the volitional aspect of human nature. Absolute idealism, in brief, was insufficiently empirical. And Sturt suggested 'empirical idealism' as an appropriate name for personal idealism. For personal life is what is closest to us and best known by us.

Needless to say, personal idealism and pragmatism are not interchangeable terms. Of the eight contributors to *Personal Idealism* some became well known outside the sphere of philosophy. R. R. Marett, the anthropologist, is an example. Others, such as G. F. Stout, were philosophers but not pragmatists. The volume contained, however, an essay by F. C. S. Schiller, who was the principal champion of pragmatism in England. And the point which we have been trying to make is that British pragmatism had a background of what we may call 'humanism'. It was to a considerable extent a protest on behalf of the human person not only against naturalism but also against the absolute idealism which was then the dominant factor in Oxford philosophy. It thus had more affinity with the pragmatism of William James than with the pragmatism of Peirce, which was essentially a method or rule for determining the meaning of concepts.

Ferdinand Canning Scott Schiller (1864–1937), came of German ancestry, though he was educated in England. In 1893 he became an instructor at Cornell University in America. In 1897 he was elected to a Tutorial Fellowship at Corpus Christi College, Oxford; and he remained a Fellow of the College until his death, though in 1929 he accepted a chair of philosophy in the University of Southern California at Los Angeles. In 1891 he published anonymously *Riddles of the Sphinx*,[69] and this was followed in 1902 by his essay, *Axioms as Postulates*, in *Personal Idealism*, the volume referred to above. *Humanism: Philosophical Essays* appeared in 1903, *Studies in Humanism* in 1907, *Plato or Protagoras?* in 1908, *Formal Logic* in 1912, *Problems of Belief* and *Tantalus, or The Future of Man* in 1924, *Eugenics and Politics* in 1926, *Logic for Use* in 1929 and *Must Philosophers Disagree? and Other Essays in Popular Philosophy* in 1934. Schiller also contributed a paper entitled *Why Humanism?* to the first series of *Contemporary British Philosophy* (1924), edited by J. H. Muirhead, and wrote the article on pragmatism for the fourteenth edition of the *Encyclopaedia Britannica* (1929).

7. As the titles of his writings suggest, Schiller's thought centres round man. In his essay *Plato or Protagoras?* he explicitly places himself on the side of Protagoras and makes his own the famous dictum that man is the measure of all things. In *Riddles of the Sphinx*, where he had attacked the absolute idealist theory of the One in the name of pluralistic personalism, he had declared that all our thinking must be anthropomorphic. But he did not at first use the term 'pragmatism' to describe his humanistic outlook. And in the preface to the first edition of *Humanism*, written after he had come under the influence of American pragmatism, especially that of William James, Schiller remarks that 'I was surprised to find that I had all along been a pragmatist myself without

knowing it, and that little but the name was lacking to my own advocacy of an essentially cognate position in 1892'.[70] But though Schiller makes frequent use of the term 'pragmatism', once he has taken it over from William James, he insists that humanism is the basic concept. Humanism, which holds that man, and not the Absolute, is the measure of all experience and the maker of the sciences, is the fundamental and permanent attitude of thought of James and himself. Pragmatism 'is in reality only the application of Humanism to the theory of knowledge'.[71] The general need is to re-humanize the universe.

Re-humanization of the universe, humanism in other words, demands in the first place a humanization of logic. This demand is in part a protest against the arid subtleties and mental gymnastics of formal logicians who treat logic as a game to be played for its own sake, a protest which, Schiller notes, was expressed by Albert Sidgwick, himself a logician, whose first work bore the title *Fallacies: A View of Logic from the Practical Side* (1883). But Schiller's demand for a humanization of logic is much more than a protest against the aridities and hair-splitting of some logicians. For it rests on the conviction that logic does not represent a realm of absolute and timeless truth which is unaffected by human interest and purposes. In Schiller's view the idea of absolute truth is an *'ignis fatuus'*,[72] in formal logic as well as in empirical science. The fundamental principles or axioms of logic are not *a priori* necessary truths; they are postulates, demands on experience,[73] which have shown themselves to possess a wider and more lasting value for the fulfilment of human purposes than is possessed by other postulates. And to bring out this aspect of the principles or axioms of logic is one of the tasks involved in the humanization of this science.

But we can go considerably further than this. The pragmatist believes that the validity of any logical procedure is shown by its successful working. But it works only in concrete contexts. And it is therefore idle to suppose that complete abstraction from all subject-matter introduces us into a realm of changeless, absolute truth. Indeed, Schiller goes so far as to say that formal logic *'is in the strictest and completest sense meaningless'*.[74] If someone says, 'it is too light' and we do not know the context, his statement is for us meaningless. For we do not know whether he is referring to the weight of an object, to the colour of something or to the quality of a lecture or a book. Similarly, we cannot abstract completely from the use of logic, from its application, 'without incurring thereby a total loss, not only of truth but also of meaning'.[75]

If, therefore, logical principles are postulates made in the light of human desires and purposes, and if their validity depends on their success in fulfilling these desires and purposes, it follows that we cannot divorce logic from psychology. 'Logical value must be found in psychological fact or nowhere. . . . Logical possibilities (or even "necessities") are nothing until they have somehow become psychologically actual and active.'[76] So much for all attempts to de-psychologize logic and to set it on its own feet.

What has been said of logical truth, namely that it is relative to human desires and aims, can be said of truth in general. Truths are in fact valuations. That is to say, to assert that a proposition is true is to say that it possesses practical value by fulfilling a certain purpose. 'Truth is the useful, efficient, workable, to which our practical experience tends to restrict our truth-valuations.'[77] Conversely, the false is the useless, what does not work. This is 'the great Pragmatist principle of selection'.[78]

Schiller sees, of course, that ' "working" is clearly a vague generic term, and it is legitimate to ask what precisely is covered by it'.[79] But he finds this a difficult question to answer. It is comparatively easy to explain what is meant by the working of a scientific hypothesis. But it is not at all so easy to explain, for example, what forms of 'working' are to be accounted relevant to assessing the truth of an ethical theory. We have to admit that 'men take up different attitudes towards different workings because they themselves are temperamentally different'.[80] In other words, no clear and precise general answer can be given to the question.

As one would expect, Schiller is anxious to show that a distinction can be made on pragmatist principles between 'all truths are useful' and 'everything useful is true'. One of his arguments is that 'useful' means useful for a particular purpose, which is determined by the general context of a statement. For example, if I were threatened with torture if I did not say that the earth is flat, it would certainly be useful for me to say this. But the utility of my statement would not make it true. For statements about the shape of the earth pertain to empirical science; and it is certainly not useful for the advancement of science to assert that the earth is flat.

Another way of dealing with the matter is to insist on social recognition. But Schiller is alive to the fact that to recognize a truth is to recognize it as true. And on his principles to recognize it as true is to recognize it as useful. Hence social recognition cannot make a proposition useful, and so true. It is accorded to propositions which have already shown their utility. 'The use-criterion selects the individual truth-valuations, and constitutes thereby the objective truth which obtains social recognition.'[81]

Schiller tends to fall back on a biological interpretation of truth and to stress the idea of survival-value.[82] There is a process of natural selection among truths. Truths of inferior value are eliminated, while truths of superior value survive. And the belief which proves to have most survival-value shows itself to be the most useful, and so the most true. But what is survival-value? It can be described as 'a sort of working, which, while wholly devoid of any rational appeal, yet exercises a far-reaching influence on our beliefs, and is capable of determining this adoption and the elimination of their contraries'.[83] So we are back once more with the admittedly imprecise and vague idea of 'working'.

As we have seen, Schiller maintains that from 'all truths are useful' it does not follow that 'any proposition which is useful is true'. This is perfectly correct, of course. But then one might quite well hold that all truths are 'useful' in some sense or other without holding that their utility constitutes their truth. If one *does* hold that truth is constituted by utility, one can hardly deny at the same time that every useful proposition is true in so far as it is useful. And if the doctrine of non-convertibility is to be maintained successfully one has to show that true propositions possess some property or properties which useful falsehoods do not. Human beings are organisms, but not all organisms are human beings. And this is so because human beings possess properties which are not possessed by all organisms. What are the properties which are peculiar to true propositions over and above a utility which can also be possessed by a proposition which is false? This is a question to which Schiller never really faces up. Mention has been made of Sturt's opinion that absolute idealism did not give sufficient recognition to the volitional side of human nature. One of the troubles with Schiller is that he accords it too much recognition.

Schiller was much less inclined than James to indulge in metaphysical speculation. He did indeed maintain that humanism, an anthropocentric outlook, demands that we should look on the world as 'wholly plastic',[84] as indefinitely modifiable, as what we can make of it. But though he allows that humanists or pragmatists will regard the efforts of metaphysicians with tolerance and will concede aesthetic value to their systems, at the same time 'metaphysics seem doomed to remain *personal guesses* at ultimate reality, and to remain inferior in objective value to the sciences, which are essentially "common" *methods* for dealing with phenomena'.[85] Here again we see the difficulty encountered by Schiller in explaining precisely what 'working' can mean outside the sphere of scientific hypotheses. So he attributes aesthetic value rather than truth-value to metaphysical theories. This is obviously because he regards scientific hypotheses as empirically verifiable whereas metaphysical systems are not. And we are back again with the question whether verification, a species of 'working', does not show an hypothesis to be true (or tend to show it) rather than constitute its truth.

Schiller's main contribution to pragmatism lay in his treatment of logic, which was more professional and detailed than that of William James. But his overall interpretation of logic cannot be said to have demonstrated its 'survival-value'.

Chapter Sixteen

THE EXPERIMENTALISM
OF JOHN DEWEY

Life and writings – Naturalistic empiricism: thought, experience and knowledge – The function of philosophy – Instrumentalism: logic and truth – Moral theory – Some implications in social and educational theory – Religion in a naturalistic philosophy – Some critical comments on Dewey's philosophy.

1. John Dewey (1859–1952) was born at Burlington, Vermont. After studying at the University of Vermont he became a high school teacher. But his interest in philosophy led him to submit to W. T. Harris an essay on the metaphysical assumptions of materialism with a view to publication in *The Journal of Speculative Philosophy*,[1] and the encouragement which he received resulted in his entering Johns Hopkins University in 1882. At the university Dewey attended courses on logic by C. S. Peirce, but the chief influence on his mind was exercised by G. S. Morris, the idealist, with whom Dewey entered into relations of personal friendship.

From 1884 until 1888 Dewey lectured at the University of Michigan, first as an instructor in philosophy and later as an assistant professor, after which he spent a year as professor at the University of Minnesota. In 1889 he returned to Michigan as head of the department of philosophy, and he occupied this post until 1894 when he went to Chicago. During this period Dewey occupied himself with logical, psychological and ethical questions, and his mind moved away from the idealism which he had learned from Morris.[2] In 1887 he published *Psychology*, in 1891 *Outlines of a Critical Theory of Ethics*, and in 1894 *The Study of Ethics: A Syllabus*.

From 1894 until 1904 Dewey was head of the department

of philosophy in the University of Chicago, where he founded his Laboratory School[3] in 1896. The publications of this period include *My Pedagogic Creed* (1897), *The School and Society* (1900), *Studies in Logical Theory* (1903) and *Logical Conditions of a Scientific Treatment of Morality* (1903).

In 1904 Dewey went as professor of philosophy to Columbia University, becoming professor emeritus in 1929.[4] In 1908 he published *Ethics*,[5] in 1910 *How We Think* and *The Influence of Darwin and Other Essays in Contemporary Thought*, in 1915 *Schools of Tomorrow*, in 1916 *Democracy and Education* and *Essays in Experimental Logic*, in 1920 *Reconstruction in Philosophy*, in 1922 *Human Nature and Conduct*, in 1925 *Experience and Nature*, and in 1929 *The Quest for Certainty*. As for later publications *Art as Experience* and *A Common Faith* appeared in 1934, *Experience and Education* and *Logic: The Theory of Inquiry* in 1938, *Theory of Valuation* in 1939, *Education Today* in 1940, *Problems of Men* in 1946 and *Knowing and The Known* in 1949.

Outside the United States at least Dewey is probably best known for his instrumentalism, his version of pragmatism. But he was certainly not the man to concern himself simply with general theories about thought and truth. As the foregoing partial list of his publications indicates, he was deeply interested in problems of value and of human conduct, of society and of education. In the last-named field especially he exercised a great influence in America. Obviously, his ideas did not win universal acceptance. But they could not be ignored. And, in general, we can say that William James and John Dewey were the two thinkers who did most to bring philosophy to the attention of the educated public in the United States.

2. Dewey often describes his philosophy as empirical naturalism or naturalistic empiricism. And the meaning of these descriptions can perhaps best be illustrated by saying something about his account of the nature and function of thought. We can begin by considering the bearing in this context of the term 'naturalism'.

In the first place thought is not for Dewey an ultimate, an absolute, a process which creates objective reality in a metaphysical sense. Nor is it something in man which represents a non-natural element, in the sense that it sets man above or over against Nature. It is in the long run a highly developed form of the active relation between a living organism and its environment. To be sure, in spite of a tendency to use behaviourist language Dewey is well aware that the intellectual life of man has its own peculiar characteristics. The point is, however, that he refuses to start, for instance, from the distinction between subject and object as from an absolute and ultimate point of departure, but sees man's intellectual life as presupposing and developing out of antecedent relations, and thus as falling wholly within the sphere of Nature. Thought is one among other natural processes or activities.

All things react in some way to their environment. But they obviously do not all react in the same way. In a given set of circumstances an inanimate thing, for example, can be said simply to react or not to react. A situation does not pose any problem which the thing can recognize as a problem and to which it can react in a selective manner. When, however, we turn to the sphere of life, we find selective responses. As living organisms become more complex, their environment becomes more ambivalent. That is to say, it becomes more uncertain what responses or actions are called for in the interests of living, what actions will best fit into a series which will sustain the continuity of life. And 'in the degree that responses take place to the doubtful *as* the doubtful, they acquire *mental* quality'.[6] Further, when such responses possess a directed tendency to change the precarious into the secure and the problematic into the resolved, 'they are *intellectual* as well as mental'.[7]

We can say therefore that for Dewey thought is a highly developed form of the relation between stimulus and response on the purely biological level. True, in its interaction with its environment the human organism, like any other organism, acts primarily according to established habits. But situations arise which reflection recognizes as problematic situations, and thus as calling for inquiry or thought, the immediate response being thus in a sense interrupted. But in another sense the response is not interrupted. For the aim of thought, stimulated by a problematic situation, is to transform or reconstruct the set of antecedent conditions which

gave rise to the problem or difficulty. In other words, it aims
at a change in the environment. 'There is no inquiry that
does not involve the making of *some* change in environing
conditions.'[8] That is to say, the conclusion at which the process of inquiry arrives is a projected action or set of actions,
a plan of possible action which will transform the problematic situation. Thought is thus instrumental and has a
practical function. It is not, however, quite accurate to say
that it subserves activity. For it is itself a form of activity.
And it can be seen as part of a total process of activity
whereby man seeks to resolve problematic situations by effecting changes in his environment, by changing an 'indeterminate' situation, one in which the elements clash or do
not harmonize and so give rise to a problem for reflection,
into a 'determinate' situation, a unified whole. In this sense,
therefore, thought does not interrupt the process of response;
for it is itself part of the total response. But the process of
inquiry presupposes recognition of a problematic situation *as*
problematic. It can thus be said to interrupt the response,
if we mean by response one that is instinctive or follows
simply in accordance with some established habit.

A man can, of course, react to a problematic situation in
an unintelligent manner. To take a simple example, he may
lose his temper and smash a tool or instrument which is not
functioning properly. But this sort of reaction is clearly un-
helpful. To solve his problem the man has to inquire into
what is wrong with the instrument and consider how to put
things right. And the conclusion at which he arrives is a plan
of possible action calculated to transform the problematic
situation.

This is an example taken from the level of common sense.
But Dewey will not allow that there is any impassable gulf
or rigid distinction between the level of common sense and
that of, say, science. Scientific inquiry may involve prolonged
operations which are not overt actions in the ordinary sense
but operations with symbols. Yet the total process of hypothesis, deduction and controlled experiment simply repro-
duces in a much more sophisticated and complex form the
process of inquiry which is stimulated by some practical problem in everyday life. Even the complicated operations with

symbols aim at transforming the problematic situation which gave rise to the hypothesis. Thus thought is always practical in some way, whether it takes place at the level of common sense or at the level of scientific theory. In both cases it is a way of dealing with a problematic situation.

It is to be noted that when Dewey speaks of effecting a change in the environment, the last-mentioned term should not be understood as referring exclusively to man's physical environment, the world of physical Nature. 'The environment in which human beings live, act and inquire, is not simply physical. It is cultural as well.'[9] And a clash of values, for example, in a given society gives rise to a problematic situation, the resolution of which would effect a change in the cultural environment.

This account of thought and its basic function corresponds with the fact that 'man who lives in a world of hazards is compelled to seek for security'.[10] And it is, of course, obvious that when man is faced with threatening and perilous situations, recognized as such, it is action which is called for, not simply thought. At the same time Dewey is, needless to say, well aware that inquiry and thought do not necessarily lead to action in the ordinary sense. For example, a scientist's inquiry may terminate in an idea or set of ideas, that is, in a scientific theory or hypothesis. Dewey's account of thought does indeed entail the view that 'ideas are anticipatory plans and designs which take effect in concrete reconstruction of antecedent conditions of existence'.[11] A scientific hypothesis is predictive, and it thus looks forward, so to speak, to verification. But the scientist may not be in a position to verify it here or now. Or he may not choose to do so. His inquiry then terminates in a set of ideas; and he does not possess warranted knowledge. But this does not alter the fact that the ideas are predictive, that they are plans for possible action.

Analogously, if a man is stimulated to inquiry or reflection by a morally problematic situation, the moral judgment which he finally makes is a plan or directive for possible action. When a man commits himself to a moral principle, he expresses his preparedness to act in certain ways in certain circumstances. But though his thought is thus directed to action, action does not necessarily follow. The judgment which he makes is a direction for possible action.

Now, there is a real sense in which each problematic situation is unique and unrepeatable. And when Dewey is thinking of this aspect of the matter, he tends to depreciate general theories. But it is obvious that the scientist works with general concepts and theories; and Dewey's recognition of the fact is shown in his insistence that a theory's connection with action is 'with *possible* ways of operation rather than with those found to be *actually* and immediately required'.[12] At the same time the tension between a tendency to depreciate general concepts and theories, in view of the fact that inquiry is stimulated by particular problematic situations and aims at transforming them, and a recognition of the fact that scientific thought operates with general ideas and constructs general theories, general solutions, shows itself in what Dewey has to say about the nature of philosophy. But this matter can be left to the next section.

We have seen that Dewey's account of thought is 'naturalistic' in the sense that it depicts thought as developing out of the relation between an organism and its environment. 'Intellectual operations are foreshadowed in behaviour of the biological kind, and the latter prepares the way for the former.'[13] Naturalism does not deny differences, of course, but it is committed to accounting for these differences without invoking any non-natural source or agent. In other words, thought must be represented as a product of evolution.

Further, Dewey's account of thought can be described as 'empiricist' in the sense that thought is depicted as starting from experiences and as leading back to experiences. The process of inquiry is set in motion when the subject encounters a problematic situation in its environment, and it terminates, whether actually or ideally, in some change in the environment, or indeed in man himself. At the same time Dewey asserts that the object of knowledge is made or constructed by thought. And as this statement seems at first sight to represent an idealist rather than an empiricist position, it stands in need of some explanation.

Experience in general is said to be a transaction, a process of doing and undergoing, an active relation between an organism and its environment. And according to Dewey primary or immediate experience is non-cognitive in character. It contains 'no division between act and material, subject and object, but contains them both in an unanalyzed totality'.[14] What is experienced is not objectified by a subject as a sign possessing significance or meaning. Distinctions such as that between subject and object arise only for reflection. And a thing assumes, or, rather, is clothed with significance only as the result of a process of inquiry or thought. A fountain pen, for example, takes on significance for me in terms of its function or functions. And it does so as the result of a process of inquiry or thought. Inasmuch, therefore, as Dewey reserves the term 'object of knowledge' for the term of this process, he can say that thought makes or constructs the object of knowledge.

On the one hand Dewey is at pains to point out that his account of the activity of knowing does not entail the conclusion that things do not exist antecedently to being experienced or to being thought about.[15] On the other hand by identifying the object of knowledge with the term of inquiry he is committed to saying that it is in some sense the product of thought. For the term of inquiry is the determinate situation which replaces an indeterminate or problematic situation. Dewey argues, however, that 'knowledge is not a distortion or perversion which confers upon *its* subject-matter traits which *do* not belong to it, but is an act which confers upon non-cognitive material traits which *did* not belong to it'.[16] The resolution of a problematic situation or the process of clothing with determinate significance is no more a distortion or perversion than is the act of the architect who confers upon stone and wood qualities and relations which they did not formerly possess.

If it is asked why Dewey adopts this odd theory of knowledge, which identifies the object of knowledge with the term of the process of inquiry, one reason is that he wishes to get rid of what he calls 'the spectator theory of knowledge'.[17] According to this theory we have on the one hand the knower and on the other the object of knowledge, which is entirely unaffected by the process of knowing. We are then faced with the problem of finding a bridge between the process of knowing which takes place wholly within the spectator-subject and the object which is indifferent to being known. If, however, we understand that the object of knowledge as such comes into being through the process of knowing, this difficulty does not arise.

The statement that the object of knowledge comes into being through the process of knowing might, considered by itself, be a tautology. For it is tautological to say that nothing is constituted an object of knowledge except by being known. But Dewey obviously does not intend the statement to be a tautology: he intends to say something more. And what he intends is to depict the process of knowing as a highly developed form of the active relation between an organism and its environment, a relation whereby a change is effected in the environment. In other words, he is concerned with giving a naturalistic account of knowledge and with excluding any concept of it as a mysterious phenomenon which is entirely *sui generis*. He is also concerned with uniting theory and practice. Hence knowledge is represented as being itself a doing or making rather than, as in the so-called spectator theory, a 'seeing'.

3. Dewey's account of thought and knowledge is obviously relevant to his concept of philosophy and to his judgments about other philosophers. For example, he is sharply opposed to the idea of philosophy as being concerned with a sphere of unchanging, timeless being and truth. We can indeed explain the genesis of this idea. 'The *world* is precarious and perilous.'[18] That is to say, the hazards to which men are exposed are objective situations. And when they are recognized as hazards, they become problematic situations which man seeks to resolve. But his means for doing so are limited. Further, in his search for security, and so for certainty, man becomes aware that the empirical world, which is a changing world, cannot provide him with absolute security and certainty. And we find Greek philosophers such as Plato making a sharp distinction between the changing, empirical world and the sphere of immutable being and truth. Theory thus becomes divorced from practice.[19] True, philosophy remains an activity. For thought is always an activity. But with Aristotle, for example, purely theoretical activity, the life of con-

templation, is exalted above the practical life, the life of action in a changing world. And it becomes necessary to recall thought to its true function of being directed to resolving indeterminate or problematic situations by effecting changes in the environment and in man himself. Thought and practice have to be once more joined together.

This union of thought and practice is seen most strikingly in the rise of modern science. In the early stages of history man either tried to control the mysterious and threatening forces of Nature by magic or personified them and sought to appease them, though he also practised simple acts such as that of agriculture. Later, as we have seen, there arose that divorce between theory and practice which was effected by philosophy, the idea of man as spectator being substituted for that of man as actor. But with the rise of modern science a new attitude to change shows itself. For the scientist sees that it is only by correlating phenomena that we can understand the process of change and, within limits, control it, bringing about the changes which we desire and preventing those which we regard as undesirable. Thought is thus no longer directed to a celestial sphere of unchanging being and truth; it is redirected to the experienced environment, though on a surer basis than it was in the early stages of humanity. And with the constant growth and progress of the sciences the whole attitude of man towards thought and knowledge has been altered. And this new attitude or vision of the function of thought and knowledge needs to be reflected in our concept of philosophy.

Now, the particular sciences are not themselves philosophy. But science has been commonly conceived as presenting us with the picture of a world which is indifferent to moral values, as eliminating from Nature all qualities and values. And 'thus is created the standing problem of modern philosophy: the relation of science to the things we prize and love and which have authority in the direction of conduct'.[20] This problem, which occupied the mind of, for example, Immanuel Kant, became 'the philosophic version of the popular conflict of science and religion'.[21] And philosophers of the spiritualistic and idealistic traditions, from the time of Kant, or rather from that of Descartes, onwards have tried to solve the problem by saying that the world of science can safely be presented as the sphere of matter and mechanism, stripped of qualities and values, because 'matter and mechanism have their foundation in immaterial mind'.[22] In other words, philosophers have tried to reconcile the scientific view of the world, as they conceived it, with an assertion of the reality of values by developing their several versions of the same sort of dichotomy or dualism which was characteristic of Platonism.

Obviously, Dewey will have nothing to do with this way of solving the problem. For in his view it amounts simply to a resuscitation of an outmoded metaphysics. But though he rejects the notion that there are immutable values, transcending the changing world, he has not the slightest intention of belittling, much less of denying, values. Hence he is committed by his naturalism to maintaining that they are in some sense comprised within Nature, and that advance in scientific knowledge constitutes no threat whatever to the reality of value. 'Why should we not proceed to employ our gains in science to improve our judgments about values, and to regulate our actions so as to make values more secure and more widely shared in existence?'[23] It is not the business of the philosopher to prove in general that there are values. For beliefs about values and value-judgments are inevitable characteristics of man; and any genuine philosophy of experience is aware of this fact. 'What is inevitable needs no proof for its existence.'[24] But man's affections, desires, purposes and devices need direction; and this is possible only through knowledge. Here philosophy can give guidance. The philosopher can examine the accepted values and ideals of a given society in the light of their consequences, and he can at the same time attempt to resolve the conflicts between values and ideals which arise within a society by pointing the way to new possibilities, thus transforming indeterminate or problematic situations in the cultural environment into determinate situations.

The function of philosophy is thus both critical and constructive or, rather, reconstructive. And it is critical with a view to reconstruction. Hence we can say that philosophy is essentially practical. And inasmuch as there is no question of the philosopher competing with the scientist on his own ground, Dewey naturally lays emphasis on moral and social philosophy and on the philosophy of education. True, the philosopher is by no means confined to these topics. As Dewey maintains in *Studies in Logical Theory*, a philosophy of experience includes within its area of inquiry all modes of human experience, including the scientific as well as the moral, religious and aesthetic, and also the social-cultural world in its organized form. And it should investigate the interrelations between these different fields. But if we are thinking of the resolution of specific problematic situations, the philosopher is obviously not in a better position than the scientist to solve scientific problems. From this point of view, therefore, it is natural that Dewey should have come to say that 'the task of future philosophy is to clarify men's ideas as to the social and moral strifes of their own day. Its aim is to become so far as is humanly possible an organ for dealing with these conflicts.'[25]

Now, if the philosopher is conceived as being called upon to throw light on specific problematic situations, it is understandable that general notions and theories should be depreciated. We can understand, for example, Dewey's assertion that whereas philosophical discussion in the past has been carried on 'in terms of *the* state, *the* individual',[26] what is really required is light upon 'this or that group of individuals, this or that concrete human being, this or that special institution or social arrangement'.[27] In other words, when he is concerned with emphasizing the practical function of philosophy, Dewey tends to depreciate general concepts and theories as divorced from concrete life and experience and as associated with a view of philosophy as a purely contemplative activity. His attitude is an expression of his protest against the divorce of theory from practice.

The reader will doubtless object that it is no more the business of the philosopher as such to solve, for instance, specific political problems than it is to solve specific scientific problems. But Dewey does not really intend to say that it is the philosopher's business to do this. What he claims is that 'the true impact of philosophical reconstruction'[28] is to be found in the development of *methods* for reconstructing spe-

cific problematic situations. In other words, Dewey is concerned with the 'transfer of experimental method from the
technical field of physical experience to the wider field of
human life'.[29] And this transfer obviously requires a general
theory of experimental method, while the use of the method
'implies direction by ideas and knowledge'.[30] True, Dewey
has not the slightest intention of encouraging the development of a method which is supposed to possess an *a priori*,
absolute and universal validity. He insists that what is needed
is an intelligent examination of the actual consequences of
inherited and traditional customs and institutions with a
view to intelligent examination of the ways in which their
customs and institutions should be modified in order to produce the consequences which we consider desirable. But this
does not alter the fact that a great part of his reflection is
devoted to developing a general logic of experience and a general theory of experimental method.

It would thus be a gross caricature of Dewey's actual practice if one were to represent him as despising all general concepts and all general theories, still more if we were to represent him as actually doing without such concepts and theories. Without them one could not be a philosopher at all. It
is true that in his contribution to a volume of essays entitled
Creative Intelligence (1917) Dewey roundly asserts that because 'reality' is a denotative term, designating indifferently
everything that happens, no general theory of reality 'is possible or needed',[31] a conclusion which does not appear to
follow from the premises. But in *Experience and Nature*
(1925) he can fairly be said to have himself developed such
a theory, though admittedly not a theory of any reality transcending Nature. Similarly, though in *Reconstruction in Philosophy* he rules out talk about 'the State', this does not
prevent him from developing a theory of the State. Again,
when he asserts that any philosophy which is not isolated
from modern life must grapple with 'the problem of restoring integration and co-operation between man's beliefs about
the world in which he lives and his beliefs about the values
and purposes that should direct his conduct',[32] he is indicating a problem which cannot possibly be discussed without
general ideas. It is not indeed a question of maintaining that

Dewey is perpetually contradicting himself. For example, one might rule out talk about 'the State', meaning by this an eternal essence, and yet make generalizations based on reflection about actual States. Rather is it a question of maintaining that Dewey's insistence on practice, as the termination of inquiry in the reconstruction of a specific problematic situation, leads him at times to speak in a way which does not square with his actual practice.

4. We have noted the stress which Dewey lays on inquiry, inquiry being defined as 'the controlled or directed transformation of an indeterminate situation into one that is so determinate in its constituent distinctions and relations as to convert the elements of the original situation into a unified whole'.[33] He calls, therefore, for a new logic of inquiry. If the Aristotelian logic is considered purely historically, in relation to Greek culture, 'it deserves the admiration it has received'.[34] For it is an admirable analysis of 'discourse in isolation from the operations in which discourse takes effect'.[35] At the same time the attempt to preserve the Aristotelian logic when the advance of science has undermined the ontological background of essences and species on which it rested is 'the main source of existing confusion in logical theory'.[36] Moreover, if this logic is retained when its ontological presuppositions have been repudiated, it inevitably becomes purely formal and quite inadequate as a logic of inquiry. True, Aristotle's logic remains a model in the sense that it combined in a unified scheme both the common sense and the science of his day. But his day is not our day. And what we need is a unified theory of inquiry which will make available for use in other fields 'the authentic pattern of experimental and operational inquiry in science'.[37] This is not to demand that all other fields of inquiry should be reduced to physical science. It is rather that the logic of inquiry has hitherto found its chief exemplification in physical science, and that it needs to be abstracted, so to speak, and turned into a general logic of inquiry which can be employed in all 'inquiries concerned with deliberate reconstruction of experience'.[38] We are thus reminded of Hume's demand that the experimental method of inquiry which had proved so fruitful in physical science or natural philosophy should be

applied in the fields of aesthetics, ethics and politics. But Dewey, unlike Hume, develops an elaborate account of this logic of inquiry.

It would be impracticable to summarize this account here. But certain features can be mentioned. In general, logic is regarded, of course, as instrumental, that is, as a means of rendering intelligent, instead of blind, the action involved in reconstructing a problematic or indeterminate situation. Intelligent action presupposes a process of thought or inquiry, and this requires symbolization and propositional formulation. Propositions in general are the necessary logical instruments for reaching a final judgment which has existential import; and the final judgment is reached through a series of intermediate judgments. Hence judgment can be described as 'a continuous process of resolving an indeterminate, unsettled situation into a determinately unified one, through operations which transform subject-matter originally given'.[39] The whole process of judgment and ratiocination can thus be considered as a phase of intelligent actions, and at the same time as instrumental to actual reconstruction of a situation. Universal propositions, for instance, are formulations of possible ways of acting or operating.[40] They are all of the 'if/then' type.

If logical thought is instrumental, its validity is shown by its success. Hence the standard of validity is 'precisely the degree in which the thinking actually disposes of the difficulty [the problematic situation] and allows us to proceed with more direct modes of experiencing that are forthwith possessed of more assured and deepened value'.[41] In accordance with this view Dewey rejects the idea of the basic principles of logic as being *a priori* truths which are fixed antecedently to all inquiry and represents them as generated in the process of inquiry itself. They represent conditions which have been found, during the continued process of inquiry, to be involved in or demanded by its success. Just as causal laws are functional in character, so are the so-called first principles of logic. Their validity is measured by their success. Instrumentalism in logic thus has a connection with Dewey's naturalism. The basic logical principles are not eternal truths, transcending the changing empirical world and to be apprehended instinctively; they are generated in the actual process of man's active relation with his environment.

In an essay on the development of American pragmatism Dewey defines instrumentalism as 'an attempt to constitute a precise logical theory of concepts, of judgments and inferences in their various forms, by considering primarily how thought functions in the experimental determinations of future consequences'.[42] But there is also an instrumentalist theory of truth. And some brief remarks must be made about this topic.

In a footnote in his *Logic* Dewey remarks that 'the best definition of *truth* from the logical standpoint which is known to me is that of Peirce',[43] namely that the true is that opinion which is fated to be ultimately accepted by all investigators. He also quotes with approval Peirce's statement that truth is the concordance of an abstract statement with the ideal limit towards which endless inquiry would tend to bring scientific belief. Elsewhere, however, Dewey insists that if it is asked what truth is here and now, so to speak, without reference to an ideal limit of all inquiry, the answer is that a statement or an hypothesis is true or false in so far as it leads us to or away from the end which we have in view. In other words, 'the hypothesis that works is the *true* one'.[44] In Dewey's opinion this view of truth follows as a matter of course from the pragmatist concept of meaning.

Dewey is careful to point out that if it is said that truth is utility or the useful, this statement is not intended to identify truth with 'some purely personal end, some profit upon which a particular individual has set his heart'.[45] The idea of utility in this context must be interpreted in relation to the process of transforming a problematic situation. And a problematic situation is something public and objective. A scientific problem, for example, is not a private neurotic worry but an objective difficulty which is resolved by appropriate objective methods. For this reason Dewey avoids speaking with James of truth as the satisfactory or that which satisfies. For this way of speaking suggests a private emotive satisfaction. And if the term 'the satisfactory' is employed, we must understand that the satisfaction in question is that of the demands of a public problematic situation, not the satisfaction of the emotive needs of any individual. For the matter of that, the solution of a scientific problem might occasion great unhappiness to the human race. Yet in so far as it worked or manifested its utility by transforming an objective problematic situation, it would be true and 'satisfactory'.

Though, however, he insists that instrumentalism does not deny the objectivity of truth by making it relative to the individual's whims, wishes and emotive needs, Dewey is, of course, well aware that his theory is opposed to that of eternal, unchanging truths. Indeed, he obviously intends this opposition. He regards the theory of eternal, unchanging truths as implying a certain metaphysics or view of reality, namely the distinction between the phenomenal sphere of becoming and the sphere of perfect and unchanging being, which is apprehended in the form of eternal truths. This metaphysics is, of course, at variance with Dewey's naturalism. Hence the so-called timeless truths have to be represented by him as being simply instruments for application in knowing the one world of becoming, instruments which constantly show their value in use. In other words, their significance is functional rather than ontological. No truth is absolutely sacrosanct, but some truths possess in practice a constant functional value.

This theory that there are no sacrosanct eternal truths, but that all statements which we believe to be true are revisible in principle or from the purely logical point of view, obviously has important implications in the fields of morals and politics. 'To generalize the recognition that the true means the verified and nothing else places upon men the responsibility for surrendering political and moral dogmas, and subjecting to the test of consequences their most cherished prejudices.'[46] In Dewey's opinion this is one of the main reasons why the instrumentalist theory of truth raises fear and hostility in many minds.

5. Passing over for the present any criticism of the instrumentalist theory of truth, we can turn to ethics which Dewey regards as concerned with intelligent conduct in view of an end, with consciously directed conduct. A moral agent is one who proposes to himself an end to be achieved by action.[47]

But Dewey insists that activity, consciously directed to an end which is thought worth while by the agent, presupposes habits as acquired dispositions to respond in certain ways to certain classes of stimuli. 'The act must come before the thought, and a habit before an ability to evoke the thought at will.'[48] As Dewey puts it, it is only the man who already has certain habits of posture and who is capable of standing erect that can form for himself the idea of an erect stance as an end to be consciously pursued. Our ideas, like our sensations, depend on experience. 'And the experience upon which they both depend is the operation of habits—originally of instincts.'[49] Our purposes and aims in action come to us through the medium of habits.

Dewey's insistence on the relevance to ethics of the psychology of habit is partly due to his conviction that habits, as demands for certain kinds of action, 'constitute the self',[50] and that 'character is the interpenetration of habits'.[51] For if such interpenetration, in the sense of an harmonious and unified integration, is something to be achieved rather than an original datum, it obviously follows that moral theory must take habits into account, in so far as it is concerned with the development of human nature.

But Dewey's emphasis on the psychology of habit is also due to his determination to include ethics in his general naturalistic interpretation of experience. Naturalism cannot accommodate such ideas as those of eternal norms, subsistent absolute values or a supernatural moral legislator. The whole moral life, while admittedly involving the appearance of fresh elements, must be represented as a development of the interaction of the human organism with its environment. Hence a study of biological and social psychology is indispensable for the moral philosopher who is concerned with the moral life as it actually exists.

It has already been noted that for Dewey environment does not mean simply the physical, non-human environment. Indeed, from the moral point of view man's relations with his social environment are of primary importance. For it is a mistake to think that morality *ought* to be social: 'morals *are* social'.[52] This is simply an empirical fact. It is true that to a considerable extent customs, which are widespread uniformities of habit, exist because individuals are faced by similar situations to which they react in similar ways. 'But to a larger extent customs persist because individuals form their personal habits under conditions set by prior customs. An individual usually acquires the morality as he inherits the speech of his social group.'[53] This may indeed be more obvious in the case of earlier forms of society. For in modern society, at least of the Western democratic type, the individual is offered a wide range of custom-patterns. But in any case, customs, as demands for certain ways of acting and as forming certain outlooks, constitute moral standards. And we can say that 'for practical purposes morals mean customs, folk-ways, established collective habits'.[54]

At the same time customs, as widespread uniformities of habit, tend to perpetuate themselves even when they no longer answer the needs of man in his relations with his environment. They tend to become matter of mechanical routine, a drag on human growth and development. And to say this is to imply that there is in man another factor, besides habit, which is relevant to morals. This factor is impulse. Indeed, habits, as acquired dispositions to act in certain ways, are secondary to unacquired or unlearned impulses.

This distinction, however, gives rise to a difficulty. On the one hand impulse represents the sphere of spontaneity and thus the possibility of reorganizing habits in accordance with the demands of new situations. On the other hand man's impulses are for the most part not definitely organized and adapted in the way in which animal instincts are organized and adapted. Hence they acquire the significance and definiteness which are required for human conduct only through being canalized into habits. Thus 'the direction of native activity depends upon acquired habits, and yet acquired habits can be modified only by redirection of impulses'.[55] How, then, can man be capable of changing his habits and customs to meet fresh situations and the new demands of a changing environment? How can he change himself?

This question can be answered only by introducing the idea of intelligence. When changing conditions in the environment render a habit useless or detrimental or when a conflict of habits occurs, impulse is liberated from the control of habit and seeks redirection. Left to itself, so to speak, it simply bursts the chains of habit asunder in a wild upsurge. In social life this means that if a society's customs have become outmoded or harmful, and if the situation is left to itself, revolution inevitably occurs, unless perhaps the society simply becomes lifeless and fossilized. The alternative is obviously the intelligent redirection of impulse into new customs and the intelligent creation of fresh institutions. In fine, a 'breach in the crust of the cake of custom releases impulses; but it is the work of intelligence to find the ways of using them'.[56]

In some sense, therefore, intelligence, when seeking to transform or reconstruct a problematic moral situation, has to deliberate about ends and means. But for Dewey there are no fixed ends which the mind can apprehend as something given from the start and perennially valid. Nor will he allow that an end is a value which lies beyond the activity which seeks to attain it. 'Ends are foreseen consequences which arise in the cause of activity and which are employed to give activity added meaning and to direct its further course.'[57] When we are dissatisfied with existing conditions, we can, of course, picture to ourselves a set of conditions which, if actualized, would afford satisfaction. But Dewey insists that an imaginary picture of this kind becomes a genuine aim or end-in-view only when it is worked out in terms of the concrete, possible process of actualizing it, that is, in terms of 'means'. We have to study the ways in which results similar to those which we desire are actually brought about by causal activity. And when we survey the proposed line of action, the distinction between means and ends arises within the series of contemplated acts.

It is obviously possible for intelligence to operate with existing moral standards. But we are considering problematic situations which demand something more than manipulating the current moral ideas and standards of a society. And in such situations it is the task of intelligence to grasp and actualize possibilities of growth, of the reconstruction of experience. Indeed, 'growth itself is the only moral "end" '.[58] Again, 'growing, or the continuous reconstruction of experience, is the only end'.[59]

A natural question to ask is, growth in what direction? Reconstruction for what purpose? But if such questions concern a final end other than growth itself, reconstruction itself, they can have no meaning in terms of Dewey's philosophy. He does indeed admit that happiness or the satisfaction of the forces of human nature is the moral end. But as happiness turns out to be living, while 'life means growth',[60] we seem to be back at the same point. The growth which is the moral end is one which makes possible further growth. In other words, growth itself is the end.

We must remember, however, that for Dewey no genuine end is separable from the means, from the process of its actualization. And he tells us that 'good consists in the meaning that is experienced to belong to an activity when conflict and entanglement of various incompatible impulses and habits terminate in a unified orderly release in action'.[61] So we can say perhaps that for Dewey the moral end is growth in the sense of the dynamic development of harmoniously integrated human nature, provided that we do not envisage a fixed and determinate state of perfection as the final end. There is for Dewey no final end save growth itself. The attainment of a definite and limited end-in-view opens up new vistas, new tasks, fresh possibilities of action. And it is in grasping and realizing these opportunities and possibilities that moral growth consists.

Dewey tries, therefore, to get rid of the concept of a realm of values distinct from the world of fact. Values are not something given; they are constituted by the act of evaluating, by the value-judgment. This is not a judgment that something is 'satisfying'. For to say this is simply to make a statement of fact, like the statement that something is sweet or white. To make a value-judgment is to say that something is 'satisfactory' in the sense that it fulfils specifiable conditions.[62] For example, does a certain activity create conditions for further growth or does it prevent them? If I say that it does, I declare the activity to be valuable or a value.

It may be objected that to say that something fulfils certain specifiable conditions is no less a statement of fact than to say that an object is satisfying, in the sense that I myself or many people or all men find it satisfying. But Dewey is aware that to ask whether something is a value is to ask whether it is 'something to be prized and cherished, *to be* enjoyed',[63] and that to say that it is a value is to say that it is something *to be* desired and enjoyed.[64] Hence the following definition. 'Judgments about values are judgments about the conditions and the results of experienced objects; judgments about that which should regulate the formation of our desires, affections and enjoyments.'[65]

The emphasis, however, is placed by Dewey on the judgment of value as the term of a process of inquiry, stimulated by a problematic situation. For this enables him to say that his theory of values does not do away with their objectivity. Something is a value if it is adapted 'to the needs and demands imposed by the situation',[66] that is to say, if it meets the demands of an objective problematic situation, in regard to its transformation or reconstruction. A judgment of value, like a scientific hypothesis, is predictive, and it is thus empirically or experimentally verifiable. 'Appraisals of courses of action as better and worse, more or less serviceable, are as experimentally justified as are non-valuative propositions about impersonal subject matter.'[67] The transfer of the experimental method from physics to ethics would mean, of course, that all judgments and beliefs about values would have to be regarded as hypotheses. But to interpret them in this way is to transfer them from the realm of the subjective into that of the objective, of the verifiable. And as much care should be devoted to their framing as is devoted to the framing of scientific hypotheses.

6. Dewey's insistence on growth obviously implies that personality is something to be achieved, something in the making. But the human person is not, of course, an isolated atom. It is not simply a question of the individual being under an obligation to consider his social environment: he *is* a social being, whether he likes it or not. And all his actions 'bear the stamp of his community as assuredly as does the language he speaks'.[68] This is true even of those courses of activity of which society in general disapproves. It is a man's relations with his fellow-men which provide him both with the opportunities for action and with the instruments for taking advantage of such opportunities. And this is verified in

the case of the burglar or the dealer in the white slave traffic no less than in that of the philanthropist.

At the same time the social environment, with its institutions, has to be organized and modified in the manner best suited for promoting the fullest possible development in desirable ways of the capacities of individuals. And at first sight we are faced with a vicious circle. On the one hand the individual is conditioned by the existing social environment in regard to his habits of action and his aims. On the other hand, if the social environment is to be changed or modified, this can be accomplished only by individuals, even though by individuals working together and sharing common aims. How, then, is it possible for the individual, who is inevitably conditioned by his social environment, to devote himself to changing that environment in a deliberate and active manner?

Dewey's answer is what one would expect, namely that when a problematic situation arises, such as a clash between man's developing needs on the one hand and existing social institutions on the other, impulse stimulates thought and inquiry directed to transforming or reconstructing the social environment. As in morals, the task-in-hand is always in the forefront of Dewey's mind. The function of political philosophy is to criticize existing institutions in the light of man's development and changing needs and to discern and point out practical possibilities for the future to meet the needs of the present. In other words, Dewey looks on political philosophy as an instrument for concrete action. This means that it is not the business of the political philosopher to construct Utopias. Nor should he allow himself to succumb to the temptation of delineating 'the State', the essential concept of a state, which is supposed to be perennially valid. For to do this is in effect to canonize, even though unconsciously, an existing state of affairs, probably one that has already been challenged and subjected to criticism. In any case inquiry is hindered rather than helped by solutions which purport to cover all situations. If, for example, we are concerned with determining the value of the institution of private property in a given society at a certain period, it is no help to be told either that private property is a sacred, inviolable and perennial right or that it is always theft.

Obviously, the process of criticizing existing social institutions and of pointing the way to fresh concrete possibilities requires some standard to which men can refer. And for Dewey the test for all such institutions, whether political, juridical or industrial, is 'the contributions they make to the all-around growth of every member of society'.[69] It is for this reason that he favours democracy, namely as founded on 'faith in the capacities of human nature, faith in human intelligence and in the power of pooled and co-operative experience'.[70] Yet 'the prime condition of a democratically organized public is a kind of knowledge and insight which does not yet exist',[71] though we can indicate some of the conditions which have to be fulfilled if it is to exist. Democracy as we know it is thus the settling for the free use of the experimental method in social inquiry and thought, which is required for the solution of concrete social, political and industrial problems.

We have seen that for Dewey the moral end is growth, and that the degree to which they facilitate growth provides a test for assessing the value of social and political institutions. The idea of growth is also the key to his educational theory. Indeed, 'the educative process is all one with the moral process'.[72] And education is 'getting from the present the degree and kind of growth there is in it'.[73] It follows that as the potentiality for growth or development does not cease with the close of adolescence, education should not be regarded as a preparation for life. It is itself a process of living.[74] In fact, 'the educational process has no end beyond itself; it is its own end'.[75] True, formal schooling comes to an end; but the educative influence of society, social relations and social institutions affects adults as well as the young. And if we take, as we should, a broad view of education, we can see the importance of effecting those social and political reforms which are judged most likely to foster the capacity for growth and to evoke those responses which facilitate further development. Morals, education and politics are closely interconnected.

Given this general view of education, Dewey naturally stresses the need of making the school as far as possible a real community, to reproduce social life in a simplified form and thus to promote the development of the child's capacity to participate in the life of society in general. Further, he emphasizes, as one would expect, the need for training children in intelligent inquiry. Struck by the contrast between the lack of interest shown by many children in their school instruction and their lively interest in those activities outside the school in which they are able to share personally and actively, he concludes that scholastic methods should be so changed as to allow the children to participate actively as much as possible in concrete processes of inquiry leading from problematic situations to the overt behaviour or actions needed to transform the situation. But we cannot enter into further details of Dewey's ideas about education in the ordinary sense. His main conviction is that education should not be simply instruction in various subjects but rather a coherent unified effort to foster the development of citizens capable of promoting the further growth of society by employing intelligence fruitfully in a social context.

7. For many years Dewey was comparatively reticent about religion. In *Human Nature and Conduct* (1922), he spoke of religion as 'a sense of the whole',[76] and remarked that 'the religious experience is a reality in so far as in the midst of effort to foresee and regulate future objects we are sustained and expanded in feebleness and failure by the sense of an enveloping whole'.[77] And in *The Quest for Certainty* (1929) we find him maintaining that Nature, including humanity, when it is considered as the source of ideals and possibilities of achievement and as the abode of all attained goods, is capable of evoking a religious attitude which can be described as a sense of the possibilities of existence and as devotion to the cause of their actualization.[78] But these were more or less incidental remarks, and it was not until 1934 that Dewey really tackled the subject of religion in *A Common Faith*, which was the published version of a series of Terry Foundation Lectures delivered at Yale University.

Although, however, Dewey had previously written little about religion, he made it clear that he himself rejected all definite creeds and religious practices. And it was indeed obvious that his empirical naturalism had no room for belief in or worship of a supernatural divine being. At the same time Dewey had also made it clear that he attached some value to what he called a religious attitude. And in A Common Faith we find him distinguishing between the noun 'religion' and the adjective 'religious'. The noun he rejects, in the sense of rejecting definite religious creeds, institutions and practices. The adjective he accepts, in the sense that he affirms the value of religion as a quality of experience.

It must be understood, however, that Dewey is not speaking of any specifically religious and mystical experience, such as might be used to support belief in a supernatural Deity. The quality which he has in mind is one which can belong to an experience that would not ordinarily be described as religious. For example, the experience or feeling of being at one with the universe, with Nature as a whole, possesses this quality. And in A Common Faith Dewey associates the quality of being 'religious' with faith in 'the unification of the self through allegiance to inclusive ideal ends, which imagination presents to us and to which the human will responds as worthy of controlling our desires and choices'.[79]

As for the word 'God', Dewey is prepared to retain it, provided that it is used to signify not an existent supernatural being but rather the unity of the ideal possibilities which man can actualize through intelligence and action. 'We are in the presence neither of ideals completely embodied in existence nor yet of ideals that are mere rootless ideals, fantasies, utopias. For there are forces in nature and society that generate and support the ideals. They are further unified by the action that gives them coherence and solidity. It is this *active* relation between ideal and actual to which I would give the name "God".'[80]

A naturalistic philosophy, in other words, can find no room for God as conceived in the Jewish, Christian and Mohammedan religions. But a philosophy of experience must find room for religion in some sense of the term. Hence the quality of being 'religious' must be detached, as it were, from specifically religious experiences, in the sense of experience which purports to have for its object a supernatural being, and reattached to other forms of experience. As Dewey notes in A Common Faith the adjective 'religious' can apply to attitudes which can be adopted towards any object or any ideal. It can apply to aesthetic, scientific or moral experience or to experience of friendship and love. In this sense religion can pervade the whole of life. But Dewey himself emphasizes the religious character of the experience of the unification of the self. As 'the self is always directed toward something beyond itself',[81] its ideal unification depends upon a harmonizing of the self with the universe, with Nature as a totality. And here Dewey stresses, as we have seen, the movement towards the realization of ideal possibilities. One might perhaps expect him to recognize an active divine principle operating in and through Nature for the realization and conservation of values. But even if much of what he says points in the direction of some such idea, his naturalism effectively prevents him from taking such a step.

8. Obviously, Dewey's philosophy is not a metaphysics if by this term we mean a study or doctrine of meta-empirical reality. But though, as has already been noted, he denies, in one place at least, that any general theory of reality is needed or even possible, it is clear enough that he develops a worldview. And world-views are generally classed under the heading of metaphysics. It would be ingenuous to say that Dewey simply takes the world as he finds it. For the plain fact is that he interprets it. For the matter of that, in spite of all that he has to say against general theories, he does not really prohibit all attempts to determine the generic traits, as he puts it, of existence of all kinds. What he does is to insist that 'the generic insight into existence which alone can define metaphysics in any empirically intelligible sense is itself an added fact of interaction, and is therefore subject to the same requirement of intelligence as any other natural occurrence: namely, inquiry into the bearings, leadings and consequences of what it discovers. The universe is no infinite self-representative series, if only because the addition within it of a representation makes it a different universe.'[82] So far as metaphysics in the sense of ontology is admitted,[83] its findings become working hypotheses, as much subject to revision as are the hypotheses of physical science. Presumably Dewey's own world-view is such a working hypothesis.

It is arguable that this world-view shows traces of its author's Hegelian past, in the sense at any rate that Nature is

substituted for Hegel's Spirit and that Dewey tends to interpret the philosophical systems of the past in relation to the
cultures which gave birth to them. This second point helps
to explain the fact that when Dewey is treating of past systems, he bothers very little, if at all, about the arguments
advanced on their behalf by their authors and dwells instead
on the inability of these systems to deal with the problematic
situations arising out of contemporary culture. This attitude
is, of course, in accordance with his instrumentalist view of
truth. But the result is that the attentive and critical reader
of his books receives the impression that the naturalistic view
of the world is assumed, not proved. And in the opinion of
the present writer this impression is justified. Dewey simply
assumes, for example, that the day of theological and metaphysical explanations is past, and that such explanations were
bogus. And the observation that such explanations do not
serve as instruments to solve, say, contemporary social problems is insufficient to show the validity of the assumption.

The reply may be made that if Dewey's philosophy of experience, his general world-view, succeeds in giving a coherent
and unified account of experiences as a whole, no further
justification is required for excluding superfluous hypotheses
which go beyond the limits of naturalism. But it is open to
question whether Dewey's philosophy as a whole is really
coherent. Consider, for example, his denial of absolute values
and fixed ends. He asserts, as we have seen, the objectivity
of values; but he regards them as relative to the problematic
situations which give rise to the processes of inquiry that terminate in value-judgments. Yet it certainly appears that
Dewey himself speaks of 'growth' as though it were an absolute value and an end in itself, an end fixed by the nature
of man and ultimately by the nature of reality. Again, Dewey
is careful to explain that he has no intention of denying the
existence of a world antecedently to human experience; and
he asserts that we experience many things *as* antecedently
prior to our experiencing them. At the same time there is a
strong tendency to interpret 'experience' in terms of the reconstruction of situations, a reconstruction which makes the
world different from what it would have been without human
operational thinking. And this points to a theory of creative

experience which tends to turn the antecedently given into a kind of mysterious thing-in-itself.

Obviously, the presence of inconsistencies in Dewey's thought does not disprove naturalism. But it does at any rate render an assumption of a naturalistic point of view more open to criticism than it would have been if Dewey had succeeded in giving a perfectly unified and coherent world-view or interpretation of experience. It is clearly not sufficient to answer that on Dewey's own premises his world-view is a working hypothesis which must be judged by its 'consequences' and not by the comparative absence of antecedent arguments in its favour. For the 'working' of a world-view is shown precisely in its ability to give us a coherent and unified conceptual mastery over the data.

If we turn to Dewey's logical theory, we again encounter difficulties of some moment. For instance, though he recognizes, of course, that there are basic logical principles which have constantly shown themselves to be objectively useful instruments in coping with problematic situations, he insists that from a purely logical point of view no principle is sacrosanct; all are revisible in principle. At the same time Dewey evidently assumes that intelligence cannot rest satisfied with a problematic situation, with an unresolved conflict or 'contradiction'. As in the philosophy of Hegel, the mind is forced on towards an overcoming of such contradictions.[84] And this seems to imply an absolute demand of the intellect, a demand which it is difficult to reconcile with the view that no logical principles are absolute.

Again, there seems to be some ambiguity in the use of the word 'consequences'. A scientific hypothesis is interpreted as predictive, and it is verified if the predicted consequences, which constitute the meaning of the hypothesis, are realized. Whether verification brings subjective satisfaction to people or not, is irrelevant. In this context Dewey is careful to avoid the objection, to which James exposes himself, that the 'satisfying' character of a proposition is the test of its truth. But when we come to the social and political spheres, we can see a tendency to slide into the interpretation of 'consequences' as desirable consequences. Dewey would probably reply that what he is talking about is 'intended' consequences. The solution to a social or political problematic situation 'intends', has as its meaning, certain consequences. And, as in the case of scientific hypotheses, verification validates the proposed solution. Whether people like the solution or not is beside the point. In both cases, in that of the social or political solution or plan as in that of the scientific hypothesis, the test of truth or validity is objective. Yet it seems fairly obvious that in practice Dewey discriminates between political plans and solutions and theories in terms of their contribution to 'growth', their promotion of an end which he considers desirable. One might, of course, apply the same criterion in an analogous sense to scientific hypotheses. For example, an hypothesis which tends to arrest further scientific inquiry and advance cannot be accepted as true. But then the test of truth is no longer simply the verification of the consequences which are said to form the meaning of the hypothesis, though it may indeed tend to coincide with Peirce's conception of truth as the ideal limit to which all inquiry converges.

The strength of Dewey's philosophy doubtless lies in the fact that its author always has his eye on empirical reality, or concrete situations and on the power of human intelligence and will to deal with these situations and to create possibilities of further development. Dewey brings philosophy down to earth and tries to show its relevance to concrete problems, moral, social and educational. And this helps to explain his great influence. He is a rather dull writer. And he is not a conspicuously precise and clear writer. His success in bringing his ideas to the attention of so many of his fellow-countrymen is not due to his literary gifts: it must be attributed in great part to the practical relevance of his ideas. Besides, his general world-view is undoubtedly capable of appealing to those who look on theological and metaphysical tenets as outmoded, and perhaps also as attempts to preserve vested interests, and who at the same time seek a forward-looking philosophy which does not appeal in any way to supernatural realities but in some sense justifies a faith in indefinite human progress.

For these reasons the activity of finding inconsistencies and ambiguities in Dewey's thought may appear to some minds a poor sort of game to play, a futile sniping at a philosophy which, by and large, is firmly rooted in the soil of experience. To others, however, it may well appear that practical relevance is bought, so to speak, at the expense of a thorough explicitation, examination and justification of the foundations of the philosophy. It may also appear that in the long run Dewey's philosophy rests on a judgment of value, the value of action. One can, of course, base a philosophy on a judgment or on judgments of value. But it is desirable that in this case the judgments should be brought into the open. Otherwise one may think, for example, that the instrumentalist theory of truth is simply the result of a dispassionate analysis.

PART V

THE REVOLT
AGAINST IDEALISM

Chapter Seventeen

REALISM IN BRITAIN AND AMERICA

An introductory remark – Some Oxford realists – Brief notes on an ethical discussion at Oxford – American neo-realism – Critical realism in America – The world-view of Samuel Alexander – A reference to A. N. Whitehead.

1. When we think of the revolt against idealism in Great Britain, the names which immediately come to mind are those of two Cambridge men, G. E. Moore and Bertrand Russell. Moore, however, is universally acknowledged to be one of the chief inspirers of the analytic movement, as it is commonly called, which has enjoyed a spectacular success in the first half of the twentieth century. And Russell, besides being another of the principal pioneers of this movement, is by far the most widely known British philosopher of this century. The present writer, therefore, has decided to postpone the brief treatment of them which is all that the scope of this volume allows and to treat first of a number of comparatively minor figures, even if this means neglecting the demands of chronological order.

2. Mention has already been made of the way in which idealism came to occupy a dominating position in the British universities, especially at Oxford, during the second half of the nineteenth century. But even at Oxford the triumph of idealism was not complete. For example, Thomas Case (1844–1925), who occupied the chair of metaphysics from

1899 until 1910 and was President of Corpus Christi College from 1904 until 1924, published *Realism in Morals* in 1877 and *Physical Realism* in 1888. It is indeed true that in itself Case's realism was opposed to subjective idealism and to phenomenalism rather than to objective or to absolute idealism. For it consisted basically in the thesis that there is a real and knowable world of things existing independently of sense-data.[1] At the same time, while in the war against materialism Case was on the side of the idealists, he regarded himself as continuing or restoring the realism of Francis Bacon and of scientists such as Newton and as an opponent of the then fashionable idealist movement.[2]

A more notable opponent of idealism was John Cook Wilson (1849-1915), who occupied the chair of logic at Oxford from 1889 until the year of his death. He published very little, his main influence being exercised as a teacher. But a two-volume collection of lectures on logic, essays and letters, together with a memoir by the editor, A. S. L. Farquharson, appeared posthumously in 1926 with the title *Statement and Inference*.

As an undergraduate Cook Wilson had been influenced by T. H. Green, and later he went to Göttingen to hear Lotze. But he gradually became a sharp critic of idealism. He did not, however, oppose to it a rival world-view. His strength lay partly in attack and partly in the way in which he selected particular problems and tried to follow them through with meticulous care and thoroughness. In this sense his thought was analytic. Further, he had an Aristotelian respect for the distinctions expressed in or implied by ordinary language. And he was convinced that logicians would do well to pay both attention and defence to the natural logic of common linguistic usage.

One of Cook Wilson's grievances against the logic of Bradley and Bosanquet is their doctrine of judgment. In his view they assume that there is one mental act, namely judging, which finds expression in every statement. And to make this assumption is to confuse mental activities, such as knowing, opining and believing, which ought to be distinguished. Further, it is a serious mistake to suppose that there is an activity called judging which is distinct from inference. 'There is no such thing.'[3] If logicians paid more attention to the ways in which we ordinarily use such terms as 'judge', they would see that to judge that something is the case is to infer it. In logic we can get along quite well with statement and inference, without introducing a fictitious separate activity, namely judging.

A statement, therefore, can express various activities. But of these knowing is fundamental. For we cannot understand what is meant by, for example, having an opinion or wondering whether something is true except by way of a contrast with knowledge. It by no means follows, however, that knowledge can be analyzed and defined. We can indeed ask how we come to know or what we know, but the question, What is knowledge itself? is absurd. For to demand an answer is to presuppose that we can estimate its truth, and it is thus presupposed that we are already aware what knowledge is. Knowledge can be exemplified but not explained or defined. Nor does it stand in need of any further justification than pointing to examples of it.

We can indeed exclude false accounts of knowledge. These take two main forms. On the one hand there is the attempt to reduce the object to the act of apprehension by interpreting knowledge as a making, a construction of the object. On the other hand there is the tendency to describe the act of apprehension in terms of the object, by maintaining that what we know is a 'copy' or representation of the object. This thesis makes knowledge impossible. For if what we know immediately is always a copy or idea, we can never compare it with the original, to see whether it tallies or not.

Refutations of false accounts of knowledge presuppose, however, that we are already well aware of what knowledge is. And we are aware of it by actually knowing something. Hence to ask, what is knowledge? as though we were ignorant, is just as much an improper question as Bradley's query, how is a relation related to its term? A relation is simply not the sort of thing which can be intelligibly said to be related. And knowledge is an indefinable and *sui generis* relation between a subject and an object. We can say what it is not, that it neither makes the object nor terminates in a copy of the object; but we cannot define what it is.

Cook Wilson's realism obviously assumes that we perceive physical objects which exist independently of the act of perception. In other words, he denies the thesis that *esse est percipi*, to be is to be perceived.[4] At the same time he finds it necessary to qualify his realism. Thus when dealing with the so-called secondary qualities he takes the example of heat and maintains that what we perceive is our own sensation of heat, while that which exists in the physical object is simply a power to cause or produce this sensation in a subject. This power 'is not perceived but inferred by a scientific theory'.[5] When, however, he is dealing with the so-called primary qualities, Cook Wilson maintains that we feel, for example, the extension of an actual body and not simply our tactual and muscular sensations. In other words, in his discussion of the relation of qualities to physical things he occupies a position close to that of Locke.

Indeed, we can say that Cook Wilson's realism involves the contention that the world which we know is simply the world as conceived by the classical Newtonian scientists. Thus he rejects the idea of non-Euclidean space or spaces. In his view mathematicians actually employ only the Euclidean concept of space, 'none other of course being possible for thought, while they imagine themselves to be talking of another kind of space'.[6]

The general outlook of Cook Wilson was shared by H. A. Prichard (1871–1947), who occupied the chair of moral philosophy at Oxford. In the first place 'it is simply *impossible* to think that any reality depends upon our knowledge of it, or upon any knowledge of it. If there is to be knowledge, there must first *be* something to be known.'[7] Obviously, the activities of Sherlock Holmes, as related by Conan Doyle, depend upon the mind in a sense in which stones and stars do not. But I could not claim to 'know' what Sherlock Holmes did unless there was first something to be known. In the second place 'knowledge is *sui generis*, and, as such, cannot be explained'.[8] For any alleged explanation necessarily presupposes that we are aware what knowledge is. In the third place secondary qualities cannot exist independently of a percipient subject, and consequently they 'cannot be qualities of things, since the qualities of a thing must exist independently of the perception of a thing'.[9]

In view of the last-mentioned point it is not surprising to find Prichard maintaining, in his posthumously published collection of essays *Knowledge and Perception* (1950), that we never actually see physical objects but only coloured and spatially related extensions, which we 'mistake' for physical bodies. If we ask how it comes about that we judge these sense-data to be physical objects, Prichard replies that it is not a case of judging at all.[10] We are naturally under the impression that what we see are physical bodies existing independently of perception. And it is only in the course of subsequent reflection that we come to infer or judge that this is not the case.

If, therefore, we start with the position of common sense or naïve realism, we must say that both Cook Wilson and Prichard modified this position, making concessions to the other side. Further concessions were made by H. W. B. Joseph (1867–1943), Fellow of New College, Oxford, and an influential teacher. Thus in a paper on Berkeley and Kant which he read to the British Academy Joseph remarks that common sense realism is badly shaken by reflection, and he suggests that though the things outside us are certainly not private in the sense in which my pain is private, they may be bound up 'with the being of knowing and perceiving minds'.[11] Joseph also suggests that reflection on the philosophies of Berkeley and Kant points to the conclusion that the conditions of our knowledge of objects may depend 'upon a reality or intelligence which shows itself in nature to itself in minds'.[12]

The last remark is clearly a concession to metaphysical idealism rather than to any form of subjective idealism. But this simply illustrates the difficulty in maintaining that in our knowledge of physical objects knowing is a relation of compresence between a subject and an object which is entirely heterogeneous to mind. As for the discussion of sense-data, a discussion which received a powerful impetus at Oxford from Professor H. H. Price's *Perception*,[13] this illustrates the difficulty in maintaining successfully a position of naïve realism. That is to say, problems arise for reflection which suggest that the position has to be modified. One way of coping with this situation is to dismiss the problems as pseudo-problems. But this was not an expedient adopted by the older Oxford philosophers whom we have been considering.

3. H. A. Prichard, who was mentioned in the last section, is probably best known for his famous essay in *Mind* (1912) on the question, 'Does Moral Philosophy rest on a Mistake?'[14] Moral philosophy is conceived by Prichard as being largely concerned with trying to find arguments to prove that what seem to be our duties really are our duties. And his own thesis is that in point of fact we simply see or intuit our duties, so that the whole attempt to prove that they are duties is mistaken. True, there can be argument in some sense. But what is called argument is simply an attempt to get people to look more closely at actions in order that they may see for themselves the characteristic of being obligatory. There are, of course, situations which give rise to what we are accustomed to call a conflict of duties. But in the case of an apparent conflict of this kind it is a mistake to try to resolve it by arguing, as so many philosophers have done, that one of the alternative actions will produce a greater good of some sort, this good being external to and a consequence of the action. The question at issue is, which action has the greater degree of obligatoriness? And the question cannot be answered in any other way than by looking closely at the actions until we *see* which is the greater obligation. This is, after all, what we are accustomed to do in practice.

This ethical intuitionism obviously implies that the concepts of right and obligation are paramount in ethics and take precedence over the concept of good. In other words, teleological ethical systems, such as the Aristotelian and the Utilitarian, rest on a fundamental mistake. And in the period after the First World War a discussion took place at Oxford on the themes raised by Prichard. It was conducted more or less independently of, though not without some reference to, the views of G. E. Moore. But we can say that it expressed a strong reaction against the type of position represented by the Cambridge philosopher. For though Moore had maintained in *Principia Ethica* (1903) that goodness is an indefinable quality,[15] he made it quite clear that in his opinion a moral obligation is an obligation to perform that action which will produce the greater amount of goodness.

In 1922 Prichard devoted his inaugural lecture as professor of moral philosophy at Oxford to the theme 'Duty and Interest', developing therein his point of view. In 1928 E. F. Carritt published *The Theory of Morals* in which he maintained that the idea of a *summum bonum*, a supreme good, is the *ignis fatuus* of moral philosophy, and that any attempt to prove that certain actions are duties because they are means to the realization of some end considered as good is foredoomed to failure. The famous Aristotelian scholar, Sir W. D. Ross, then Provost of Oriel College, Oxford, contributed to the discussion by his book on *The Right and The Good* (1930). And this was followed in 1931 by Joseph's *Some Problems in Ethics*, in which the author characteristically tried to combine admission of the thesis that obligation is not derived from the goodness of the consequences of an action with the thesis that obligation is none the less not independent of any relation to goodness.

In other words, Joseph attempted to compromise between Prichard's view and the Aristotelian tradition. And in his little work *Rule and End in Morals* (1932), which was intended as a summing-up of the Oxford discussions, Professor J. H. Muirhead of the University of Birmingham drew attention to signs of a return, welcomed by himself, towards an Aristotelian-idealist view of ethics. But in 1936 there appeared *Language, Truth and Logic*, the celebrated logical positivist manifesto by A. J. Ayer, in which a statement such as 'actions of type X are wrong' was interpreted, not as the expression of any intuition, but as an utterance expressing an emotive attitude towards actions of type X and as also calculated to arouse a similar emotive attitude in others. And though the emotive theory of ethics certainly cannot be said to have won the universal assent of British moral philosophers, it stimulated a new phase of discussion in ethical theory, a phase which lies outside the scope of this volume.[16] Hence when Sir David Ross published *The Foundations of Ethics* in 1939, his intuitionism seemed to some at any rate to belong to a past phase of thought. However, on looking back we can see how the discussion by Prichard, Ross, Joseph and others of concepts such as those of the right and the good represented an analytic approach to moral philosophy which was different from the idealist tendency to treat ethics as a subordinate theme dependent on a metaphysical world-view. Yet we can also see how in the subsequent phase of ethical discussion philosophers have at length been led to doubt whether ethics can profitably be confined in a water-tight compartment as a study of the language of morals.[17]

4. To turn now to realism in the United States of America. In March 1901 William Pepperell Montague (1873–1953) published in *The Philosophical Review* an article entitled 'Professor Royce's Refutation of Realism'. And in October of the same year Ralph Barton Perry (1876–1957) published in *The Monist* a paper on 'Professor Royce's Refutation of Realism and Pluralism'. Both articles, therefore, were answers to Royce's attack on realism as destructive of the possibility of knowledge. And in 1910 the two writers, together with E. B. Holt (1873–1946), W. T. Marvin (1872–1944), W. B. Pitkin (1878–1953), and E. G. Spaulding (1873–1940), published in the *Journal of Philosophy* 'The Program and First Platform of Six Realists'.[18] This was followed by the publication in 1912 of a volume of essays by these authors under the title, *The New Realism: Co-operative Studies in Philosophy*.

As was stated in the 1910 programme and as the sub-title of *The New Realism* indicates, this group of philosophers aimed at making philosophy a genuine co-operative pursuit, at least among those thinkers who were prepared to accept the basic tenets of realism. They insisted on a scrupulous care of language as the instrument of all philosophy, on analysis considered as 'the careful, systematic and exhaustive examination of any topic of discourse',[19] on separating vague complex problems into definite questions which should be dealt with separately, and on a close association with the special sciences. By this approach to philosophy the new realist hoped, therefore, to overcome the subjectivism, looseness of thought and language, and disregard of science which in their opinion had tended to bring philosophy into disrepute. In other words, a reform of philosophy in general was to go hand in hand with the development of a realist line of thought.

The new realists were at any rate agreed on the truth of a basic tenet, namely that, as Pitkin expressed it, 'things known are not products of the knowing relation nor essentially dependent for their existence or behaviour upon that relation'.[20] This tenet corresponds with our natural spontaneous belief, and it is demanded by the sciences. Hence the burden of proof rests fairly and squarely on the shoulders of those who deny it. But the disproofs offered by the idealists are fallacious. For instance, they slide from a truism, that it is only when objects are known that we know that they exist, or from the tautology 'no object without a subject', to a substantial but unproven conclusion, namely that we know that objects exist only as objects, that is, only when they are known, as terms of the knowing relation.

This obviously implies that knowledge is an external relation. As Spaulding puts it, knowledge is 'eliminable',[21] in the sense that a thing can exist when it is not known and that, when not known, it can be precisely what it is when it is known, with the obvious difference that it is then not the term of the external relation of knowing. There must thus be at least one kind of external relation. And we can say in general that the new realists accepted the theory of relations as external to their terms. This view obviously favoured pluralism rather than monism in metaphysics. And it also pointed to the impossibility of deducing the world-system *a priori*.

The ordinary man's spontaneous reaction to the basic tenet of realism would undoubtedly be one of unqualified acceptance. For he is obviously accustomed to think of physical objects as existing quite independently of the knowing relation and as being entirely unaffected by this relation in their natures or characteristics. But reflection shows us that some account has to be taken of illusions, hallucinations and such like phenomena. Are they to be described as objects of knowledge? If so, can they reasonably be said to be real independently of the subject? And what of apparently converging railway-lines, sticks which appear bent when half immersed in water, and so on? Can we say that such percepts exist independently of perception? Must we not at any rate modify realism in such a way as to be able to assert that some objects of consciousness exist independently while others do not?

Holt's way of dealing with the matter is to make a distinction between being and reality. Realism does not commit us to holding that all perceived things are real. 'While all perceived things are things, *not* all perceived things are *real* things.'[22] It does not follow, however, that 'unreal' objects of perception or of thought are to be described as 'subjective' in character. On the contrary, the unreal has being and 'subsists of its own right in the all-inclusive universe of being'.[23] In fine, 'the universe is not all real; but the universe all is'.[24]

Obviously, some explanation of this use of terms is required. And in the first place what does Holt mean by reality? The answer, 'as to what reality is, I take no great interest',[25] is not very promising. But Holt goes on to say that, if challenged, he would 'hazard the guess that perhaps reality is some very comprehensive system of terms in relation. . . . This would make reality closely related to what logic knows as "existence" '.[26] This suggests that an hallucinatory object, for example, is unreal in the sense that it cannot be fitted, without contradiction, into the most universal system of related terms. But Holt remarks that 'I shall not call an hallucinatory object necessarily "unreal" '.[27] The point on which he insists, however, is that unreality does not exclude objectivity. If, for instance, I assume certain geometrical premisses at will and deduce a consistent system, the system is 'objective', even if it is described as 'unreal'. And to say that the unreal is objective, not subjective, is what Holt means by saying that it has being.

As for converging railway lines, sticks which appear bent in water and so on, Holt maintains that a physical object has innumerable projective properties, with which there correspond different specific responses in the nervous systems of different percipient organisms. Hence if we abstract from the particular purpose or purposes which lead us to select one appearance as a thing's 'real' appearance, we can say that all its appearances are on the same footing. They are all objective, and they subsist as projective properties. We are thus offered the picture of 'a general universe of being in which all things physical, mental, and logical, propositions and terms, existent and non-existent, false and true, good and evil, real and unreal *subsist*'.[28]

As Montague was afterwards to point out when discussing the differences between himself and some of his colleagues in the neo-realist group, there are considerable objections to putting all these things on the same footing. In the first place, the relations between objects of perception can be asymmetrical. For instance, on the assumption that the stick partly immersed in water is straight, we can easily explain why it appears bent. But if we assume that it is bent, we cannot explain why it appears straight in the circumstances in which it does appear to be straight. And this difficulty is certainly not overcome by saying that the stick is bent when it is partly immersed in water, while it is straight when it is out of the water. Again, some objects can produce effects only indirectly by means of the subject which conceives them, while other objects can also produce effects directly. For example, a dragon, as object of thought, might conceivably stimulate a man to make a voyage of exploration; but it could not produce the effects which can be produced by a lion. And we need to be able to make clear distinctions between the ontological statuses of these different classes of objects.

The new realists also concerned themselves with discussing the nature of consciousness. Holt and Perry, partly under the influence of William James, accepted the doctrine of neutral monism, according to which there is no ultimate substantial difference between mind and matter. And they tried to eliminate consciousness as a peculiar entity by explaining awareness of an object as a specific response by an organism. Montague interpreted this as meaning that the response consists of a motion of particles. And he asked how this theory, which he described as behaviourism, could possibly explain, for example, our awareness of past events. He himself identified the specific response which constitutes consciousness with 'the relation of self-transcending implication, which the brain-states sustain to their extra-organic causes'.[29] But it is not at all clear how brain-states can exercise any such self-transcending function. Nor does it help very much to be told that the possibility of the cortical states transcending themselves and providing awareness of objects is 'a matter for psychology rather than epistemology'.[30]

However, it is at any rate clear that the new realists were intent on maintaining that, as Montague put it, 'cognition is a peculiar type of relation which may subsist between a living being and any entity . . . [that it] belongs to the same world as that of its objects . . . [and that] there is nothing transcendental or supernatural about it'.[31] They also rejected all forms of representationalism. In perception and knowledge the subject is related directly to the object, not indirectly by means of an image or some sort of mental copy which constitutes the immediate term of the relation.

5. This rejection by the neo-realists of all representationalism seemed to some other philosophers to be naïve and uncritical. It was this rejection which led to physical and hallucinatory objects being placed on the same footing. And it made it impossible to explain, for instance, our perception of a distant star when the star has ceased to exist. Thus there soon arose a movement of critical realism, formed by philosophers who agreed with the neo-realists in rejecting idealism but who found themselves unable to accept their thoroughgoing rejection of representationalism.

Like neo-realism, critical realism found expression in a joint-volume, *Essays in Critical Realism: A Co-operative Study of the Problems of Knowledge*, which appeared in 1920. The contributors were D. Drake (1898–1933), A. O. Lovejoy (1873–1962), J. B. Pratt (1875–1944), A. K. Rogers (1868–1936), G. Santayana (1863–1952), R. W. Sellars (b. 1880), and C. A. Strong (1862–1940).

The strength of critical realism lay in attack. For example, in *The Revolt against Dualism* (1930), Lovejoy argued that while neo-realists originally appealed to common sense in their rejection of representationalism, they then proceeded to give an account of objects which was incompatible with the common sense point of view. For to maintain with Holt that all the appearances of a thing are on the same footing as its objective projective properties is to commit oneself to saying that railway lines are both parallel and convergent, and that the surface of, say, a penny is both circular and elliptical.

In expounding their own doctrine, however, the critical realists encountered considerable difficulties. We can say that they were agreed in maintaining that what we directly perceive is some character-complex or immediate datum which functions as a sign of or guide to an independently existing thing. But they were not in full agreement about the nature of the immediate datum. Some were prepared to speak about such data as mental states.[32] And in this case they would presumably be in the mind. Others, such as Santayana, believed that the immediate data of consciousness are essences, and ruled out any question as to their whereabouts on the ground that they exist only as exemplified. In any case, if representationalism is once admitted, it seems to follow that the existence of physical objects is inferred. And there then arises the problem of justifying this inference. What reason have I for supposing that what I actually perceive represents something other than itself? Further, if we never perceive physical objects directly, how can we discriminate between the representative values of different sense-data?

The critical realists tried to answer the first question by maintaining that from the very start and by their very nature the immediate data of perception point to physical objects beyond themselves. But they differed in their accounts of this external reference. Santayana, for instance, appealed to animal faith, to the force of instinctive belief in the external reference of our percepts, a belief which we share with the animals, while Sellars relied on psychology to explain how our awareness of externality develops and grows in definiteness.

As for the question, how can we discriminate between the representative values of sense-data if we never perceive physical objects directly? one may be tempted to answer, 'In the way that we actually do discriminate, namely by verification'. And this may be an excellent answer from the practical point of view. After all, travellers in the desert, interpreting a mirage as a prediction that they will find water ahead of them, find by bitter experience that the prediction is not verified. At the same time a theoretical difficulty still remains for the representationalist to solve. For on his premises the process of verification terminates in sensory experience or the having of sense-data and is not a magic wand which, when waved, gives us direct access to what lies beyond sense-data. True, if what we are seeking is the sensory experience of a slaking of thirst, having this experience is all that is required from the practical point of view. But from the point of view of the theory of knowledge the representationalist seems to remain immersed in the world of 'representation'.

The fact of the matter is, of course, that on the level of common sense and practical life we can get along perfectly well. And in ordinary language we have developed distinctions which are quite sufficient to cope for all practical purposes with sticks partially immersed in water, converging railway lines, pink rats, and so on. But once we start to reflect on the epistemological problems to which such phenomena appear to give rise, there is the temptation to embrace some overall solution, either by saying that all the objects of awareness are objective and on the same footing or by saying that they are all subjective mental states or sense-data which are somehow neither subjective nor objective. In the first case we have neo-realism, in the second critical realism, provided, of course, that the immediate data are regarded as representative of or in some way related to independent physical objects. Both positions can be regarded as attempts to reform ordinary language. And though this enterprise cannot be ruled out *a priori*, the fact that both positions give rise to serious difficulties may well prompt us, with the late Professor J. L. Austin, to take another look at ordinary language.

The word 'realism' can have different shades of meaning. In this chapter it has as its basic meaning the view that knowledge is not a construction of the object, that knowing is a relation of compresence between a subject and an object, which makes no difference to the object. We have seen, however, that in the realist movement problems arose about the immediate objects of perception and knowledge. At the same time we do not wish to give the quite erroneous impression that the American philosophers who belonged to the two groups which have been mentioned were exclusively concerned with the problems to which attention has been drawn in this and the preceding sections. Among the neo-realists Perry, for example, became well known as a moral philoso-

pher,[33] and also devoted himself to political and social
themes. Among the critical realists Santayana developed a
general philosophy,[34] while Strong and Drake expounded a
panpsychistic ontology, taking introspection as a key to the
nature of reality.[35] Sellars defended a naturalistic philosophy,[36] based on the idea of emergent evolution with irreducible levels and comprising a theory of perception as an
interpretative operation. Lovejoy exercised a considerable influence by his studies in the history of ideas.[37]

6. A realist theory of knowledge, in the sense already described, obviously does not exclude the construction of a
metaphysical system or world-view. All that is excluded is a
metaphysics based on the theory that knowledge is a construction of the object or on the theory that creative thought
or experience is the basic, primary reality. And in point of
fact there have been a considerable number of world-views
in modern philosophy, which presupposed a realist theory of
knowledge. To mention them all is, however, out of the question. And I propose to confine myself to making some remarks
about the world-view of Samuel Alexander.

Samuel Alexander (1859–1938) was born in Sydney, Aus-
tralia, but went to Oxford in 1877, where he came under the
influence of Green and Bradley. This influence, however, was
supplanted by that of the idea of evolution, as well as by an
interest in empirical psychology, which was scarcely a characteristic of Oxford at the time.[38] Later on Alexander received stimulus from the realism of Moore and Russell and
came to approach, though he did not altogether accept, the
position of American neo-realism. But he regarded the theory
of knowledge as preparatory to metaphysical synthesis. And
it may well be true that his impulse to metaphysical construction, though not the actual content of his system, was
due in some measure to the early influence of idealism on
his mind.

In 1882 Alexander was elected a Fellow of Lincoln College, Oxford. And the influence of evolutionary thought can
be seen in the book which he published in 1889, *Moral Order
and Progress: An Analysis of Ethical Conceptions*. As the title
of the book indicates, Alexander considered ethics to be concerned with the analysis of moral concepts, such as good and

evil, right and wrong. But he also regarded it as a normative science. In his interpretation of the moral life and of moral concepts he carried on the line of thought represented by Herbert Spencer and Sir Leslie Stephen. Thus in his view the struggle for survival in the biological sphere takes the form in the ethical sphere of a struggle between rival moral ideals. And the law of natural selection, as applying in the moral field, means that that set of moral ideals tends to prevail which most conduces to the production of a state of equilibrium or harmony between the various elements and forces in the individual, between the individual and society, and between man and his environment. There is thus an ultimate and overall ideal of harmony which in Alexander's view includes within itself the ideals upheld by other ethical systems, such as happiness and self-realization. At the same time the conditions of life, physical and social, are constantly changing, with the result that the concrete meaning of equilibrium or harmony assumes fresh forms. Hence, even though there is in a real sense an ultimate end of moral progress, it cannot be actually attained in a fixed and unalterable shape, and ethics cannot be expressed in the form of a set of static principles which are incapable of modification or change.

To turn to Alexander's realism.[39] His basic idea of knowledge is that it is simply a relation of compresence or togetherness between some object and a conscious being. The object, in the sense of the thing known, is what it is whether it is known or not. Further, Alexander rejects all forms of representationalism. We can, of course, direct our attention explicitly to our mental acts or states. But they do not serve as copies or signs of external things which are known only indirectly. Rather do we 'enjoy' our mental acts while knowing directly objects which are other than the acts by which we know them. Nor are sense-data intermediate objects between consciousness and physical things, they are perspectives of things. Even a so-called illusion is a perspective of the real world, though it is referred by the mind to a context to which it does not belong.[40] Further, in knowing the past by memory we really do know the past. That is to say, pastness is a direct object of experience.

In 1893 Alexander was appointed professor of philosophy

in the University of Manchester. In the years 1916–18 he delivered the Gifford Lectures at Glasgow, and the published version appeared in 1920 under the title *Space, Time and Deity*. In this work we are told that metaphysics is concerned with the world as a whole, thus carrying comprehensiveness to its furthest limits. In Aristotelian language we can say that it is the science of being and its essential attributes, investigating 'the ultimate nature of existence if it has any, and those pervasive characters of things, or categories'.[41] But though metaphysics has a wider subject-matter than any special science, its method is empirical, in the sense that, like the sciences, it uses 'hypotheses by which to bring its data into verifiable connection'.[42] At the same time the pervasive and essential attributes of things can be described as non-empirical or *a priori* provided that we understand that the distinction between the empirical and the non-empirical lies within the experienced and is not equivalent to a distinction between experience and what transcends all experience. Bearing this in mind, we can define metaphysics as 'the experiential or empirical study of the non-empirical or *a priori*, and of such questions as arise out of the relation of the empirical to the *a priori*'.[43]

According to Alexander, ultimate reality, the basic matrix of all things, is space-time. Precisely how he arrived at this notion, it is difficult to say. He mentions, for example, the idea of a world in space and time formulated by H. Minkowski in 1908. And he refers to Lorentz and Einstein. Further, he speaks with approval of Bergson's concept of real time, though with disapproval of the French philosopher's subordination of space to time. In any case Alexander's notion of space-time as the ultimate reality is obviously opposed to Bradley's relegation of space and time to the sphere of appearance and to McTaggart's theory of the unreality of time. Alexander is concerned with constructing a naturalistic metaphysics or world-view; and he begins with what is for him both the ultimate and, when considered purely in itself, the primitive phase of the evolutionary process.

The naïve way of conceiving space and time is as receptacles or containers. And a natural corrective to this crude image is to depict them as relations between individual entities, relations respectively of co-existence and succession. But this view clearly implies that individual entities are logically prior to space and time, whereas the hypothesis embraced by Alexander is that space and time constitute 'the stuff or matrix (or matrices) out of which things or events are made, the medium in which they are precipitated and crystallized'.[44] If we consider either space or time by itself, its elements or parts are indistinguishable. But 'each point of space is determined and distinguished by an instant in time, and each instant of time by its position in space'.[45] In other words, space and time together constitute one reality, 'an infinite continuum of pure events or point-instants'.[46] And empirical things are groupings or complexes of such events.

Alexander proceeds to discuss the pervasive categories or fundamental properties of space-time, such as identity, diversity and existence, universal and particular, relation, causality and so on. The stage is thus set for an examination of the emergence of qualities and of levels of empirical reality, from matter up to conscious mental activity. We cannot discuss all these themes here. But it is worth drawing attention to Alexander's doctrine of 'tertiary qualities'.

The tertiary qualities are values, such as truth and goodness. They are called 'tertiary' to distinguish them from the primary and secondary qualities of traditional philosophy. But as applied to values the term 'qualities' should really be placed in inverted commas, to indicate that 'these values are not qualities of reality in the same sense as colour, or form, or life'.[47] To speak of them as objective qualities of reality can be misleading. For instance, reality is not, properly speaking, either true or false: it is simply reality. Truth and falsity are properly predicated of propositions as believed, that is, in relation to the mind which believes them, not of things, nor even of propositions when considered simply as mental facts. Similarly, a thing is good, according to Alexander, only in relation to a purpose, as when we speak of a good tool. Again, though a red rose is red whether anyone perceives it or not, it is beautiful only in relation to the mind which appreciates its 'coherence'. But it by no means follows that we are entitled to speak of the tertiary qualities or values as purely subjective or as unreal. They emerge as real features of the universe, though only in relation to minds or conscious subjects. They are, in fine, 'subject-object determinations',[48] which 'imply the amalgamation of the object with the human appreciation of it'.[49]

The relation between subject and object is not, however, invariable. In the case of truth, for example, appreciation by the subject is determined by the object. For in knowledge reality is discovered, not made. But in the case of goodness the quality of being good is determined primarily by the subject, that is, by purpose, by the will. There is, however, a common factor which must be noted, namely that the appreciation of values in general arises in a social context, out of the community of minds. For instance, it is in relation to the judgment of others that I become aware that a proposition is false; and in my judgments about truth or falsity I represent what we can call the collective mind. 'It is social intercourse, therefore, which makes us aware that there is a reality compounded of ourselves and the object, and that in that relation the object has a character which it would not have except for that relation.'[50]

This doctrine of the emergence of tertiary qualities enables Alexander to insist that evolution is not indifferent to values. 'Darwinism is sometimes thought to be indifferent to value. It is in fact the history of how values come into existence in the world of life.'[51] We thus have the general picture of a process of evolution in which different levels of finite being emerge, each level possessing its own characteristic empirical quality. 'The highest of these empirical qualities known to us is mind or consciousness.'[52] And at this level the tertiary qualities or values emerge as real features of the universe, though this reality involves a relation to the subject, the human mind.

Now, Alexander's work is entitled *Space, Time and Deity*. Hence the question arises, how does Deity fit into this scheme or world-view? The philosopher's answer is that 'Deity is the next higher empirical quality to the highest we know'.[53] We obviously cannot say what this quality is. But we know that it is not any quality with which we are already acquainted. For that it should be any such quality is ruled out by definition.

Does it follow from this that God exists only in the future, so to speak, being identifiable with the next level of finite being to emerge in the process of evolution? To this question Alexander gives a negative answer. As an actually existent being, God is the universe, the whole space-time continuum. 'God is the whole world as possessing the quality of deity. . . . As an actual existent, God is the infinite world with its nisus towards deity, or, to adapt a phrase of Leibniz, as big or in travail with deity.'[54]

Alexander was of Jewish origin and it is not unreasonable to see in his view of God a dynamic version of Spinoza's pantheism, adapted to the theory of evolution. But there is an obvious difficulty in maintaining both that God is the whole world as possessing the quality of Deity and that this quality is a future emergent. Alexander is aware of this, of course. And he concludes that 'God as an actual existent is always becoming deity but never attains it. He is the ideal God in embryo.'[55] As for religion, it can be described as 'the sentiment in us that we are drawn towards Him [God], and caught in the movement of the world to a higher level of existence'.[56]

Given his premisses, Alexander's position is understandable. On the one hand, if Deity is the quality of a future level of being, and if God were identifiable with the actual bearer of this quality, he would be finite. On the other hand, the religious consciousness, Alexander assumes, demands a God who is not only existent but also infinite. Hence God must be identified with the infinite universe as striving after the quality of Deity. But to say this is really to do no more than to apply a label, 'God', to the evolving universe, the space-time continuum. To be sure, there is some similarity between Alexander's view and that of Hegel. At the same time Hegel's Absolute is defined as Spirit, whereas Alexander's is defined as Space-Time. And this renders the label 'God' even more inappropriate. What is appropriate is the description of religion as a 'sentiment'. For in a naturalistic philosophy this is precisely what religion becomes, namely some kind of cosmic emotion.

7. Owing to the development and spread of a current of thought which has been accompanied by a marked distrust

of all comprehensive world-views, little attention has been paid to Alexander's philosophy.[57] In any case, in the field of speculative philosophy his star has been completely eclipsed by that of Alfred North Whitehead (1861–1947), the greatest English metaphysical philosopher since Bradley. True, it can hardly be claimed that the influence of Whitehead as a speculative philosopher on recent British philosophy has been extensive or profound. Given the prevailing climate of philosophical thought, one would hardly expect it to have been. Whitehead's influence has in fact been greater in America, where he worked from 1924 until his death, than in his native land. In the last few years, however, interest in his thought has shown itself in a considerable number of books and articles published in Great Britain.[58] And his name has become increasingly known in Europe. In other words, Whitehead is recognized as a major thinker, whereas Alexander tends to be forgotten.

From one point of view, Whitehead's philosophy certainly qualifies for inclusion in this chapter. True, he himself drew attention to the affinity between the results of his philosophizing and absolute idealism. Thus in his preface to *Process and Reality* he notes that 'though throughout the main body of the work I am in sharp disagreement with Bradley, the final outcome is after all not so greatly different'.[59] At the same time Whitehead, who came from mathematics to the philosophy of science and Nature, and thence to metaphysics, intended to return to a pre-idealist attitude and point of departure. That is to say, just as some of the pre-Kantian philosophers had philosophized in close association with the science of their time, Whitehead considered that the new physics demanded a fresh effort in speculative philosophy. He did not start from the subject-object relation or from the idea of creative thought, but rather from reflection on the world as presented in modern science. His categories are not simply imposed by the *a priori* constitution of the human mind; they belong to reality, as pervasive features of it, in much the same sense as Aristotle's categories belonged to reality. Again, Whitehead gives a naturalistic interpretation of consciousness, in the sense that it is depicted as a developed, emergent form of the relation of 'prehension' which is found between all actual entities. Hence when he notes the affinity between the results of his speculative philosophy and some features of absolute idealism he also suggests that his type of thought may be 'a transformation of some main doctrines of Absolute Idealism on to a realistic basis'.[60]

But though Whitehead's philosophy, as standing on what he calls a realistic basis, certainly qualifies for consideration in this chapter, it is far too complicated to summarize in a few paragraphs. And after some consideration the present writer has decided not to make the attempt. It is, however, worth noting that Whitehead was convinced of the inevitability of speculative or metaphysical philosophy. That is to say, unless a philosopher deliberately breaks off at a certain point the process of understanding the world and of generalization, he is inevitably led to 'the endeavour to frame a coherent, logical, necessary system of general ideas in terms of which every element of our experience can be interpreted'.[61] Moreover, it is not simply a question of synthesizing the sciences. For the analysis of any particular fact and the determination of the status of any entity require in the long run a view of the general principles and categories which the fact embodies and of the entity's status in the whole universe. Linguistically speaking, every proposition stating a particular fact requires for its complete analysis an exhibition of the general character of the universe as exemplified in this fact. Ontologically speaking, 'every definite entity requires a systematic universe to supply its requisite status'.[62] Wherever we start, therefore, we are led to metaphysics, provided that we do not break off the process of understanding on the way.

This point of view assumes, of course, that the universe is an organic system. And it is Whitehead's sustained attempt to show that the universe is in fact a unified dynamic process, a plurality-in-unity which is to be interpreted as a creative advance into novelty, that constitutes his philosophical system. As already noted, the total result of his speculation bears some resemblance to absolute idealism. But the world as presented by Whitehead is certainly not the dialectical working-out of an absolute Idea. The total universe, comprising both God and the world, is said to be caught 'in the grip of the ultimate metaphysical ground, the creative advance into novelty'.[63] It is 'creativity',[64] not thought, which is for him the ultimate factor.

Chapter Eighteen

G. E. MOORE AND ANALYSIS

Life and writings – Common sense realism – Some remarks on Moore's ethical ideas – Moore on analysis – The sense-datum theory as an illustration of Moore's practice of analysis.

1. In the last chapter we had occasion to consider briefly some Oxford realists. But when one thinks of the collapse of idealism in England and of the rise of a new dominating current of thought, one's mind naturally turns to the analytic movement which had its origins at Cambridge and which in the course of time established itself firmly at Oxford and in other universities. It is true that in its later phase it has become commonly known as 'Oxford philosophy'; but this does not alter the fact that the three great pioneers of and stimulative influences in the movement, Moore, Russell and Wittgenstein, were all Cambridge men.

George Edward Moore (1873–1958) went up to Cambridge in 1892, where he began by studying classics. He has remarked that he does not think that the world or the sciences would ever have suggested to him philosophical problems. In other words, left to himself he tended to take the world as he found it and as it was presented by the sciences. He appears to have been entirely free from Bradley's dissatisfaction with all our ordinary ways of conceiving the world, and he did not hanker after some superior way of viewing it. Still less was he tortured by the problems which beset Kierkegaard, Jaspers, Camus and such-like thinkers. At the same time Moore became interested in the queer things which philosophers have said about the world and the sciences; for example, that time is unreal or that scientific knowledge is not really knowledge. And he was diverted from classics to philosophy, partly under the influence of his younger contemporary, Bertrand Russell.

In 1898 Moore was awarded a Prize-Fellowship at Trinity College, Cambridge. And in 1903 he published *Principia Ethica*. After an absence from Cambridge he was appointed Lecturer in Moral Science in 1911; and in the following year he published his little work, *Ethics*, in the Home University Library Series. In 1921 he succeeded G. F. Stout as editor of *Mind*; and in 1922 he published *Philosophical Studies*, consisting for the most part of reprinted articles. In 1925 Moore was elected to the Chair of Philosophy at Cambridge on the retirement of James Ward. In 1951 he was awarded the *Order of Merit*; and in 1953 he published *Some Main Problems of Philosophy. Philosophical Papers*, a collection of essays prepared for publication by Moore himself, appeared posthumously in 1959, while his *Commonplace Book*, 1919–53, a selection from his notes and jottings, was published in 1962.

2. According to Bertrand Russell, it was Moore who led the rebellion against idealism. And Moore's early realism can be illustrated by reference to an article on the nature of judgment, which he published in *Mind* during the year 1899.

In this article Moore takes as his text Bradley's statement that truth and falsity depend on the relation between ideas and reality, and he refers with approval to Bradley's explanation that the term 'ideas' does not signify mental states but rather universal meanings.[1] Moore then proceeds to substitute 'concept' for 'idea' and 'proposition' for 'judgment', and to maintain that what is asserted in a proposition is a specific relation between concepts. In his view this holds good also of existential judgments. For 'existence is itself a concept'.[2] But Moore rejects the theory that a proposition is true or false in virtue of its correspondence or lack of correspondence with a reality or state of affairs other than itself. On the contrary, the truth of a proposition is an identifiable property of the proposition itself, belonging to it in virtue of the relation obtaining, within the proposition, between the concepts which compose it. 'What kind of relation makes a proposition true, what false, cannot be further defined, but must be immediately recognized.'[3] It is not, however, a relation between the proposition and something outside it.

Now, as Moore says that concepts are 'the only objects of knowledge',[4] and as propositions assert relations between concepts and are true or false simply in virtue of the relation asserted, it looks at first sight as though he were expounding a theory which is the reverse of anything which could reasonably be described as realism. That is to say, it looks as though Moore were creating an unbridgeable gulf between the world of propositions, which is the sphere of truth and falsity, and the world of non-propositional reality or fact.

We have to understand, however, that for Moore concepts are not abstractions, mental constructs formed on the basis of the material provided by sense-data, but rather objective realities, as with Meinong. Further, we are invited 'to regard the world as formed of concepts'.[5] That is to say, an existent thing is a complex of concepts, of universals such as whiteness for example, 'standing in a unique relation to the concept of existence'.[6] To say this is not to reduce the world of existing things to mental states. On the contrary, it is to eliminate the opposition between concepts and things. And to say that concepts are the objects of knowledge is to say that we know reality directly. When, therefore, Moore says of concepts that they must *be* something before they can enter into a relation with a cognitive subject and that 'it is indifferent to their nature whether anybody thinks them or not',[7] we can see what he means. He is saying that knowledge makes no difference to the object. It doubtless has its causes and effects; but 'these are to be found only in the subject'.[8] Construction of the object is certainly not one of the effects of knowing.

If a proposition consists of concepts standing in a specific relation to one another, and if concepts are identical with the realities conceived, it obviously follows that a true proposition must be identical with the reality which it is commonly considered as representing and with which it is commonly said to correspond. And in an article on truth,[9] Moore did not hesitate to maintain that the proposition 'I exist' does not differ from the reality 'my existence'.

As Moore was well aware at the time of writing, this theory sounds extremely odd. But what is more serious than its oddity is the difficulty in seeing how it does not eliminate the distinction between true and false propositions. Suppose, for example, that I believe that the earth is flat. If what I believe is a proposition, it seems to follow from the account of propositions explained above, that the earth being flat is a reality. Moore, therefore, came to throw overboard the idea that what we believe is propositions. In fact he came to jettison the idea of propositions at all, at any rate in the sense in which he had formerly postulated them. At the same time he clung to a realist view of knowledge as a unique unanalyzable relation between a cognitive subject and an object, a relation which makes no difference to the nature of the object. As for the truth or falsity of beliefs, he came to admit that this must depend in some sense on correspondence or the lack of it, though he felt unable to give any clear account of the nature of this correspondence.

Now, if being the term of the unique and indefinable relation in which knowledge consists makes no difference to the nature of the object, there must be at any rate one external relation. And in point of fact Moore, having ascribed to the idealists the view that no relation is purely external, in the sense that there is no relation which does not affect the natures or essences of the terms, proceeds to reject it. Thus in an article on the concept of the relative[10] he distinguishes between the terms 'relative' and 'related' and asserts that the former term, when predicated of a thing, implies that the relation or relations referred to are essential to the subject of which the term is predicated. But this implies that the relation of something which is a whole to something else is identical with or a part of the whole. And this notion, Moore maintains, is self-contradictory. In other words, a thing is what it is, and it is not definable in terms of its relations to anything else. Hence a thing's nature cannot be constituted by the nature of the system to which it belongs; and idealist monism is thus deprived of one of its main foundations.

Moore's best-known criticism of idealism is, of course, his article entitled *The Refutation of Idealism*.[11] In it he maintains that if modern idealism makes any general assertion at all about the universe, it is that the universe is spiritual. But it is not at all clear what this statement means. And it is thus very difficult to discuss the question whether the universe is or is not spiritual. When we examine the matter, however, we find that there is a large number of different propositions which the idealist has to prove if he is to establish the truth of his general conclusion. And we can inquire into the weight of his arguments. Obviously, the statement that the universe is spiritual in character might still be true even if all the arguments advanced by idealists to prove its truth were fallacious. At the same time to show that the arguments were fallacious would be at any rate to show that the general conclusion was entirely unproved.

According to Moore, every argument used to prove that reality is spiritual has as one of its premisses the proposition *esse est percipi*, to be is to be perceived. And one's natural reaction to this contention is to comment that belief in the truth of *esse est percipi* is characteristic of Berkeley's idealism, and that it should not be attributed to Hegel, for instance, or to Bradley. But Moore understands *percipi* as including 'that other type of mental fact, which is called "thought"',[12] and as meaning, in general, to be experienced. And on this interpretation of *percipi* Bradley could be counted as subscribing to the thesis *esse est percipi*, inasmuch as everything is for him a constituent element in one all-comprehensive absolute experience.

As Moore understands *esse est percipi* in such a broad sense, it is not surprising that he finds the thesis ambiguous and capable of being interpreted in several ways. However, let us take it that acceptance of the thesis commits one to holding, among other things, that the object of a sensation cannot be distinguished from the sensation itself, or that, insofar as a distinction is made, it is the result of illegitimate abstraction from an organic unity. Moore undertakes to show that this view is false.

In the first place we are all aware, for example, that the sensation of blue differs from that of green. Yet if they are both sensations, they must have something in common. And Moore calls this common element 'consciousness', while the differentiating elements in the two sensations he calls their respective 'objects'. Thus 'blue is one object of sensation and green is another, and consciousness, which both sensations have in common, is different from either'.[13] On the one hand, as consciousness can co-exist with other objects of sensation besides blue, we obviously cannot legitimately claim that blue is the same thing as consciousness alone. On the other hand, we cannot legitimately claim that blue is the same thing as blue together with consciousness. For if we could, the statement that blue exists would have the same meaning as the statement that blue co-exists with consciousness. And this cannot be the case. For if, as has already been admitted, consciousness and blue are distinct elements in the sensation of blue, it makes sense to ask whether blue can exist without consciousness. And it would not make sense if the statement that blue exists and the statement that blue co-exists with consciousness had exactly the same meaning.

It may be objected that by using the term 'object' instead of 'content' this line of argument simply begs the question. In point of fact blue is the content, rather than the object, of the sensation of blue. And any distinction which we may make between the elements of content and consciousness or awareness is the result of an operation of abstraction performed on an organic unity.

For Moore, however, an appeal to the concept of organic unity is tantamount to an attempt to have things both ways. That is to say, a distinction is allowed and prohibited at the same time. In any case Moore is not prepared to admit that 'content' is a more appropriate term than 'object'. It is legitimate to speak of blue as part of the content of a blue flower. But a sensation of blue is not itself blue: it is awareness or consciousness of blue as an object. And 'this relation is just that which we mean in every case by "knowing"'.[14] To know or be aware of blue is not to have in the mind a representative image of which blue is the content or part of the content; it is to be directly aware of the object 'blue'.

According to Moore, therefore, the awareness which is included in sensation is the same unique relation which basically constitutes every kind of knowledge. And the problem of getting out of the subjective sphere or circle of our sensations, images and ideas is a pseudo-problem. For 'merely to have a sensation is already to *be* outside that circle. It is to know something which is as truly and really *not* a part of *my* experience, as anything which I can ever know.'[15]

It can be added, with reference to the idealist thesis that reality is spiritual, that according to Moore we possess precisely the same evidence for saying that there are material things as we possess for saying that we have sensations. Hence to doubt the existence of material things entails doubting the existence of our sensations, and of experience in general. To say this is not to say, or even to suggest, that nothing is spiritual. It is to say that if the statement that reality is spiritual entails denying the existence of material things, we have no possible reason for making the statement. For 'the only *reasonable* alternative to the admission that matter exists *as well as* spirit, is absolute scepticism—that, as likely as not, *nothing* exists at all'.[16] And this is not a position which we can consistently propose and maintain.

In his discussion of sensation and perception, a discussion to which we shall have to return presently, Moore can be said to be concerned with phenomenological analysis. But it is obvious that his general attitude is founded on a common sense realism. And this element in his thought comes out clearly in the famous essay entitled A *Defence of Common sense*,[17] where he maintains that there are a number of propositions, the truth of which is known with certainty. Thus I know that there is at present a living human body which is my body. I know also that there are other living bodies besides my own. I know too that the earth has existed for many years. Further, I know that there are other people, each of whom knows that there is a living body which is his own body, that there are other living bodies besides his own, and that the earth has existed for many years. Again, I know not only that these people are aware of the truth of these propositions but also that each of them knows that there are other people who are aware of the same truths. Such propositions belong to the common sense view of the world. And it follows, according to Moore, that they are true. There may indeed be differences of opinion about whether a given proposition belongs or not to the common sense view of the world. But if it does, it is true. And if it is known to belong, it is known to be true. And it is known to be true because of the reasons which we actually have for stating that it is true, not for any supposedly better reasons which philosophers may claim to be able to provide. It is no more the philosopher's business to prove the truth of propositions which we already know to be true than it is his business to disprove them.

Moore's defence of common sense has been referred to here simply as an illustration of one aspect of his realism. We shall have to return to the subject in connection with his conception of analysis. Meanwhile we can profitably take a glance at some of his ethical ideas, which, apart from their intrinsic interest, seem to illustrate the fact that his realism is not a 'naturalistic' realism.

3. Some moral philosophers, Moore remarks, have considered adequate the description of ethics as being concerned with what is good and what is bad in human conduct. In point of fact this description is too narrow. For other things besides human conduct can be good, and ethics can be described as 'the general inquiry into what is good'.[18] In any case, before we ask the question 'what is good?', meaning 'what things and which kinds of conduct possess the property of being good?', it seems logically proper to ask and answer the question, 'what is good?', meaning 'how is good to be defined?', 'what is goodness in itself?' For unless we know the answer to this question, it may be argued, how can we discriminate between good and bad conduct and say what things possess the property of goodness?

Moore insists that when he raises the question, 'how is good to be defined?', he is not looking for a purely verbal definition, the sort of definition which consists simply in substituting other words for the word to be defined. Nor is he concerned with establishing or with justifying the common usage of the word 'good'. 'My business is solely with that object or idea, which I hold, rightly or wrongly, that the word is generally used to stand for. What I want to discover is the nature of that object or idea.'[19] In other words, Moore is concerned with phenomenological rather than with linguistic analysis.

Having raised the question, Moore proceeds to assert that

it cannot be answered, not because good is some mysterious, occult and unrecognizable quality but because the idea of good is a simple notion, like that of yellow. Definitions which describe the real nature of an object are only possible when the object is complex. When the object is simple, no such definition is possible. Hence good is indefinable. This does not entail the conclusion that the things which are good are indefinable. All that is being maintained is that the notion of good as such is a simple notion and hence 'incapable of any definition, in the most important sense of that word'.[20]

From this doctrine of good as an indefinable property or quality there follow some important conclusions. Suppose, for example, that someone says that pleasure is the good. Pleasure may be one of the things which possess the property of being good; but if, as is probably the case, the speaker imagines that he is giving a definition of good, what he says cannot possibly be true. If good is an indefinable property, we cannot substitute for it some other property, such as pleasurable. For even if we admitted, for the sake of argument, that all those things which possess the property of being good also possess the property of being pleasurable, pleasure would still not be, and could not be, the same as good. And anyone who imagines that it is or could be the same, is guilty of the 'naturalistic fallacy'.[21]

Now, the fallacy in question is basically 'the failure to distinguish clearly that unique and indefinable quality which we mean by good'.[22] Anyone who identifies goodness with some other quality or thing, whether it be pleasure or self-perception or virtue or love, saying that this is what 'good' *means*, is guilty of this fallacy. These things may perfectly well possess the quality of goodness in the sense, for example, that what is pleasurable also possesses the quality of being good. But it no more follows that to be pleasurable is the same thing as to be good than it would follow, on the supposition that all primroses are yellow, that to be a primrose and to be yellow are the same thing.

But, it may well be asked, why should this fallacy be described as 'naturalistic'? The only real reason for so describing it would obviously be the belief that goodness is a 'non-natural' quality. Given this belief, it would follow that those who identify goodness with a 'natural' quality are guilty of a naturalistic fallacy. But though in *Principia Ethica* Moore does indeed maintain that goodness is a non-natural quality, he greatly complicates matters by distinguishing between two groups of philosophers who are both said to be guilty of the naturalistic fallacy. The first group consists of those who uphold some form of naturalistic ethics by defining good in terms of 'some one property of things, which exists in time'.[23] Hedonism, which identifies pleasure and goodness, would be an example. The second group consists of those who base ethics on metaphysics and define good in metaphysical terms, in terms of or by reference to a supersensible reality which transcends Nature and does not exist in time. According to Moore, Spinoza is an example, when he tells us that we become perfect in proportion as we are united with Absolute Substance by what he calls the intellectual love of God. Another example is provided by those who say that our final end, the supreme good, is the realization of our 'true' selves, the 'true' self not being anything which exists here and now in Nature. What, then, is meant by saying that good is a 'non-natural' quality, if at the same time those who define good in terms of or with reference to a 'non-natural' reality or quality or experience are said to be guilty of the naturalistic fallacy?

The answer which immediately suggests itself is that there is no incompatibility between asserting that good is an indefinable non-natural quality and denying that it can be defined in terms of some other non-natural quality. Indeed, the assertion entails the denial. But this consideration by itself does not tell us in what sense good is a non-natural quality. In *Principia Ethica* Moore makes it clear that he has not the slightest intention of denying that good can be a property of natural objects. 'And yet I have said that "good" itself is not a natural property.'[24] What, then, is meant by saying that good can be, and indeed is, a non-natural property of at least some natural objects?

The answer provided in *Principia Ethica* is extremely odd. A natural property, or at any rate most natural properties, can exist by themselves in time, whereas good cannot. 'Can we imagine "good" as existing *by itself* in time, and not merely as a property of some natural object?'[25] No, we certainly cannot imagine this. But neither can we imagine a natural quality such as being brave existing *by itself* in time. And when Professor C. D. Broad, for example, pointed this out, Moore said that he completely agreed. It is not surprising, therefore, to find him eventually admitting roundly that 'in *Principia* I did not give any tenable explanation of what I meant by saying that "good" was not a natural property'.[26]

In his essay on the conception of intrinsic value in *Philosophical Studies* Moore gave another account of the distinction between natural and non-natural properties. He later admitted that this account was really two accounts; but he maintained that one of them might possibly be true. If one ascribes to a thing a natural intrinsic quality, one is always describing it to some extent. But if one ascribes to a thing a non-natural intrinsic quality, one is not describing the thing at all.

Obviously, if good is a non-natural intrinsic quality, and if to ascribe this quality to an object is not to describe the object in any way at all, the temptation immediately arises to conclude that the term 'good' expresses an evaluative attitude, so to speak, and that to call a thing good is to express this attitude and at the same time a desire that others should share this attitude. But if this conclusion is drawn, the view that goodness is an intrinsic quality of things has to be abandoned. And Moore was not prepared to abandon it. He believed that we can recognize what things possess the quality of being good, though we cannot define the quality. And when he wrote *Principia Ethica*, he was convinced that it is one of the main tasks of moral philosophy to determine values in this sense, namely to determine what things possess the quality of goodness and what things possess it in a higher degree than others.[27]

Obligation was defined by Moore in terms of the production of good. 'Our "duty", therefore, can be defined as that action which will cause more good to exist in the Universe than any possible alternative.'[28] Indeed, in *Principia Ethica* Moore went so far as to say that it is demonstrably certain that the assertion that one is morally bound to perform an action is identical with the assertion that this action will produce the greatest possible amount of good in the Universe. When, however, he came to write *Ethics*, he was no longer prepared to claim that the two statements were identical. And later on he recognized the necessity of distinguishing clearly between the statement that that action is morally obligatory which will produce the greatest amount of good as an effect *subsequent* to the action and the statement that that action is morally obligatory which, by reason of its being performed, by reason of its intrinsic nature, makes the Universe intrinsically better than it would be if some other action were performed. In any case the point to notice is that Moore does not regard his theory of good as an indefinable non-natural property as being in any way incompatible with a teleological view of ethics, which interprets obligation in terms of the production of good, that is, in terms of the production of things or experiences possessing the intrinsic quality of goodness. Nor in fact does there appear to be any incompatibility.

From this theory of obligation it does not follow, however, that in any set of circumstances whatsoever we are morally obliged to perform a certain action. For there might be two or more possible actions which, as far as we can see, would be equally productive of good. We can then describe these actions as right or morally permissible, but not as morally obligatory, even though we were obliged to perform either the one or the other.

Moore certainly assumed and implied that if a man passes a specifically moral judgment or an action, his statement, considered precisely as a moral judgment, is capable of being true or false. Take, for example, the assertion that it was right of Brutus to stab Julius Caesar. If this assertion is intended in a specifically ethical sense, it is reducible neither to the statement that the speaker has a subjective attitude of approval towards Brutus's action nor to the statement that as a matter of historical fact Brutus stabbed Caesar. And in its irreducible moral character it is either true or false. Hence the dispute between the man who says that Brutus's action was right and the man who says that it was wrong is a dispute about the truth or falsity of a moral proposition.

When, however, he was confronted with the so-called emotive theory of ethics, Moore began to feel doubt about the truth of the position which he had hitherto adopted. As can be seen from his 'A Reply to My Critics', he conceded that Professor C. L. Stevenson might be right in maintaining that the man who says that Brutus's action was right, when the word 'right' is being used in a specifically ethical sense, is not saying anything of which truth or falsity can be predicated, except perhaps that Brutus actually did stab Caesar, a statement which is clearly historical and not ethical. Further, Moore conceded that if one man says that Brutus's action was right while another says that it was wrong, 'I feel some inclination to think that their disagreement *is* merely a disagreement in attitude, like that between the man who says "Let's play poker" and the other who says, "No; let's listen to a record": and I do not know that I am not *as much* inclined to think this as to think that they are making incompatible assertions'.[29] At the same time Moore confessed that he was also inclined to think that his old view was true; and he maintained that in any case Stevenson had not shown that it was false. 'Right', 'wrong', 'ought', may have merely emotive meaning. And in this case the same must be said of 'good' too. 'I am *inclined* to think that this is so, but I am also inclined to think that it is not so; and I do not know which way I am inclined most strongly.'[30]

These hesitations can reasonably be described as typical of Moore. He was, as has often been remarked, a great questioner. He raised a problem, tried to define it precisely and offered a solution. But when he was faced with criticism, he never brushed it aside. When he thought that it was based on misunderstanding of what he had said, he tried to explain his meaning more clearly. When, however, the criticism was substantial and not simply the fruit of misunderstanding, it was his habit to give serious consideration to the critic's remarks and to give due weight to his point of view. Moore never assumed that what he had said must be true and what the other fellow said must be false. And he did not hesitate to give a candid expression to his reflections and perplexities. We have to remember, therefore, that he is thinking aloud, so to speak, and that his hesitations are not necessarily to be taken as a definite retraction of his former views. He is engaged in weighing a new point of view, suggested to him by a critic, and in trying to estimate the amount of truth in it. Further, as we have seen, he is extremely frank about his subjective impressions, letting his readers know, without any attempt at concealment, that he is inclined to accept the new point of view, while at the same time he is inclined to stick to his own former view. Moore never felt that he was irretrievably committed to his own past, that is, to what he had said in the past. And when he became convinced that he had been wrong, he said so plainly.

In regard, however, to the question whether truth and falsity can legitimately be predicated of moral judgments, we are not entitled to say that Moore became *convinced* that his former view had been wrong. In any case the ethical theses which are for ever associated with his name are those of the indefinability of good, considered as a non-natural intrinsic quality, and of the need for avoiding any form of the so-called naturalistic fallacy. Moore's ethical position, especially as developed in *Principia Ethica*, can be said to be realist but not naturalistic; realist in the sense that good is regarded as an objective and recognizable intrinsic quality, not naturalistic in the sense that this quality is described as non-natural. But Moore never succeeded in explaining satisfactorily what was meant by saying, for example, that good is a non-natural quality of natural objects. And it is understandable that the emotive theory of ethics eventually came to the fore in philosophical discussion. After all, this theory can itself claim to be free from the 'naturalistic fallacy' and can use this claim as a weapon for dealing blows at rival theories. At the same time the theory is immune from the accusation of committing what Moore called the naturalistic fallacy only because 'good' is removed altogether from the sphere of objective intrinsic qualities.[31]

4. Mention has already been made of the fact that as an undergraduate at Cambridge Moore was struck by some of the odd things which philosophers have said about the world. McTaggart's denial of the reality of time was a case in point. What, Moore wondered, could McTaggart possibly mean by this? Was he using the term 'unreal' in some pe-

culiar sense which would deprive the statement that time is unreal of its paradoxical character? Or was he seriously suggesting that it is untrue to say that we have our lunch after we have had our breakfast? If so, the statement that time is unreal would be exciting but at the same time preposterous: it could not possibly be true. In any case, how can we profitably discuss the question whether time is real or unreal unless we first know precisely what is being asked? Similarly, according to Bradley reality is spiritual. But it is not at all clear what it means to say that reality is spiritual. Perhaps several different propositions are involved. And before we start discussing whether reality is spiritual or not, we must not only clarify the question but make sure that it is not really several separate questions. For if it is, these questions will have to be treated in turn.

It is important to understand that Moore had no intention whatsoever of suggesting that all philosophical problems are pseudo-problems. He was suggesting that the reason why philosophical problems are often so difficult to answer is sometimes that it is not clear in the first place precisely what is being asked. Again, when, as so often happens, disputants find themselves at cross-purposes, the reason may sometimes be that the question under discussion is not really one question but several. Such suggestions have nothing at all to do with any general dogma about the meaninglessness of philosophical problems. They represent an appeal for clarity and accuracy from the start, an appeal prompted by enlightened common sense. They express, of course, the predominantly analytic turn of Moore's mind; but they do not make him a positivist, which he certainly was not.

When, however, we think of Moore's idea of philosophical analysis, we generally think of it in connection with his contention that there are common sense propositions which we all know to be true. If we know them to be true, it is absurd for the philosopher to try to show that they are not true. For he too knows that they are true. Nor is it the business of the philosopher, according to Moore, to attempt to prove, for example, that there are material things outside the mind. For there is no good reason to suppose that the philosopher can provide better reasons than those which we already have for saying that there are material things external to the mind. What, however, the philosopher can do is to analyze propositions, the truth or the falsity of which is established by other than specifically philosophical argument. The philosopher can, of course, try to make explicit the reasons which we already have for accepting some common sense propositions. But this does not turn the reasons into specifically philosophical reasons, in the sense that they have been added, as it were, by the philosopher to our stock of reasons.[32]

The question arises, therefore, what is meant by analyzing a proposition? It obviously cannot signify simply 'giving the meaning'. For if I know that a proposition is true, I must know what it means. Normally at any rate we would not be prepared to say that a man knew, or could know, that a proposition was true, if at the same time he had to admit that he did not know what the proposition meant.[33] And from this we can infer that analysis, as envisaged by Moore, does not consist simply in putting what has been said into other words. For instance, if an Italian asks me what it means to say 'John is the brother of James' and I reply that it means 'Giovanni è il fratello di Giacomo', I have explained to the Italian what the English sentence means, but I can hardly be said to have analyzed a proposition. I have not analyzed anything.

Analysis means for Moore conceptual analysis. He admitted later that he had sometimes spoken as though to give the analysis of a proposition was to give its 'meaning'. But he insisted that what he really had in mind was the analysis of concepts. The use of the word 'means' implies that analysis is concerned with verbal expression, with defining words, whereas it is really concerned with defining concepts. The *analyzandum*, that which is to be analyzed, is a concept, and the *analyzans*, the analysis, must also be a concept. The expression used for the *analyzans* must be different from the expression used for the *analyzandum*, and it must be different in that it explicitly means or expresses a concept or concepts not explicitly mentioned by the expression used for the *analyzandum*. For instance, to give an example employed by Moore himself, 'x is a male sibling' would be an analysis of 'x is a brother'. It is not a question of merely substituting

one verbal expression for another in the sense in which
'fratello' can be substituted for 'brother'. 'Male sibling' is
indeed a different verbal expression from 'brother', but at
the same time it explicitly mentions a concept which is not
explicitly mentioned in 'x is a brother'.

And yet, of course, as Moore admits, if the analysis is
correct, the concepts in the *analyzandum* and the *analyzans*,
in the proposition to be analyzed and in its analysis, must
be in some sense the same. But in what sense? If they are
the same in the sense that no distinction can be made between them except in terms of verbal expression, analysis
seems to be concerned simply with the substitution of one
verbal expression for another. But Moore has said that this is
not the case. He is therefore faced with the task of explaining
in what sense the concepts in *analyzandum* and *analyzans*
must be the same if the analysis is to be correct, and in
what sense they must be distinct if analysis is to be more
than the mere substitution of an equivalent verbal expression
for a given verbal expression. But Moore does not feel able
to give a really clear explanation.

In a general way it is, of course, easy enough to give a
cash-value to the idea of philosophical analysis. True, if we
are told that 'x is a male sibling' is an analysis of 'x is a
brother', we may be inclined to wonder what possible philosophical relevance analysis of this kind can possess. But consider the non-philosopher who knows perfectly well how to
use causal expressions in concrete contexts. If someone tells
him that the banging of the door was caused by a sudden
gust of wind through the open window, he knows perfectly
well what is meant. He can distinguish between cases of *post
hoc* and cases of *propter hoc*, and he can recognize particular causal relations. In a sense, therefore, he is well aware
what causality means. But if the non-philosopher were asked
to give an abstract analysis of the concept of causality, he
would find himself at a loss. Like Socrates's young friends
in a similar situation, he would probably mention instances
of the causal relation and be unable to do anything more.
Yet philosophers from Plato and Aristotle onwards have tried
to give abstract analyses of concepts such as causality. And
we can call this sort of thing philosophical analysis.

Though, however, this idea of philosophical analysis seems at first sight to be plain sailing, it can be and has been challenged. Thus those who sympathize with the attitude expressed in certain remarks in Wittgenstein's *Philosophical Investigations* would maintain that if one is asked what causality is, the proper answer is precisely to mention examples of the causal relation. It is a mistake to look for one single and profounder 'meaning' of the term. Either we already know what causality is (how the word is used) or we do not. And if we do not, we can be informed by having examples of the causal relation pointed out to us. Similarly, it is a mistake to suppose that because we describe a variety of things as beautiful, there must necessarily be one single 'real' meaning, one genuine analysis of a unitary concept, which the philosopher can, as it were, dig out. We can, of course, say that we are looking for a definition. But one can be found in the dictionary. And if this is not what we are looking for, then what we really need is to be reminded of the ways in which the word in question is actually used in human language. We shall then know what is 'means'. And this is the only 'analysis' which is really required.

It is not the intention of the present writer to defend this more 'linguistic' idea of analysis. His sympathies lie rather with the older idea of philosophical analysis, provided, of course, that we avoid the fallacy of 'one word, one meaning'. At the same time the notion of conceptual analysis is not at all so clear as it may seem to be at first sight. Difficulties arise which require to be considered and, if possible, met. But we cannot find any adequate answers to such difficulties in Moore's account of analysis.

This is not, however, surprising. For the fact of the matter is that Moore devoted himself for the most part to the *practice* of philosophical analysis. That is to say, he concerned himself with the analysis of particular propositions rather than with analyzing the concept of analysis. And when he was challenged to give an abstract account of his method and its aims, he felt able to remove some misunderstandings but unable to answer all questions to his own satisfaction. With his characteristic honesty, he did not hesitate to say so openly.

Obviously, therefore, to obtain some concrete idea of what Moore understood by analysis we have to look primarily at his actual practice. But before we turn to a line of analysis which occupied a great deal of his attention, there are two points which must be emphasized. In the first place Moore never said, and never intended to say, that philosophy and analysis are the same thing, and that the philosopher can do nothing more than analyze propositions or concepts. And when this view was attributed to him, he explicitly rejected it. The bent of his mind was indeed predominantly analytic; but he never laid down any dogma about the limits of philosophy. Other people may have done so, but not Moore. In the second place he never suggested that all concepts are analyzable. We have already seen, for example, that according to him the concept of good is simple and unanalyzable. And the same can be said of the concept of knowing.

5. In his well-known paper *Proof of an External World*, which he read to the British Academy in 1939,[34] Moore maintained that it is a good argument for, and indeed sufficient proof of, the existence of physical objects external to the mind if we can indicate one or more such objects. And he proceeded to claim that he could prove that two hands exist by the simple expedient of holding up his two hands, making a gesture with the right hand while saying 'here is one hand' and then making a gesture with the left hand while saying 'and here is the other'.

This may sound extremely naïve. But, as someone has said, Moore always had the courage to appear naïve. The trouble is, however, that while we may all come to believe that there is an external world by becoming aware of external objects, the only person who can possibly need a proof of the existence of an external world is the person who professes to doubt it. And if he professes to doubt, his doubt covers the existence of an extra-mental physical object. Hence he is not likely to be impressed when Moore, or anyone else, exhibits two hands. He will simply say that he doubts whether what he sees, when he is shown two hands, are really external physical objects.

And yet, of course, Moore's position is not really as naïve

as it appears to be at first sight. For the determined sceptic is not going to be convinced by any proof. And what Moore is saying to the sceptic is more or less this: 'The only evidence which I can offer you is the evidence which we already have. And this is sufficient evidence. But you are looking for evidence or proof which we have not got, and which in my opinion we can never have. For I see no reason to believe that the philosopher can offer better evidence than the evidence we have. What you are really demanding is something which can never be provided, namely proof that the existence of an external world is a necessary truth. But it is not a necessary truth. Hence it is futile to look for the sort of evidence or proof which you insist on demanding.' This is clearly a reasonable point of view.

Now, as we have already indicated, while thinking that it is not the philosopher's job to try to prove by some special means of his own the truth of such a proposition as 'there are material things' or 'there are extra-mental physical objects', Moore believes that analysis of such propositions does form part of the philosopher's job. For while the truth of a proposition may be certain, its correct analysis may not be at all certain. But the correct analysis of such general propositions such as those just mentioned 'depends on the question how propositions of another and simpler type are to be analyzed'.[35] And an example of a simpler proposition would be 'I am perceiving a human hand'.

This proposition, however, is itself a deduction from two simpler propositions which can be expressed as 'I am perceiving *this*' and '*this* is a human hand'. But what is '*this*'? In Moore's opinion it is a sense-datum. That is to say, what I directly apprehend when I perceive a human hand is a sense-datum. And a sense-datum, even if we assume it to be somehow part of a human hand, cannot be identified with the hand. For the hand is in any case much more than what I actually see at a given moment. Hence a correct analysis of 'I perceive a human hand' involves one in specifying the nature of a sense-datum and its relation to the relevant physical object.

In a paper entitled *The Nature and Reality of Objects of Perception* which he read to the Aristotelian Society in 1905

Moore maintained that if we look at a red book and a blue book standing side by side on a shelf, what we really see are red and blue patches of colour of certain sizes and shapes, 'having to one another the spatial relation which we express by saying they are side by side'.[36] Such objects of direct perception he called 'sense-contents'. In the lectures which he gave in the winter of 1910–11[37] Moore used the term 'sense-data'. True, in a paper entitled *The Status of Sense-Data*, which he read to the Aristotelian Society during the session 1913–14, Moore admitted that the term 'sense-datum' is ambiguous. For it suggests that the objects to which this term is applied can exist only when they are given, a view to which Moore did not wish to commit himself. Hence he proposed as 'more convenient'[38] the use of the term 'sensible'. But to all intents and purposes 'sense-data' is Moore's name for the immediate objects of direct perception. And in *A Defence of Common Sense* we find him saying that 'there is no doubt at all that there are sense-data, in the sense in which I am now using the term,'[39] that is, in a sense which makes it true to say that what we directly perceive when we look at a hand or at an envelope is a sense-datum but which leaves open the question whether this sense-datum is or is not part of the physical object which in ordinary language we are said to be seeing.

Now, Moore was careful to distinguish between sensations and sense-data. When, for example, I see a colour, the *seeing* the colour is the sensation and *what* is seen, the object, is the sense-datum. It therefore makes sense, at any rate at first sight, to ask whether sense-data can exist when they are unperceived. It would hardly make sense to ask whether a 'seeing' can exist when no sentient subject is seeing. But it does make sense to ask whether a colour exists when it is not perceived. If, of course, sense-data were described as existing 'in the mind', it would hardly make sense to ask whether they can exist unperceived. But Moore was unwilling to describe sense-data in this way, namely as being 'in the mind'.

But if sense-data are not 'in the mind', *where* are they? Provided that sense-data exist, and do not exist in the mind, the question arises whether or not they exist when they are not objects of perception. Do they then exist in a public physical space? One difficulty in saying this is the following. When two men look at a white envelope, we commonly say that they are seeing the same object. But according to the sense-datum theory there must be two sense-data. Further, the shape and spatial relations of one man's sense-datum do not seem to be precisely the same as those of the other man's sense-datum. If, therefore, we take it that the shape and size and spatial relations of a physical object existing in public space are the same for all, must we not say that the one man's sense-datum exists in one private space and the other man's sense-datum in another private space?

Further, what is the relation between a sense-datum and the relevant physical object? For example, if I look at a coin from such an angle of vision that its surface appears to me as elliptical, is my sense-datum a part of the coin as a physical object, the surface of which we take to be roughly circular? Ordinary language suggests that it is. For I should normally be said to be seeing the coin. But if I look at the coin at another moment from a different position, or if another man looks at the same coin at the same moment as I do, there are different sense-data. And they differ not merely numerically but also qualitatively or in content. Are all these sense-data parts of the physical object? If they are, this suggests that the surface of a coin can be both elliptical and circular at the same time. If they are not, how are we to describe the relations between the sense-data and the physical object? Indeed, how do we know that there is a physical object for the sense-data to be related to?

These are the sort of problems with which Moore grappled on and off throughout his life. But he did not succeed in solving them to his own satisfaction. For example, we have already seen that in his attack on idealism Moore denied the truth of 'to be is to be perceived'; and his natural inclination was to claim that sense-data can exist even when they are unperceived. But though this point of view may appear reasonable when it is a question of a visual sense-datum such as a colour, it by no means appears reasonable if a toothache, for instance, is admitted into the category of sense-data, nor perhaps if sweet and bitter are taken as examples of sense-data rather than colour, size and shape. And in 'A Reply to My Critics' we find Moore saying that while he had once certainly suggested that sense-data such as blue and bitter could exist unperceived, 'I am inclined to think that it is as impossible that anything which has the sensible quality "blue", and more generally, *anything whatever which is directly apprehended*, any *sense-datum*, that is, should exist unperceived, as it is that a headache should exist unfelt'.⁴⁰

In this case, of course, as Moore notes, it follows that no sense-datum can possibly be identical with or part of the surface of a physical object. And to say this is to say that no physical surface can be directly perceived. The question, therefore, of how we know that there are physical objects distinct from sense-data becomes acute. Needless to say, Moore is well aware of the fact. But he is certainly not prepared to jettison his conviction that we do know the truth of the propositions which he regards as propositions of common sense. He is not prepared to throw overboard what, in *A Defence of Common Sense*, he called 'the Common Sense view of the world'.⁴¹ And in a lecture entitled *Four Forms of Scepticism*, which Moore delivered on various occasions in the United States during the period 1940–4, we find a characteristic denial of Russell's contention that 'I do not know for certain that this is a pencil or that you are conscious'.⁴² I call the denial 'characteristic' for this reason. Moore remarks that Russell's contention seems to rest on four distinct assumptions; that one does not know these things (that this is a pencil or that you are conscious) immediately; that they do not follow logically from anything which one does know immediately; that, in this case, one's knowledge of or belief in the propositions in question must be based on an analogical or inductive argument; and that no such argument can yield certain knowledge. Moore then proceeds to say that he agrees that the first three assumptions are true. At the same time 'of no one even of these three do I feel *as* certain as that I do know for certain that this is a pencil. Nay more: I do not think it is *rational* to be as certain of any one of these four propositions, as of the proposition that I do know that this is a pencil.'⁴³

It is, of course, open to anyone to say that in his opinion

the sense-datum theory as expounded by Moore leads logically to scepticism or at any rate to agnosticism in regard to the physical world as distinct from sense-data. But it is certainly not correct to speak of Moore as a sceptic. He was no such thing. He started, as we have seen, with the assumption that we know with certainty that there are external physical objects or material things; but he was doubtful of the correct analysis of such a proposition. And though his analysis may have led him into a position which was difficult to reconcile with his initial conviction, he did not abandon this conviction.

It has not been possible here to follow Moore through all his struggles with the theory of sense-data and its implications. The fulfilment of such a task would require a whole book. The theme has been discussed in brief primarily in order to illustrate Moore's practice of analysis. But what sort of analysis is it? In a sense, of course, it is concerned with language. For Moore is out to analyze propositions, such as 'I see a human hand' or 'I see a penny'. But to describe his analysis as being concerned 'simply with words', as though it were a case of choosing between two sets of linguistic conventions, would be grossly misleading. Part at any rate of what he does can best be described, I think, as phenomenological analysis. For example, he raises the question, what exactly is it that happens when, as would ordinarily be said, we see a material object? He then explains that he is in no way concerned with the physical processes 'which occur in the eye and the optic nerves and the brain'.[44] What he is concerned with is 'the mental occurrence—the act of consciousness—which occurs (as is supposed) as a consequence of or accompaniment—of these bodily processes'.[45] Sense-data are introduced as objects of this act of consciousness. Or, rather, they are 'discovered', as Moore believes, as its immediate objects. And the process by which they are discovered is phenomenological analysis. But sense-data are not, of course, confined to visual sense-data. Hence we can say that Moore is concerned with the phenomenological analysis of sense-perception in general.

It is not my intention to suggest that this is all that Moore is concerned with, even within the restricted context of the sense-datum theory. For if we assume that sense-data can properly be said to exist, the question of their relation to physical objects can be described as an ontological question. Further, Moore concerns himself with epistemological questions; how do we know this or that? But part at any rate of his activity can better be described as phenomenological analysis than as linguistic analysis. And though the stock of the sense-datum theory has slumped greatly in recent years,[46] the judgment of Dr. Rudolf Metz was not entirely unreasonable, that in comparison with Moore's meticulous phenomenological analysis of perception 'all earlier studies of the problem seem to be coarse and rudimentary'.[47]

Chapter Nineteen

BERTRAND RUSSELL (1)

Introductory remarks – Life and writings up to the publication of Principia Mathematica; *Russell's idealist phase and his reaction against it, the theory of types, the theory of descriptions, the reduction of mathematics to logic – Ockham's razor and reductive analysis as applied to physical objects and to minds – Logical atomism and the influence of Wittgenstein – Neutral monism – The problem of solipsism.*

1. We have already had occasion to remark that of all present-day British philosophers Bertrand Russell is by far the best known to the world at large. This is partly due to the fact that he has published a very considerable number of books and essays on moral, social and political topics which are salted with amusing and provocative remarks and are written at a level which can be understood by a public that is scarcely capable of appreciating his more technical contributions to philosophical thought. And it is largely this class of publications which has made of Russell a prophet of liberal humanism, a hero of those who regard themselves as rationalists,

free from the shackles of religious and metaphysical dogma and yet at the same time devoted to the cause of human freedom, as against totalitarianism, and of social and political progress according to rational principles. We can also mention, as a contributing cause to Russell's fame, his active self-commitment at various periods of his life to a particular side, sometimes an unpopular side, in issues of general concern and importance. He has always had the courage of his convictions. And the combination of aristocrat, philosopher, Voltairean essayist and ardent campaigner has naturally made an impact on the imagination of the public.

It scarcely needs to be said that the fame of a philosopher during his lifetime is not an infallible indication of the value of his thought, especially if his general reputation is largely due to his more ephemeral writings. In any case the varied character of Russell's writing creates a special difficulty in estimating his status as a philosopher. On the one hand he is justly renowned for his work in the field of mathematical logic. But he himself regards this subject as belonging to mathematics rather than to philosophy. On the other hand it is not fair to Russell to estimate his status as a thinker in terms of his popular writings on concrete moral issues or on social and political topics. For though in view of the traditional and common view of the word 'philosophy' he recognizes that he has to resign himself to having his moral writings labelled as philosophical works, he has said that the only ethical topic which he regards as belonging properly to philosophy is the analysis of the ethical proposition as such. Concrete judgments of value should, strictly speaking, be excluded from philosophy. And if such judgments express, as Russell believes that they do, basic emotive attitudes, he is doubtless entitled to express his own emotive attitudes with a vehemence which would be out of place in discussing problems which, in principle at least, can be solved by logical argument.

If we exclude from philosophy mathematical logic on the one hand and concrete moral, valuational and political judgments on the other, we are left with what can perhaps be called Russell's general philosophy, consisting, for example, of discussions of epistemological and metaphysical questions.

This general philosophy has passed through a series of phases and mutations, and it represents a strange mixture of acute analysis and of blindness to important relevant factors. But it is unified by his analytic method or methods. And the changes are hardly so great as to justify a literal interpretation of Professor C. D. Broad's humorous remark that, 'as we all know, Mr. Russell produces a different system of philosophy every few years.'[1] In any case Russell's general philosophy represents an interesting development of British empiricism in the light of later ways of thought, to which he himself made an important contribution.

In the following pages we shall be concerned mainly, though not exclusively, with Russell's idea and practice of analysis. But a thorough treatment, even of this limited theme, will not be possible. Nor indeed could it legitimately be expected in a general history of western philosophy.

2. (i) Bertrand Arthur William Russell was born in 1872. His parents, Lord and Lady Amberley, died when he was a small child,[2] and he was brought up in the house of his grandfather, Lord John Russell, afterwards Earl Russell.[3] At the age of eighteen he went up to Cambridge, where he at first concentrated on mathematics. But in his fourth year at the university he turned to philosophy, and McTaggart and Stout taught him to regard British empiricism as crude and to look instead to the Hegelian tradition. Indeed, Russell tells us of the admiration which he felt for Bradley. And from 1894, the year in which he went down from Cambridge, until 1898 he continued to think that metaphysics was capable of proving beliefs about the universe which 'religious' feeling led him to think important.[4]

For a short while in 1894 Russell acted as an honorary attaché at the British Embassy in Paris. In 1895 he devoted himself to the study of economics and German social democracy at Berlin. The outcome was the publication of *German Social Democracy* in 1896. Most of his early essays were indeed on mathematical and logical topics, but it is worth noting that his first book was concerned with social theory.

Russell tells us that at this period he was influenced by both Kant and Hegel but sided with the latter when the two were in conflict.[5] He has described as 'unadulterated Hegel'[6] a paper on the relations of number and quantity which he published in *Mind* in 1896. And of *An Essay on the Foundations of Geometry* (1897), an elaboration of his Fellowship dissertation for Trinity College, Cambridge, he has said that the theory of geometry which he presented was 'mainly Kantian',[7] though it was afterwards swept away by Einstein's theory of relativity.

In the course of the year 1898 Russell reacted strongly against idealism. For one thing, a reading of Hegel's *Logic* convinced him that what the author had to say on the subject of mathematics was nonsense. For another thing, while lecturing on Leibniz at Cambridge in place of McTaggart, who was abroad, he came to the conclusion that the arguments advanced by Bradley against the reality of relations were fallacious. But Russell has laid most emphasis on the influence of his friend G. E. Moore. Together with Moore he adhered to the belief that, whatever Bradley or McTaggart might say to the contrary, all that common sense takes to be real is real. Indeed, in the period in question Russell carried realism considerably further than he was later to do. It was not simply a question of embracing pluralism and the theory of external relations, nor even of believing in the reality of secondary qualities. Russell also believed that points of space and instants of time are existent entities, and that there is a timeless world of Platonic ideas or essences, including numbers. He thus had, as he has put it, a very full or luxuriant universe.

The lectures on Leibniz, to which reference has been made above, resulted in the publication in 1900 of Russell's notable work *A Critical Exposition of the Philosophy of Leibniz*. In it he maintained that Leibniz's metaphysics was in part a reflection of his logical studies and in part a popular or exoteric doctrine expounded with a view to edification and at variance with the philosopher's real convictions.[8] From then on Russell remained convinced that the substance-attribute metaphysics is a reflection of the subject-predicate mode of expression.

(ii) Considerable importance is attached by Russell to his becoming acquainted at an international congress at Paris in 1900 with the work of Giuseppe Peano (1858–1932), the

Italian mathematician. For many years, in fact since he began to study geometry, Russell had been perplexed by the problem of the foundations of mathematics. At this time he did not know the work of Frege, who had already attempted to reduce arithmetic to logic. But the writings of Peano provided him with the stimulus for tackling his problem afresh. And the immediate result of his reflections was *The Principles of Mathematics*, which appeared in 1903.

But there were weeds in the mathematical garden. Russell finished the first draft of *The Principles of Mathematics* at the end of 1900, and early in 1901 he came upon what seemed to him to be an antinomy or paradox in the logic of classes. As he defined number in terms of the logic of classes, a cardinal number being 'the class of all classes similar to the given class',[9] the antinomy evidently affected mathematics. And Russell had either to solve it or to admit an insoluble antinomy within the mathematical field.

The antinomy can be illustrated in this way. The class of pigs is evidently not itself a pig. That is to say, it is not a member of itself. But consider the notion of the class of all classes which are not members of themselves. Let us call this class X and ask whether X is a member of itself or not. On the one hand, it seems that it cannot be a member of itself. For if we assume that it is, it follows logically that X has the defining property of its members. And this defining property is that any class of which it is a property is not a member of itself. Hence X cannot be a member of itself. On the other hand, it seems that X must be a member of itself. For if we begin by assuming that it is not a member of itself, it follows logically that it is not a member of those classes which are not members of themselves. And to say this is to say that X is a member of itself. Hence whether we begin by assuming that X is a member of itself or that it is not a member of itself, we seem in either case to be involved in self-contradiction.

Russell communicated this antinomy or paradox to Frege, who replied that arithmetic was tottering. But after some struggles Russell hit upon what seemed to him to be a solution. This was the doctrine or theory of types, a preliminary version of which was presented in *Appendix B* in *The Prin-*

ciples of Mathematics. Every propositional function, Russell maintained, 'has in addition to its range of truth, a range of significance.'[10] For example, in the propositional function 'X is mortal', we can obviously substitute for the variable X a range of values such that the resultant propositions are true. Thus 'Socrates is mortal' is true. But there are also values which, if substituted for X, would make the resultant propositions neither true nor false but meaningless. For instance, 'the class of men is mortal' is meaningless. For the class of men is not a thing or object of which either mortality or immortality can be meaningfully predicated. From 'if X is a man, X is mortal' we can infer 'if Socrates is a man, Socrates is mortal'; but we cannot infer that the class of men is mortal. For the class of men neither is nor could be a man. In other words, the class of men cannot be a member of itself: in fact it is really nonsense to speak of its either being or not being a member of itself. For the very idea of a class being a member of itself is nonsensical. To take an example given by Russell,[11] a club is a class of individuals. And it can be a member of a class of another type, such as an association of clubs, which would be a class of classes. But neither the class nor the class of classes could possibly be a member of itself. And if the distinctions between types are observed, the antinomy or paradox in the logic of classes does not arise.

To deal with further difficulties Russell produced a 'branching' or ramified theory of types. But we cannot discuss it here. Instead we can draw attention to the following point. Having made it clear that a class of things is not itself a thing, Russell goes on in *Principia Mathematica* to what he has called 'the abolition of classes'.[12] That is to say, he interprets classes as 'merely symbolic or linguistic conveniences'[13] as incomplete symbols. And it is not surprising to find him later on adopting a sympathetic attitude towards a linguistic interpretation of the theory of types and saying, for example, that 'difference of type means difference of syntactical function'.[14] Having once implied that differences between types are differences between types of entities, Russell came to recognize that the differences lie between different types of symbols, which 'acquire their type-status through the syntactical rules to which they are subject'.[15] In any case it is safe to say that one of the general effects of Russell's theory of types was to encourage belief in the relevance to philosophy of 'linguistic analysis'.

The theory of types has, of course, a variety of possible applications. Thus in his introduction to Ludwig Wittgenstein's *Tractatus Logico-Philosophicus* Russell, writing in 1922, suggested that Wittgenstein's difficulty about not being able to say anything within a given language about the structure of this language could be met by the idea of a hierarchy of languages. Thus even if one were unable to say anything within language A about its structure, one might be able to do so within language B, when they belong to different types, A being a first-order language, so to speak, and B a second-order language. If Wittgenstein were to reply that his theory of the inexpressible in language applies to the totality of languages,[16] the retort could be made that there is not, and cannot be, such a thing as a totality of languages.[17] The hierarchy is without limit.

What Russell has to say in developing the theory of types also has its application in metaphysics. For example, if we once accept the definition of the world as the class of all finite entities, we are debarred from speaking of it as being itself a contingent entity or being, even if we regard contingency as belonging necessarily to every finite being. For to speak in this way would be to make a class a member of itself. It does not follow, however, that the world must be described as a 'necessary entity'. For if the world is to be defined as the class of entities, it cannot itself be an entity, whether contingent or necessary.

(iii) It has already been mentioned, by way of anticipation, that in *Principia Mathematica* Russell maintains that the symbols for classes are incomplete symbols. 'Their *uses* are defined, but they themselves are not assumed to mean anything at all.'[18] That is to say, the symbols for classes undoubtedly possess a definable use or function in sentences, but, taken by themselves, they do not denote entities. Rather are they ways of referring to other entities. In this respect the symbols for classes are 'like those of descriptions'.[19] And something must now be said about Russell's theory of descriptions, which he developed between the writing of *The*

Principles of Mathematics and the publication of *Principia Mathematica*.[20]

Let us consider the sentence 'the golden mountain is very high'. The phrase 'the golden mountain' functions as the grammatical subject of the sentence. And it may appear that as we can say something about the golden mountain, namely that it is very high, the phrase must denote an entity of some sort. True, it does not denote any existing entity. For though it is not logically impossible for there to be a golden mountain, we have no evidence that there is one. Yet even if we say 'the golden mountain does not exist', we seem to be saying something intelligible *about* it, namely that it does not exist. And in this case it appears to follow that 'the golden mountain' must denote an entity, not indeed an actually existing entity, but none the less a reality of some sort.

This line of reasoning can be applied, of course, to the grammatical subjects in sentences such as 'the king of France is bald' (uttered or written when there is no king of France) or 'Sherlock Holmes wore a deerstalker's cap'. We thus get the sort of overpopulated, or at any rate very well populated, universe in which Russell originally believed in the first flush of his realist reaction against the way in which idealists such as Bradley and McTaggart described as unreal several factors in the universe which common sense spontaneously regards as real. It is understandable, therefore, that Russell devoted himself to the study of Meinong, who also accepted a luxuriant universe in which room was found for entities which do not actually exist but which are none the less realities in some sense. At the same time it was precisely his study of Meinong which raised serious doubts in Russell's mind about the validity of the principle that phrases such as 'the golden mountain', which can function as grammatical subjects in sentences, denote entities of some sort. Indeed, when taken by themselves, have such phrases as 'the golden mountain', 'the king of France' and so on any 'meaning'? It was one of the functions of the theory of descriptions to show that they have not.

According to this theory such phrases are not 'names', denoting entities, but 'descriptions'. In his *Introduction to Mathematical Philosophy* (1919) Russell distinguishes be-

tween two sorts of descriptions, indefinite and definite.[21]
Phrases such as 'the golden mountain' and 'the king of
France' are definite descriptions; and we can confine our attention here to this class. The theory of descriptions purports to show that they are incomplete symbols, and though
they can function as grammatical subjects in sentences, these
sentences can be restated according to their logical form in
such a way that it becomes clear that the phrases in question
are not the real logical subjects in the sentences in which
they occur as grammatical subjects. When this has become
clear, the temptation to think that they must denote entities
should vanish. For it is then understood that, taken by themselves, the phrases in question have no denoting function.
The phrase 'the golden mountain', for example, does not
denote anything at all.

Let us take the sentence 'the golden mountain does not
exist'. If this is translated as 'the propositional function "X
is golden and a mountain" is false for all values of X', the
meaning of the original sentence is revealed in such a way
that the phrase 'the golden mountain' disappears and, with
it, the temptation to postulate a subsisting non-actual entity.
For we are no longer involved in the awkward situation which
arises in view of the fact that the statement 'the golden
mountain does not exist' can prompt the question 'what does
not exist?', implying that the golden mountain must have
some sort of reality if we can say of it significantly that it
does not exist.

This is all very well, it may be said, but it is extremely odd
to claim, in regard to descriptions in general, that they have
no meaning when they are taken by themselves. It seems
indeed to be true that 'the golden mountain' does not mean
anything, provided that by meaning one understands denoting an entity. But what about a phrase such as 'the author
of *Waverley*'? According to Russell, it is a description, not a
proper name. But is it not evident that it means Scott?

If 'the author of *Waverley*' meant Scott, Russell replies,
'Scott is the author of *Waverley*' would be a tautology, de-
claring that Scott is Scott. But it is evidently not a tautology.
If, however, 'the author of *Waverley*' meant anything else
but Scott, 'Scott is the author of *Waverley*' would be false,

which it is not. The only thing to say is, therefore, 'the author of *Waverley*' means nothing. That is to say, taken in isolation it does not denote anyone. And the statement 'Scott is the author of *Waverley*' can be restated in such a way that the phrase 'the author of *Waverley*' is eliminated. For example, 'for all values of X, "X wrote *Waverley*" is equivalent to "X is Scott" '.[22]

It seems indeed that we can very well say 'the author of *Waverley* is Scotch', and that in this case we are predicating an attribute, namely being Scotch, of an entity, namely the author of *Waverley*. Russell, however, maintained that 'the author of *Waverley* is Scotch' implies and is defined by three distinct propositions; 'at least one person wrote *Waverley*', 'at most one person wrote *Waverley*', and 'whosoever wrote *Waverley* was Scotch'.[23] And this can be stated formally as 'there is a term c such that "X wrote *Waverley*" is equivalent, for all values of X, to "X is c", and "c is Scotch" '.

Needless to say, Russell has no doubt that the author of *Waverley* was Scotch, in the sense that Sir Walter Scott wrote *Waverley* and was a Scotsman. The point is, however, that if the descriptive term 'the author of *Waverley*' is not a proper name and does not denote anyone, the same can be said of such a descriptive term as 'the king of France'. 'The author of *Waverley* was Scotch' can be restated in such a way that the translation is a true proposition but does not contain the descriptive phrase 'the author of *Waverley*', and 'the king of France is bald' can be restated in such a way that the translation does not contain the descriptive phrase 'the king of France' but is a false, though significant proposition. It is thus in no way necessary to postulate any non-actual entity denoted by 'the king of France'.

It is understandable that Russell's theory of descriptions has been subjected to criticism. For example, G. E. Moore has objected[24] that if in 1700 an Englishman had made the statement 'the king of France is wise', it would certainly have been correct to say that 'the king of France' denoted an entity, namely Louis XIV. In this case, therefore, 'the king of France' would not have been an incomplete symbol. But in other circumstances it might be. There can be sentences in which 'the king of France' does not denote anyone; but, equally, there can be sentences in which it does denote someone.

It seems to the present writer that in his criticism of Russell's theory of descriptions Moore is appealing to ordinary linguistic usage. This is, of course, the strength of his criticism. Russell himself, however, is concerned not so much with mapping-out ordinary language as with constructing a theory which will deprive of its linguistic basis the notion that it is necessary to postulate non-existent but real entities such as 'the golden mountain', 'the king of France' (when there is no king of France), and so on. It is perfectly legitimate criticism, it seems to me, to object that the theory involves an interpretation of such phrases which is too narrow to square with actual linguistic usage.[25] But in the present context it is more important to draw attention to Russell's aim, to what he thinks that he is accomplishing by means of his theory.

It would obviously be a great mistake to suppose that Russell imagines that translation of 'the golden mountain is very high' into a sentence in which the descriptive phrase 'the golden mountain' does not occur proves that there is no golden mountain. Whether there is or is not a golden mountain in the world is an empirical question; and Russell is perfectly well aware of the fact. Indeed, if the translation to which reference has just been made proved that there is in fact no golden mountain, then the fact that 'the author of *The Principles of Mathematics* is English' can be restated in such a way that the descriptive phrase 'the author of *The Principles of Mathematics*' disappears would prove that there is no Bertrand Russell.

It would also be a mistake to suppose that according to Russell the ordinary man, the non-philosopher, is misled into thinking that there must be some sort of non-existing but real object corresponding to the phrase 'the golden mountain' because we can say 'the golden mountain does not exist'. Russell is not attributing any mistakes of this kind to the ordinary man. His point is that for philosophers, who reflect on the implications or apparent implications of linguistic expressions, descriptive phrases such as 'the golden mountain' may occasion, and in Russell's opinion have occasioned, the temptation to postulate entities with a queer status between actual existence and non-entity. And the function of the theory of descriptions is to remove this temptation by showing that descriptive phrases are incomplete symbols which, according to Russell, mean nothing, that is, do not denote any entity. The paradoxical aspect of the theory of descriptions is that, because of its generality, it applies equally both to phrases such as 'the golden mountain' or 'the king of France' and to phrases such as 'the author of *The Principles of Mathematics*', not to speak of the other class of phrases such as 'the round square'. But its function is to contribute to clearing away the fictitious entities with which certain philosophers, not the man in the street, have over-populated the universe. It thus serves the purpose of Ockham's razor and can be brought under the general heading of reductive analysis, a theme to which we shall have to return.

A final point. We have noted that when a phrase such as 'the golden mountain' or 'the author of *Waverley*' occurs as the grammatical subject of a sentence, Russell maintains that it is not the logical subject. The same line of reasoning can, of course, be applied to grammatical objects. In 'I saw nobody on the road' the grammatical object is 'nobody'. But 'nobody' is not a special kind of 'somebody'. And the sentence can be restated in such a way (for example, 'it is not the case that I saw any person on the road') that the word 'nobody' disappears. In general, therefore, Russell's contention is that the grammatical form of a sentence is by no means the same as its logical form, and that philosophers can be seriously misled if they do not understand this fact. But though Russell may have generalized this idea, it is historically inaccurate to suggest that he was the first man to make this discovery.[26] For example, in the twelfth century St. Anselm pointed out that to say that God created the world out of nothing is not to say that the world was created out of nothing as some kind of pre-existing material. It is to say that God did not create the world out of anything, that is, out of any pre-existing material.

(iv) The three volumes of *Principia Mathematica*, which were the fruit of the joint work of Russell and A. N. Whitehead, appeared in 1910–13. The point which aroused most interest was the attempt to show that pure mathematics is reducible to logic, in the sense that it can be shown to follow from purely logical premisses and employs only concepts which are capable of being defined in logical terms.[27] In practice, of course, we cannot simply take a complicated mathematical formula at random and express it without more ado in purely logical terms. But in principle the whole of pure mathematics is ultimately derivable from logical premisses, mathematics being, as Russell has put it, the manhood of logic.

As Russell believed that in *Principia Mathematica* he had demonstrated the truth of his thesis, he also believed that he had provided a decisive refutation of Kantian theories of mathematics. For example, if geometry is derivable from purely logical premisses, to postulate an *a priori* intuition of space is entirely superfluous.

Russell and Whitehead had, needless to say, their predecessors. George Boole (1815–64)[28] had attempted to 'algebraicize' logic and had developed a calculus of classes. But he regarded logic as subordinate to mathematics, whereas William Stanley Jevons (1835–82)[29] was convinced that logic is the fundamental science. John Venn (1834–1923),[30] however, while attempting to remedy the defects in Boole's system and to overcome the contemporary chaos in symbolic notation, looked on logic and mathematics as separate branches of symbolic language, neither being subordinate to the other. In America C. S. Peirce modified and developed the logical algebra of Boole and showed how it could accommodate a revised version of the logic of relations formulated by Augustus De Morgan (1806–71).

In Germany Friedrich Wilhelm Schröder (1841–1902) gave a classical formulation to Boole's logical algebra as modified by Peirce. More important, Gottlob Frege (1848–1925) attempted to derive arithmetic from logic in his works *Die Grundlagen der Arithmetik* (1884) and *Grundgesetze der Arithmetik* (1893–1903). As has been mentioned, Russell was not at first aware that he had rediscovered for himself ideas which had already been proposed by Frege. But when he became aware of Frege's work, he drew attention to it,[31] though it was not until a considerably later period that the German mathematician's studies obtained general recognition in England.

In Italy Peano and his collaborators tried to show, in their *Formulaires de mathématiques* (1895–1908), that arithmetic and algebra can be derived from certain logical ideas, such as those of a class and of membership of a class, three primitive mathematical concepts and six primitive propositions. As we have seen, Russell became acquainted with Peano's work in 1900. And he and Whitehead made use of Peano's logical symbolism or notation in the construction of *Principia Mathematica*, which carried further the work of both Peano and Frege.

The present writer is not competent to pass any judgment on the contents of *Principia Mathematica*. It must suffice to say that though the thesis of the reducibility of mathematics to logic has by no means won the consent of all mathematicians,[32] nobody would question the historic importance of the work in the development of mathematical logic. Indeed, it stands out above all other English contributions to the subject.[33] In any case, though Russell himself may understandably regret that more attention was not paid to the mathematical techniques evolved in the work, the present writer's principal aim in drawing attention here to *Principia Mathematica* is to illustrate the background to Russell's conception of reductive analysis. For example, to say that mathematics is reducible to logic obviously does not mean that there is no such thing as mathematics. Nor is it tantamount to a denial that there are any differences between logic and mathematics as they actually exist or have actually been developed. Rather does it mean that pure mathematics can in principle be derived from certain fundamental logical concepts and certain primitive indemonstrable propositions, and that, in principle, mathematical propositions could be translated into logical propositions with equivalent truth-values.

Before we pass on to Russell's general idea of reductive analysis, it is worth noting that the reducibility of mathematics to logic does not mean that mathematics is based on laws of thought in the psychological sense of laws governing human thinking. In the earlier years of this century Russell believed that mathematics carries us beyond what is human 'into the region of absolute necessity, to which not only the actual world, but every possible world, must conform'.[34] In this ideal world mathematics forms an eternal edifice of truth; and in the contemplation of its serene beauty man can find refuge from a world full of evil and suffering. Gradually, however, though reluctantly, Russell came to accept Wittgenstein's view that pure mathematics consists of 'tautologies'. This change of mind he has described as 'a gradual retreat from Pythagoras'.[35] One effect of the First World War on Russell's mind was to turn it away from the idea of an eternal realm of abstract truth, where one can take refuge in the contemplation of timeless and non-human beauty, to concentration on the actual concrete world. And this meant, in part at least, a turning away from purely logical studies to the theory of knowledge and to the parts of psychology and linguistics which seemed to be relevant to epistemology.

3. We have seen Russell getting rid of superfluous entities such as 'the golden mountain'. And in the course of writing *Principia Mathematica* he found that the definition of cardinal numbers as classes of classes, together with the interpretation of class-symbols as incomplete symbols, rendered it unnecessary to regard cardinal numbers as entities of any kind. But there remained, for example, points, instants and particles as factors in the physical world. And these figured in *The Problems of Philosophy* (1912), which can be said to represent Russell's incursion into the general philosophical field, as distinct from the more restricted sphere of logical and mathematical theory. Whitehead, however, woke him from his 'dogmatic slumbers' by inventing a way of constructing points, instants and particles as sets of events, or as logical constructions out of sets of events.[36]

The technique of reductive analysis as illustrated in the case of points, instants and particles was regarded by Russell as an application of the method already employed in *Principia Mathematica*. In this work the task was to find for mathematics a minimum vocabulary in which no symbol would be definable in terms of the others. And the result of the inquiry was the conclusion that the minimum vocabulary for mathematics is the same as that for logic. In this sense mathematics was found to be reducible to logic. If a similar technique, Russell came to think, is applied to the language used to describe the physical world, it will be found that points, instants and particles do not appear in the minimum vocabulary.

Now, talk about finding a minimum vocabulary tends to suggest that the operation in question is purely linguistic, in the sense of being concerned only with words. But in the context of propositions about the physical world finding a minimum vocabulary means for Russell discovering by analysis the uneliminable entities in terms of which inferred entities can be defined. If, for example, we find that the inferred non-empirical entity, or putative entity, X can be defined in terms of a series of empirical entities a, b, c, and d, X is said to be a logical construction out of a, b, c, and d. This reductive analysis as applied to X has indeed a linguistic aspect. For it means that a proposition in which X is mentioned can be translated into a set of propositions in which there is no mention of X but only of a, b, c, and d, the relation between the original proposition and the translation being such that if the former is true (or false) the latter is true (or false) and *vice versa*. But the reductive analysis has at the same time an ontological aspect. True, if X can be interpreted as a logical construction out of a, b, c, and d, we are not necessarily committed to denying the existence of X as a non-empirical entity distinct from or over and above a, b, c, and d. But it is unnecessary to postulate the existence of such an entity. Hence the principle of parsimony (or economy) or Ockham's razor forbids us to *assert* the existence of X as an inferred non-empirical entity. And the principle itself can be stated in this form: 'whenever possible logical constructions are to be substituted for inferred entities'.[37]

This quotation is taken from a paper on the relation of sense-data to physics, which Russell wrote at the beginning of 1914. In this paper he maintains that physical objects can be defined as functions of sense-data, a sense-datum being a particular object, such as a particular patch of colour, of which a subject is directly aware. Sense-data, therefore, are not to be confused with sensations, that is, with the acts of awareness of which they are the object.[38] Nor are they mental entities, in the sense of being purely within the mind. We must thus admit, to speak paradoxically, sense-data which are not actual data, not objects of actual awareness on the part of a subject. But the paradox can be avoided by calling these unsensed sense-data *sensibilia*, potential sense-data. And the physical objects of common sense and of science are to be interpreted as functions of sense-data and *sensibilia* or, to put the matter in another way, as the classes of their appearances.

There is, however, a major difficulty in admitting *sensibilia* as being on the same level, so to speak, as actual sense-data. For Russell's programme demands that the physical objects of common sense and of science should be interpreted, if possible, as logical constructions out of purely empirical, non-inferred entities. But *sensibilia* are inferred entities. The only relevant non-inferred entities are *actual* sense-data. Hence it is not surprising to find Russell saying, in his paper on the relation of sense-data to physics, that 'a complete application of the method which substitutes constructions for inferences would exhibit matter wholly in terms of sense-data, and even, we may add, of the sense-data of a single person, since the sense-data of others cannot be known without some element of inference'.[39] But he goes on to add that the carrying out of this programme is extremely difficult, and that he proposes to allow himself two kinds of inferred entities, the sense-data of other people and *sensibilia*.

In *Our Knowledge of the External World* (1914) Russell depicts the physical objects of common sense and science as logical constructions out of actual sense-data, *sensibilia* or possible sense-data being defined with reference to them. At any rate 'I think it may be laid down quite generally that, *in so far* as physics or common sense is verifiable, it must be capable of interpretation in terms of actual sense-data alone'.[40] However, in a lecture on the ultimate constituents of matter which he delivered early in 1915, Russell remarks that while the particles of mathematical physics are logical constructions, useful symbolic fictions, 'the actual data in sensation, the immediate objects of sight or touch or hearing, are extra-mental, purely physical, and among the ultimate constituents of matter'.[41] Similarly, 'sense-data are merely those among the ultimate constituents of the physical world, of which we happen to be immediately aware'.[42] Whether the statement that sense-data are 'among' the ultimate constituents of the physical world is equivalent to the admission of *sensibilia* as members of this class, or whether it means simply that sense-data are the only ultimate constituents of which we are directly aware, is not quite clear. In any case, if the world of common sense and of science is to be regarded as a logical construction, or hierarchy of logical constructions, out of the actual sense-data of a single person, it is difficult to see how solipsism can be successfully avoided. However, it was not long before Russell abandoned the doctrine of sense-data as here presented. And his ideas on solipsism will be considered later.

So far we have been concerned only with analysis of the physical objects of common sense and science. But what of the subject or mind which is aware of objects? When Russell rejected monism and embraced pluralism, he made a sharp distinction between the act of awareness and its object. Originally indeed, as he himself tells us, he accepted the view of Brentano that in sensation there are three distinct elements, 'act, content and object'.[43] He then came to think that the distinction between content and object is superfluous; but he continued to believe in the relational character of sensation, that is to say, that in sensation a subject is aware of an object. And this belief found expression in, for example, *The Problems of Philosophy* (1912). In this work Russell admitted, even if tentatively, that the subject can be known by acquaintance. It does not follow, of course, that he accepted the idea of a permanent mental substance. But he held at any rate that we are acquainted with what one might perhaps call the momentary self, the self precisely as apprehending an object in a given act of awareness. In other words, it was a question of the phenomenological analysis of consciousness rather than of metaphysical theory.

When, however, we turn to an essay on the nature of acquaintance, which Russell wrote in 1914, we find him expressing his agreement with Hume that the subject is not acquainted with itself. He does indeed define acquaintance as 'a dual relation between a subject and an object which need not have any community of nature'.[44] But the term 'subject', instead of denoting an entity with which we can be acquainted, becomes a description. In other words, the self or mind becomes a logical construction; and in his 1915 address on the ultimate constituents of matter Russell suggests that 'we might regard the mind as an assemblage of particulars, namely, what would be called "states of mind", which belong together in virtue of some specific common quality. The common quality of all states of mind would be the quality designated by the word "mental".'[45] This suggestion is indeed advanced only in the context of a discussion of the theory, rejected by Russell, that sense-data are 'in the mind'. But it is clear that the subject, considered as a single entity, has become a class of particulars. At the same time these particulars possess a quality which marks them off as mental. In other words, an element of dualism is still retained by Russell. He has not yet adopted the neutral monism, of which something will be said presently.

Needless to say, the theory of logical constructions is not intended to imply that we ought to give up talking about minds on the one hand and the physical objects of common sense and science on the other. To say, for example, that sentences in which a table is mentioned can in principle be translated into sentences in which only sense-data are referred to and the word 'table' does not occur is not equivalent to a denial of the utility of talking about tables. Indeed, within the context of ordinary language and its purposes it is perfectly true to say that there are tables, though from the point of view of the analytic philosopher a table is a logical construction out of sense-data. The language of atomic physics, for instance, does not render ordinary language illegitimate. For the purposes of ordinary life we are perfectly entitled to go on talking about trees and stones; we do not have to talk about atoms instead. And if philosophical analysis leads us to regard the entities of physical science, such as atoms, as logical constructions, this does not render illegitimate the language of physical science. The different levels of language can co-exist and are employed for different purposes, within different contexts. They should not, of course, be confused; but the one level does not exclude the other levels.

It is thus easy to understand the contention that the issue between the sense-datum theory and the common sense view of the world is a purely linguistic matter; that is, that it is simply a question of choosing between two alternative languages. But, as has already been indicated, this contention does not adequately represent Russell's point of view. Obviously, analysis as he practises it takes different forms.[46] Sometimes it is predominantly a logical analysis which has ontological implications only in the sense that it removes the ground for postulating superfluous entities. But in its application to the physical objects of common sense and science it professes to reveal the ultimate constituents of such objects. In other words it professes to increase our understanding not only of language but also of extra-linguistic reality. To be sure, Russell has at times expressed a very sceptical view about the knowledge which is actually attainable in philosophy. But his aim at any rate has been that of attaining impersonal truth. And the primary method of doing so is for him analysis. His point of view is thus opposed to that of Bradley, who thought that analysis, the breaking-up of a whole into its constituent elements, distorts reality and leads us away from the truth which is, as Hegel said, the whole. Later on, especially when treating of the relation of philosophy to the empirical sciences, Russell is ready to emphasize the role of synthesis, of bold and wide philosophical hypotheses about the universe. But at the period of which we have been writing the emphasis is placed on analysis. And it would be extremely misleading to describe analysis, as practised by Russell, as being purely 'linguistic'.

This point can also be illustrated in the following way. In *The Problems of Philosophy* Russell accepted universals as ultimate conceptual constituents of reality, universals being said 'to *subsist* or *have being*, where "being" is opposed to "existence" as being timeless'.[47] And though he has progressively depopulated the world of universals, he has never entirely rejected his former view. For he has continued to believe not only that a minimum vocabulary for the description of the world requires some universal term or terms but also that this fact shows something about the world itself, even if he has ended by being uncertain about precisely what it shows.

4. In *My Philosophical Development*,[48] Russell tells us that from August 1914 until the end of 1917 he was wholly occupied with matters arising out of his opposition to the war. These matters presumably cover *Principles of Social Reconstruction* and *Justice in War-Time*, both of which appeared in 1916, in addition to a number of articles and addresses relating to the war. However, during the period 1914–19 Russell published an important series of philosophical articles in *The Monist*.[49] In 1918 he published *Mysticism and Logic and Other Essays* and *Roads to Freedom: Socialism, Anarchism and Syndicalism*. His *Introduction to Mathematical Philosophy*, to which reference has already been made, was written in 1918, during his six months imprisonment,[50] and was published in 1919.

Shortly before the First World War Wittgenstein gave Russell some notes on various logical points. And these, together with the conversations which the two men had had during Wittgenstein's first sojourn at Cambridge, 1912–13, affected Russell's thought during the years when he was cut off from contact with his friend and former pupil.[51] In fact he prefaced his 1918 lectures on the philosophy of logical atomism with the remark that they were largely concerned with ideas which he had learned from Wittgenstein.

As for the term 'atomism' in 'logical atomism' Russell says that he wishes to arrive at the ultimate constituent elements of reality in a manner analogous to that in which in *Principia Mathematica* he worked back from 'result' to the uneliminable logical 'premisses'. But he is looking, of course, for logical and not physical atoms. Hence the use of the term 'logical'. 'The point is that the atom I wish to arrive at is the atom of logical analysis, not the atom of physical analysis.'[52] The atom of physical analysis (or, more accurately, whatever physical science at a given time takes to be ultimate physical constituents of matter) is itself subject to logical analysis. But though in his final lecture on logical atomism Russell makes what he calls an excursus into metaphysics and introduces the idea of logical constructions or, as he puts it, logical fictions, he is mainly concerned with discussing propositions and facts.

We can, of course, understand the meaning of a proposition without knowing whether it is true or false. But a proposition which asserts or denies a fact is either true or false; and it is its relation to a fact which makes it true or false.[53] As we have seen, the grammatical form of a sentence may be different from its logical form. But in a logically perfect language 'the words in a proposition would correspond one by one with the components of the corresponding fact, with the exception of such words as "or", "not", "if", "then", which have a different function'.[54] In such a language therefore there would be an identity of structure between the fact asserted or denied and its symbolic representation, the proposition. Hence if there are atomic facts, there can be atomic propositions.

The simplest imaginable kind of fact, according to Russell, is that which consists in the possession of a quality by a particular, the quality being called a 'monadic relation'. This kind of fact is an atomic fact, though not the only kind. For it is not required, in order that a fact should be atomic, that it should comprise only one term and a monadic relation. There can be a hierarchy of atomic facts; facts which comprise two particulars and a (dyadic) relation, facts which comprise three particulars and a (triadic) relation, and so on. It must be understood, however, that 'particulars', defined by Russell as the terms of relations in atomic facts, are to be understood in the sense of what would be for him genuine particulars, such as actual sense-data, not in the sense of logical constructions. 'This is white' would thus be an atomic proposition, provided that 'this' functions as a proper name denoting a sense-datum. So would 'these are white', provided again that 'these' denotes genuine particulars.

Now, an atomic proposition contains a single verb or verbal phrase. But by the use of words such as 'and', 'or' and 'if', we can construct complex or molecular propositions.[55] It would appear to follow, therefore, that there are molecular facts. But Russell shows hesitation on this point. Let us suppose, for example, that 'either today is Sunday or I made a mistake in coming here' is a molecular proposition. Does it make any sense to speak of a disjunctive fact? However, though Russell expresses some doubt about molecular facts, he admits 'general facts'. For instance, if we could enumerate all the atomic facts in the world, the proposition 'these are all the atomic facts there are' would express a general fact. Russell is also prepared to admit negative facts, even if with some hesitation. He suggests, for example, that 'Socrates is not alive' expresses an objective negative fact, an objective feature of the world.

We cannot refer to all the topics mentioned by Russell in his lectures on logical atomism. But there are two points to which attention can profitably be drawn. The first is the doctrine that every genuine particular is completely self-subsistent, in the sense that it is logically independent of every other particular. 'There is no reason why you should not have a universe consisting of one particular and nothing else.'[56] True, it is an empirical fact that there is a multitude of particulars. But it is not logically necessary that this should be the case. Hence it would not be possible, given knowledge of one particular, to deduce from it the whole system of the universe.

The second point is Russell's analysis of existence-propositions. I know, for example, that there are men in Canton; but I cannot mention any individual who lives there. Hence, Russell argues, the proposition 'there are men in Canton' cannot be about actual individuals. 'Existence is essentially a property of a propositional function.'[57] If we say 'there are men' or 'men exist', this means that there is at least one value of X for which it is true to say 'X is a man'. At the same time Russell recognizes 'existence-facts', such as that corresponding to 'there are men', as distinct from atomic facts.

It has already been mentioned that according to Russell's own explicit declaration his 1918 lectures on logical atomism were partly concerned with explaining theories suggested to him by Wittgenstein. But at that time, of course, he was acquainted with Wittgenstein's ideas only in a preliminary or immature form. Shortly after the armistice, however, Russell received from Wittgenstein the typescript of the *Tractatus Logico-Philosophicus*. And though he found himself in agreement with some of the ideas expressed in it, there were others which he was unable to accept. For example, at that time Russell accepted Wittgenstein's picture-theory of the proposition,[58] his view that atomic propositions are all logically independent of one another, and his doctrine that the propositions of logic and pure mathematics are 'tautologies' which, in themselves,[59] neither say anything about the actual existing world nor reveal to us another world of subsistent entities and timeless truths. But Russell did not accept, for instance, Wittgenstein's contention that the form which a true proposition has in common with the corresponding fact cannot be 'said' but can only be 'shown'. For Russell, as we have already noted, believed in a hierarchy of languages. Even if in language *a* nothing can be said *about* this language, there is nothing to prevent us employing language *b* to talk about *a*. Again, Wittgenstein's denial that anything can be said about the world as a whole, for example about 'all the things that there are in the world,' was more than Russell could stomach.[60]

Every student of recent British philosophy is aware that Russell has shown a marked lack of sympathy with Wittgenstein's later ideas, as expressed above all in *Philosophical Investigations*. But he admired the *Tractatus*; and in spite of the important points on which he disagreed with its author, his own logical atomism was, as we have seen, influenced by Wittgenstein's ideas. It does not follow, however, that the approaches of the two men were precisely the same. Wittgenstein thought of himself as writing simply as a logician. He thought that logical analysis demanded elementary propositions, atomic facts and the simple objects which enter into atomic facts and are named in elementary propositions.[61] But he did not think that it was his business as a logician to give any examples of simple objects, atomic facts or elementary propositions. Nor did he give any. Russell, however, while approaching analysis by way of mathematical logic rather than from the point of view of classical empiricism, very soon became interested in discovering the actual ultimate constituents of the world. And, as we have seen, he did not hesitate to give examples of atomic facts. 'This is white' would be an example, when 'this' denotes an actual sense-datum. Similarly, while in the *Tractatus* Wittgenstein described psychology as a natural science and so as having nothing to do with philosophy, Russell, in his lectures on logical atomism, applied reductive analysis not only to the physical objects of common sense and science but also to the human person. 'A person is a certain series of experiences',[62] the members of the series having a certain relation R between them, so that a person can be defined as the class of all those experiences which are serially related by R.

It is true that while he had previously regarded the goal of analysis as a knowledge of simple particulars, Russell later came to think that while many things can be known to be complex, nothing can be *known* to be simple.[63] But the reason why he came to think this was because in science what was formerly thought to be simple has often turned out to be complex. And the conclusion which he drew was simply that the logical analyst should refrain from any dogmatic assertion that he has arrived at a knowledge of what is simple. In other words, though Russell undoubtedly approached logical atomism with a background of mathematical logic, his attitude was much more empirical than that of Wittgenstein as manifested in the *Tractatus*. And in the application of reductive analysis to physical objects and minds he carried on the tradition of British empiricism, a tradition which hardly figured in Wittgenstein's mental furniture.

5. After the First World War Russell found his mind turning to the theory of knowledge and relevant topics, mathematical logic remaining more or less a past interest. This is not to say that his interest in social and political subjects abated. In 1920 he visited Russia, though his impressions were unfavourable, as is clear from *The Practice and Theory of Bolshevism* (1920). A succeeding visit to China bore fruit in *The Problems of China* (1922). Meanwhile he had published in 1921 *The Analysis of Mind*,[64] one of his best known books in the field of philosophy as he understands the term.

When Russell embraced pluralism in 1898, he accepted a dualist position. And, as we have seen, this position was maintained for some time, even if in an attenuated form. Russell was indeed acquainted with William James's theory of neutral monism, according to which the mental and physical are composed of the same material, so to speak, and differ only in arrangement and context.[65] But in his 1914 essay on the nature of acquaintance he first quoted passages from Mach and James and then expressed his disagreement with neutral monism as being incapable of explaining the phenomenon of acquaintance, which involves a relation between subject and object.

In the 1918 lectures on logical atomism, however, the sharpness of Russell's rejection of neutral monism is greatly diminished. In fact he states roundly that 'I feel more and more inclined to think that it may be true'.[66] He is indeed conscious of difficulties in accepting a view which does not distinguish between a particular and experiencing it. At the same time he is no longer sure that the difficulties are insuperable. And it is clear that while he has not yet embraced neutral monism, he would like to be able to do so.

It is thus no matter for surprise if in *The Analysis of Mind* we find Russell announcing his conversion to neutral monism,[67] which is conceived as providing a harmonization of two conflicting tendencies in contemporary thought. On the one hand many psychologists emphasize more and more the dependence of mental on physical phenomena; and one can see a definite tendency, especially among the behaviourists, to a form of methodological materialism. Obviously psychologists of this kind really consider physics, which has made a much greater advance than psychology, as the basic science. On the other hand there is a tendency among the physicists, particularly with Einstein and other exponents of the theory of relativity, to regard the matter of old-fashioned materialism as a logical fiction, a construction out of events. These two apparently conflicting tendencies can be harmonized in neutral monism, that is, by recognizing that 'physics and psychology are not distinguished by their material'.[68] Both mind and matter are logical constructions out of particulars which are neither mental nor material but neutral.

Obviously, Russell has now to abandon his former sharp distinction between the sense-datum and awareness of it. He mentions Brentano's theory of the intentionality of consciousness,[69] the theory that all consciousness is consciousness 'of' (an object), and Meinong's distinction between act, content and object. And he then remarks that 'the *act* seems unnecessary and fictitious. . . . Empirically, I cannot discover anything corresponding to the supposed act; and theoretically I cannot see that it is indispensable.'[70] Russell also tries to get rid of the distinction between content and object, when the content is supposed to be something in the external physical world. In fine, 'my own belief is that James was right in rejecting consciousness as an entity'.[71] Russell admits, of course, that he formerly maintained that a sense-datum, a patch of colour for example, is something physical, not psychical or mental. But he now holds that 'the patch of colour may be both physical and psychical',[72] and that 'the patch of colour and our sensation in seeing it are identical'.[73]

How, then, are the spheres of physics and psychology to be distinguished? One way of doing so is by distinguishing between different methods of correlating particulars. On the one hand we can correlate or group together all those particulars which common sense would regard as the appearances of a physical thing in different places. This leads to the construction of physical objects as sets of such appearances. On the other hand we can correlate or group together all events in a given place, that is, events which common sense would regard as the appearances of different objects as viewed from a given place. This gives us a perspective. And it is correlation according to perspectives which is relevant to psychology. When the place concerned is the human brain, the perspective 'consists of all the perceptions of a certain man at a given time'.[74]

Now, we have spoken of Russell's 'conversion' to neutral monism. It must be added, however, that this conversion was not complete. For example, while accepting the idea that sensation can be described in terms of a neutral material which in itself is neither mental nor material, he adds that in his opinion 'images belong only to the mental world, while those occurrences (if any) which do not form part of any "experience" belong only to the physical world'.[75] Russell does indeed say that he would be 'glad to be convinced that images can be reduced to sensations of a peculiar kind';[76] but this does not alter the fact that in *The Analysis of Mind* he maintains, even if hesitantly, that images are purely mental. Again, when discussing differentiation between physics and psychology in terms of causal laws, Russell is prepared to admit that 'it is by no means certain that the peculiar causal laws which govern mental events are not really physiological';[77] but at the same time he expresses his belief that images are subject to peculiar psychological laws, which he calls 'mnemic' and that the unperceived entities of physics cannot be brought under psychological causal laws. Further, though, as we have seen, Russell expresses agreement with James in rejecting consciousness as an entity, he clearly feels some hesitation on the point, as well he might. Thus he remarks that whatever the term 'consciousness' may mean, consciousness is 'a complex and far from universal characteristic of mental phenomena'.[78] It thus cannot be used to distinguish the psychical from the physical. And we ought to try to exhibit its derivative character. But to say this is not quite the same thing as to deny the existence of consciousness.

In 1924 Russell published a well-known essay on logical atomism, his contribution to the First Series of *Contemporary British Philosophy*, edited by J. H. Muirhead. The ultimate constituents of the world are there said to be 'events',[79] each of which stands to a certain number of other events in a relation of compresence. The mind is defined as 'a track of sets of compresent events in a region of space-time where there is matter peculiarly liable to form habits'.[80] As this refers especially to the brain, the definition is more or less the same as the provisional definition offered in 1927 in *An Outline of Philosophy*.[81] But though both minds and physical objects are interpreted as logical constructions out of events, the former are constructed out of sensations and images, while the latter are constructions out of sensations and unperceived events.[82] And we have seen that Russell finds difficulty in regarding images as being anything else but purely mental, and unperceived events as anything else but purely physical.

Reviewing the course of his reflections in *My Philosophical Development* (1959) Russell remarks that 'in *The Analysis of Mind* (1921), I explicitly abandoned "sense-data"'.[83] That is to say, he abandoned the relational theory of sensation, according to which sensation is a cognitive act, sense-data being physical objects of psychical awareness. This meant that there was not the same need as before to regard physical and psychical occurrences as fundamentally different; and to this extent he was able to embrace neutral monism. He adds, however, that when dualism has been got rid of at one point, it is very difficult not to re-introduce it at another, and that it is necessary to re-interpret and re-define such terms as 'awareness', 'acquaintance' and 'experience'. An effort in this direction was made in *An Inquiry into Meaning and Truth* (1940);[84] but Russell does not pretend to have solved all his problems. It is thus not quite accurate to say that Russell embraced neutral monism only to reject it. It is rather that he has found himself unable in practice to carry through the requisite programme of re-interpretation, without, however, being prepared to assert that it could not be carried through.

6. Now, if the physical objects of common sense and science are first interpreted as logical constructions out of sense-data, and if sense-data, considered as extra-mental objects of awareness, are then eliminated, it seems to follow that we have no direct knowledge or awareness of any external object. For example, when the occurrence takes place which would ordinarily be called seeing the sun, the direct object of my awareness seems to be an event or events, sensations, which are in some sense 'in me'.[85] And the same must be said about my awareness of other persons. We are then faced with the difficulty that the direct objects of experience or awareness are not the physical objects of common sense and of science, while at the same time it is only what we directly experience that gives us any real reason for believing that there are such objects.

Of the possible ways of dealing with this problem 'the simplest is that of solipsism',[86] which Russell is prepared to admit as a logically possible position. For example, after saying that in his opinion the universe in itself is without unity and continuity he remarks, 'indeed there is little but prejudice and habit to be said for the view that there is a world at all'.[87] Similarly, though as a matter of fact my experience leads me to believe in the existence of other minds, 'as a matter of pure logic, it would be possible for me to have these experiences even if other minds did not exist'.[88] One can, of course, appeal to causal inference. But even at best such inference cannot provide demonstrative certainty and thus cannot show that solipsism is utterly untenable.

Though, however, solipsism may be logically possible, it is hardly credible. If it is taken as involving the dogmatic assertion that 'I alone exist', nobody really believes it. If it is taken to mean simply that there is no valid reason either for asserting or denying anything except one's own experiences, consistency demands that one should doubt whether one has had a past and whether one will have a future. For we have no better reason for believing that we have had experiences in the past than we have for believing in external objects. Both beliefs depend on inference. And if we doubt the second, we should also doubt the first. But 'no solipsist has ever gone as far as this'.[89] In other words, no solipsist is ever consistent.

The alternative to what Russell calls 'solipsism of the moment',[90] the hypothesis that the whole of my knowledge is limited to what I am now noticing at this moment, is the hypothesis that there are principles of non-deductive inference which justify our belief in the existence of the external world and of other people. When these two alternatives are clearly presented, nobody, Russell argues, would honestly and sincerely choose solipsism. He is doubtless right. But in this case an examination of the relevant principles of inference becomes a matter of importance.[91]

Chapter Twenty

BERTRAND RUSSELL (2)

The postulates of non-demonstrative inference and the limits of empiricism – Language; the complexity of language and the idea of a hierarchy of languages, meaning and significance, truth and falsity – Language as a guide to the structure of the world.

1. Russell has drawn attention to three books in particular as representing the outcome of his reflections in the years after the First World War on the theory of knowledge and relevant subjects.[1] These are *The Analysis of Mind* (1921), *An Inquiry into Meaning and Truth* (1940), and *Human Knowledge: Its Scope and Limits* (1948). In this section, where we shall be considering Russell's ideas about non-demonstrative inference, we shall be referring mainly to the last-named book.[2]

If we assume with Russell that the physical objects of common sense and of science are logical constructions out of events and that each event is a logically self-sufficient entity, it follows that from one event or group of events we cannot infer with certainty the occurrence of any other event or group of events. Demonstrative inference belongs to logic and pure mathematics, not to the empirical sciences. Indeed, on the face of it it appears that we have no real ground for making any inferences at all in science. At the same time we are all convinced that valid inferences, leading to conclusions which possess varying degrees of probability, can be made both on the level of common sense and in science. To be sure, not all inferences are valid. Many scientific hypotheses have had to be discarded. But this does not alter the fact that no sane man doubts that by and large science has increased and is increasing human knowledge. On this assumption, therefore, the question arises, how can scientific inference be theoretically justified?

Some philosophers would say, and the plain man would probably be inclined to agree with them, that scientific inference stands in need of no other justification than a pragmatic one, namely its success. Scientists can and do make successful predictions. Science works. And the philosopher who looks for a further justification is looking for what cannot be had and is in any case not required.

In Russell's opinion this attitude is equivalent to blocking inquiry from the outset. He is, needless to say, as well aware as anyone else that by and large science delivers the goods.

But he is also acutely aware of the fact that purely empiricist premises lead to the conclusion that the factual success of scientific inference is simply fortuitous. Yet nobody really believes that this is the case. Hence we must look for some justification of scientific inference other than its factual success. To attempt to block inquiry at the outset is unworthy of a genuine philosopher. And if inquiry leads us to the conclusion that pure empiricism is an inadequate theory of knowledge, we just have to accept the fact and not shut our eyes to it.

Russell regards his task as that of finding 'the minimum principles required to justify scientific inference'.[3] Such principles or premises[4] must state something about the world. For inference from the observed to the unobserved or from one group of events to another can be justified only 'if the world has certain characteristics which are not logically necessary'.[5] It is not a question of logically necessary principles which are known to possess absolute validity independently of all experience. For scientific inference is non-demonstrative inference. Rather is it a question of reflecting on actual scientific inference and discovering the minimum number of principles, premises or postulates which are required to justify them.

The matter has, however, to be expressed more precisely. There is obviously no question of justifying all inferences and generalizations. For, as we know by experience, some generalizations are false. What we are looking for is the minimum number of principles which will confer an antecedent finite probability on certain inferences and generalizations and not on others. In other words, we have to examine what are universally regarded as genuine instances of scientific inference and generalization and discover the principles which are required in order to justify these types of inference and generalization by conferring on them an antecedent finite probability that is not conferred on the types which experience has taught us to reject as inherently fallacious and unscientific.[6]

To cut a long story short, Russell finds five principles or premises of scientific inference. But he lays no particular emphasis upon the number five. He considers indeed that the principles which he enunciates are sufficient; but he allows for the possibility that the number might be reduced. Further, he does not insist on his actual formulation of the principles.[7] Greater precision might well be possible. It is to be noted, however, that all the principles state probabilities only, not certainties, and that they are conceived as conferring a finite antecedent probability on certain types of inductive inference.

The first principle, described by Russell as the postulate of quasi-permanence, states that, given any event A, it frequently happens that an event very similar to A occurs in a neighbouring place at a neighbouring time. This postulate enables us to operate, for instance, with the common sense concepts of person and thing without introducing the metaphysical notion of substance. For the 'very similar' event can be regarded as part of the history of the series of events which constitutes the person or thing.

The second principle, the postulate of separable causal lines, states that it is often possible to form a series of events such that from one or two members of the series we can infer something about the other members. This principle or postulate is clearly essential for scientific inference. For it is only on the basis of the idea of causal lines that we can infer distant from near events.

The third principle, the postulate of spatio-temporal continuity, which presupposes the second principle and refers to causal lines, denies action at a distance and states that when there is a causal connection between non-contiguous events, there will be found to be intermediate links in the chain.

The fourth principle, 'the structural postulate', states that when a number of structurally similar complex events occur around a centre from which they are not too widely separated, it is generally the case that all are members of causal lines which have their origin in an event of similar structure at the centre. Suppose, for example, that a number of persons are situated in different parts of a public square where an orator is holding forth or a radio is blaring, and that they have similar auditory experiences. This postulate confers antecedent probability on the inference that their similar experiences are causally related to the sounds made by the orator or radio.[8]

The fifth principle, the postulate of analogy, states that if, when two classes of events, A and B, are observed, there is reason to believe that A causes B, then if, in a given case, A occurs but we cannot observe whether B occurs or not, it is probable that it does occur. Similarly, if the occurrence of B is observed while the occurrence of A cannot be observed, it is probable that A has occurred. According to Russell, an important function of this postulate is to justify belief in other minds.

This doctrine of the principles of non-demonstrative inference is partly intended to solve a problem raised by J. M. Keynes (1883–1946) in his *Treatise on Probability* (1921).[9] But the point to which we wish to draw attention here is the unprovability of the principles. They are not offered as eternal truths which can be intuited *a priori*. Nor are they supposed to be deducible from such truths. At the same time they cannot be proved nor even rendered probable by empirical arguments. For they are the very principles on which the validity of such arguments rests. If we tried to justify them by appealing to scientific inference, we should be involved in a vicious circle. Hence the principles must necessarily be described as 'postulates' of scientific inference.

In view of the fact that these postulates cannot be proved, nor even rendered probable, by empirical argument, Russell explicitly admits the failure of empiricism, in the sense that it is inadequate as a theory of knowledge and is unable to justify the presuppositions on which all inferred empirical knowledge depends for its validity. It has therefore sometimes been said that he approaches a Kantian position. But the similarity is limited to a common recognition of the limitations of pure empiricism. Russell is very far from developing a theory of the *a priori* on the lines of Kant's first *Critique*. Instead he proceeds to give a biological-psychological account of the origins of the postulates of non-demonstrative inference. If, for example, an animal has a habit of such a kind that in the presence of an instance of A it behaves in a manner in which, before acquiring the habit, it behaved in the presence of an instance of B, it can be said to have 'inferred' and to 'believe' that every instance of A is usually followed by an instance of B. This is, of course, an anthropomorphic way of speaking. The animal does not consciously make inferences. None the less there is such a thing as animal inference. It is a feature of the process of adaptation to environment, and there is continuity between it and inference in man. That is to say, our 'knowledge' of the principles or postulates of non-demonstrative inference 'exists at first solely in the form of a propensity to inferences of the kind that they justify'.[10] Man, unlike the animal, is capable of reflecting on examples of these inferences, of making the postulates explicit and of using logical technique to improve their foundations. But the relatively *a priori* character[11] of the principles is explicable in terms of a propensity to make inferences in accordance with them, a propensity which is continuous with that manifested in animal inference.

Now, we have seen that Russell set out to discover a theoretical justification of scientific inference. But though he justifies scientific inference in terms of certain postulates, the postulates themselves are then explained through a biological-psychological account of their origin. And this account, which goes back ultimately to the process of adaptation to environment, appears to be quite compatible with the theory of what Nietzsche called biologically useful fictions. In other words, it is arguable that Russell does not in fact fulfil his programme of providing a theoretical justification of non-demonstrative inference, not at least if to justify this inference theoretically means to supply premisses which warrant the assertion that it is theoretically valid.

It may appear, therefore, that in the long run we are thrown back on a pragmatic justification, on an appeal to the fact that the postulates work, that 'their verifiable consequences are such as experience will confirm'.[12] Indeed, Russell explicitly says that the postulates 'are justified by the fact that they are implied in inferences which we all accept as valid, and that, although they cannot be proved in any formal sense, the whole system of science and everyday knowledge, out of which they have been distilled, is, within limits, self-confirmatory'.[13] The fact that the postulates or principles lead to results which are in conformity with experience 'does not logically suffice to make the principles even probable'.[14] At the same time the whole system of science, of probable knowledge, which rests on the postulates, is self-confirmatory, self-justifying in a pragmatic sense. Hence Russell can say that while he does not accept the idealist coherence theory of truth, there is, in an important sense, a valid coherence theory of probability.[15]

In this case we may be inclined to ask why Russell does not accept from the start the position of those who claim that scientific inference is sufficiently justified by its results, by the fact that it leads to verifiable predictions. But Russell would presumably answer that to content oneself with this position from the start is equivalent to suppressing a real problem, to shutting one's eyes to it. Consideration of the problem leads to a recognition of the indemonstrable postulates of scientific inference, and thus to a recognition of the limitations and inadequacy of pure empiricism as a theory of knowledge. Recognition of these facts is a real intellectual gain; and it cannot be obtained if the attempt to discover a theoretical justification of non-demonstrative inference is prohibited from the outset.

The comment might be made, of course, that though this attitude is reasonable enough when considered within the framework of Russell's general empiricist analysis of the world, the fact remains that while explicitly recognizing the limitations of pure empiricism as a theory of knowledge he does not really go beyond it. His biological explanation of the origin of a propensity to make inferences in accordance with certain implicit postulates or expectations can be seen as a continuation and development of Hume's doctrine of natural beliefs. But to go beyond empiricism, in the sense of substituting for it a genuinely non-empiricist theory of knowledge, would obviously have demanded a much more radical revision of his opinions than Russell was prepared either to undertake or to recognize as justified.

2. We have noted Russell's statement that after the First World War his thoughts turned to the theory of knowledge and to the relevant parts of psychology and linguistics. It is appropriate, therefore, to say something about the last-mentioned theme, Russell's theory of language. Reference has already been made, however, to the theory of the relation between language and fact as expounded in the 1918 lectures

on logical atomism. And we can confine ourselves here mainly to Russell's ideas as set out in *An Inquiry into Meaning and Truth* and as repeated or modified in *Human Knowledge*.[16]

(i) Philosophers, Russell remarks, have been chiefly interested in language as a means of making statements and conveying information. But 'what is the purpose of language to a sergeant-major?'[17] The purpose of commands is obviously to influence the behaviour of others rather than to state facts or convey information. Besides, the sergeant-major's language is also sometimes directed to expressing emotive attitudes. Language, in other words, has a variety of functions.

Though, however, Russell recognizes the complex and flexible character of language, he himself is chiefly interested, like the philosophers to whom he vaguely refers, in descriptive language. This is indeed only to be expected. For Russell regards philosophy as an attempt to understand the world. And his attention is thus naturally centred on language as an instrument in fulfilling this task.[18] This is indeed one reason for his marked lack of sympathy with any tendency to treat language as though it were an autonomous, self-sufficient entity, which can be profitably studied by the philosopher without reference to its relation to non-linguistic fact.[19]

Reference has already been made to Russell's idea of a hierarchy of languages, an idea which is connected with the theory of types. In *An Inquiry into Meaning and Truth* he assumes this idea and maintains that though the hierarchy extends indefinitely upwards, it cannot extend indefinitely downwards. In other words, there must be a basic or lowest-type language. And Russell proceeds to discuss one possible form of such a language, though he does not claim that it is the only possible form.

The basic or primary language suggested by Russell is an object-language, consisting, that is to say, of object-words. A word of this type can be defined in two ways. Logically, it is a word which has meaning in isolation. Hence the class of object-words would not include terms such as 'or'. Psychologically, an object-word is one the use of which can be learned without its being necessary to have previously learned the uses or meanings of other words. That is to say, it is a word the meaning of which can be learned by ostensive definition, as when one says to a child 'pig', while pointing to an example of this kind of animal.

It does not follow, however, that an object-language of this kind would be confined to nouns. For it would admit verbs such as 'run' and 'hit' and adjectives such as 'red' and 'hard'. And, according to Russell, 'theoretically, given sufficient capacity, we could express in the object-language every non-linguistic occurrence',[20] though this would admittedly involve translating complicated sentences into a kind of 'pidgin'.

Now, meaningful statements expressed in this primary language would *be* either true or false. But we should not be able to *say*, within the limits of the primary language, that any statement expressed in it was true or false. For these logical terms would not be available. It would be necessary to use a second-order language for this purpose. Actual language, of course, includes both object-words and logical words. But the artificial isolation of a possible object-language serves to illustrate the idea of a hierarchy of languages and shows how we can cope with any difficulty arising out of the contention that nothing can be said within a given language *about* this language.[21]

(ii) Truth and falsity obviously presuppose meaning. We could not properly say of a meaningless statement that it was either true or false. For there would be nothing to which these terms could apply. But it does not follow that every meaningful utterance is either true or false. 'Right turn!' and 'Are you feeling better?' are meaningful utterances, but we would not say of either that it is true or false. The range of meaning is thus wider than the range of logical truth and falsity.[22] And in the *Inquiry* Russell tells us that indicative sentences 'alone are true or false',[23] though subsequently we are told that 'truth and falsehood, in so far as they are public, are attributes of sentences, either in the indicative or in the subjective or conditional'.[24]

Hitherto we have attributed 'meaning' both to object-words and to sentences. But Russell tends, though without uniform consistency, to restrict the term 'meaning' to object-words and to speak of sentences as having 'significance'. And we can say that 'although meanings must be derived from experience, significance need not'.[25] That is to say, we can understand the significance of a sentence which refers to something which we have never experienced, provided that we know the meanings of the words and that the sentence observes the rules of syntax.

Meaning, when attributed to object-words, signifies reference. And it is said to be fundamental. For it is through the meanings of object-words, learned by experience, that 'language is connected with non-linguistic occurrences in the way that makes it capable of expressing empirical truth or falsehood'.[26] But whereas we might expect a purely logical definition of meaning in this sense, Russell introduces psychological considerations based on what he believes to be the way in which a child, for example, comes to acquire the habit of using certain words correctly. Thus we are told that a word is said to mean an object 'if the sensible presence of the object causes the utterance of the word, and the hearing of the word has effects analogous, in certain respects, to the sensible presence of the object'.[27]

This methodological, though not dogmatic, behaviourism can be found also in, for instance, Russell's account of imperatives. An uttered imperative 'expresses' something in the speaker, a desire coupled with an idea of the intended effect, while it 'means' the external effect intended and commanded. And the heard imperative is understood 'when it causes a certain kind of bodily movement, or an impulse towards such a movement'.[28]

Imperative sentences, however, though significant, are not said to be true or false. So let us consider indicative sentences, which are said to indicate fact. Russell also calls them assertions, maintaining that 'an assertion has two sides, subjective and objective'.[29] Subjectively, an assertion expresses a state of the person who makes the assertion, a state which can be called a belief.[30] Objectively, the assertion is related to something which makes it true or false. An assertion is false if it intends to indicate a fact but fails to do so, true if it succeeds. But true and false assertions are equally meaningful. Hence the significance of an assertion cannot be equated with actual indication of a fact, but lies rather in what the assertion expresses, namely a certain belief or, more accurately, the object of this belief, what is believed. And a heard assertion is said to be significant, from a psychological point of view, if it can cause belief, disbelief or doubt in the hearer.

Russell's insistence on studying language in the context of human life is doubtless largely responsible for his introducing a number of perhaps somewhat confusing psychological considerations. But the main issue can be simplified in this way. The significance of a sentence is that which is common to a sentence in one language and its translation into another language. For example, 'I am hungry' and 'J'ai faim' have a common element which constitutes the significance of the sentence. This common element is the 'proposition'. We cannot ask, therefore, if a proposition is significant. For it *is* the significance. But in the case of indicative sentences at any rate we can properly ask whether the proposition is true or false. Significance is thus independent of truth.

Now, we have noted Russell's insistence that, given certain conditions, we can understand the significance of an assertion which refers to something which we have not personally experienced. It can now be added that he does not wish to tie down the significance of assertions or statements even to the experienceable. And this naturally leads him to adopt a critical attitude towards the logical positivist criterion of meaning. True, in some respects he regards logical positivism with a benevolent eye, chiefly perhaps because of its interpretation of logic and pure mathematics and its serious concern with empirical science. But though he agrees with the positivists in rejecting the idea of 'ineffable knowledge',[31] he has consistently refused to accept the criterion of meaning, according to which the meaning of a factual proposition is identical with the mode of its verification.

In general, Russell argues, the logical positivist criterion of meaning implies two things. First, what cannot be verified or falsified is meaningless. Secondly, two propositions verified by the same occurrences have the same meaning or significance. 'I reject both.'[32] In regard to the first point, the propositions which are most nearly certain, namely judgments of perception, cannot be verified, 'since it is they that constitute the verification of all other empirical propositions that can be in any degree known. If Schlick were right, we should be committed to an endless regress.'[33] In regard to the second point, the hypothesis that the stars exist continuously and the hypothesis that they exist only when I see them are identical in their testable consequences. But they do not have the same significance. Of course, the principle of verifiability can be modified and interpreted as claiming that a factual statement is meaningful if we can imagine sensible experiences which would verify it, if it were true. But Russell comments that in his opinion this is a sufficient but not a necessary criterion of significance.[34]

(iii) In 1906–9 Russell wrote four essays dealing with the subject of truth, especially in relation to pragmatism, which were reprinted in *Philosophical Essays*. At a later date he took up the subject again, the results of this second phase of reflection being embodied in the *Inquiry*. The topic is also treated in *Human Knowledge*. And in *My Philosophical Development* Russell devotes the fifteenth chapter to a review of the course of his investigations.

A certain looseness in the use of terminology is characteristic of Russell. Thus in different places we are told that truth and falsity are predicated of indicative sentences, of sentences in the indicative or in the subjunctive or conditional, of assertions, of propositions and of beliefs. But it does not follow, of course, that all these ways of speaking are mutually incompatible. The significance of a sentence is a proposition; but propositions, according to Russell, express states of belief. Hence we can say that 'it is in fact primarily beliefs that are true or false; sentences only become so through the fact that they can express beliefs'.[35] In any case the main lines of Russell's theory of truth are clear enough.

In the first place Russell rejects the idealist interpretation of truth as coherence. In an early article he argued that if every particular true judgment, when isolated from the total system of truth, is only partially true, and if what would normally be called false judgments are partially true and have their place in the complete system of truth, it follows that the statement 'Bishop Stubbs was hanged for murder' is not completely false but forms part of the whole truth.[36] But this is incredible. And, in general, the coherence theory simply blurs the distinction between truth and falsehood.

In the second place Russell rejects the pragmatist theory of truth. When he paraphrased William James's statement that the true is only the expedient in our way of thinking as 'a truth is anything which it pays to believe', he was accused of gross misinterpretation. Russell retorted, however, that James's explanation of the real meaning of the statement was even sillier than what he, Russell, had taken the statement to mean. Russell did indeed owe a number of important ideas to James; but he had no sympathy with the American philosopher's account of truth.

In the third place Russell protests against any confusion between truth and knowledge. Obviously, if I can properly be said to know that something is the case, the statement which expresses my knowledge is true. But it by no means follows that a true proposition must be known to be true. Indeed, Russell is prepared to admit the possibility of propositions which are true, though we cannot know them to be true. And if it is objected that this admission is tantamount to an abandonment of pure empiricism, he replies that 'pure empiricism is believed by no one'.[37]

We are left, therefore, with the correspondence theory of truth, according to which 'when a sentence or belief is "true", it is so in virtue of some relation to one or more facts'.[38] These facts are called by Russell 'verifiers'. To know what an assertion or statement means, I must, of course, have some idea of the state of affairs which would make it true. But I need not know that it is true. For the relation between statement and verifier or verifiers is an objective one, independent of my knowledge of it. Indeed, in Russell's opinion I need not be able to mention any particular instance of a verifier in order to know that a statement is meaningful and that it is thus either true or false. And this thesis enables him to maintain that a statement such as 'there are facts which I cannot imagine' is meaningful and either true or false. In Russell's view at any rate I could not mention any particular instance of a fact which cannot be imagined. At the same time I can conceive 'general circumstances'[39] which would verify the belief that there are facts which I cannot imagine. And this is sufficient to render the statement intelligible and capable of being true or false. Whether it *is* true or false, however, depends on a relation which is independent of my knowledge of it. In popular language the statement either corresponds or does not correspond with the facts. And the relation which actually obtains is unaffected by my knowing or not knowing it.

The theory of truth as correspondence with fact does not apply, of course, to the analytic propositions of logic and pure mathematics. For in their case truth 'follows from the form of the sentence'.[40] But in its application to empirical statements or assertions the theory can be said to represent a common sense position. The ordinary man would certainly argue that an empirical factual statement is made true or false by its relation to a fact or facts.[41] Difficulty arises only when we try to give a precise and adequate account of the idea of correspondence in this context. What precisely is meant by it? Russell is conscious of this difficulty. But he tells us that 'every belief which is not merely an impulse to action is in the nature of a picture, combined with a yes-feeling or a no-feeling; in the case of a yes-feeling it is "true" if there is a fact having to the picture the kind of similarity that a prototype has to an image; in the case of a no-feeling it is "true" if there is no such fact. A belief which is not true is called "false". This is a definition of "truth" and "falsehood".'[42]

In the opinion of the present writer the introduction of terms such as 'yes-feeling' and 'no-feeling' into a definition of truth is hardly felicitous. This point apart, however, it is clear that correspondence is conceived by Russell according to the analogy of pictorial representation. But though we may perhaps speak of true and false pictures, that which is strictly speaking true or false is not the picture but the statement that it does or does not correspond with an object or set of objects. So presumably the relation of correspondence which makes a statement true must be, as in Wittgenstein's *Tractatus*, a structural correspondence between the proposition and the fact or facts which count as its verifier or verifiers. Russell notes, however, that the relation is by no means always simple or of one invariable type.

3. It scarcely needs saying that no amount of inspection of a belief, as Russell puts it, or of an empirical statement will tell us whether it is true or false. To ascertain this we have to consider the factual evidence. But Russell has claimed that in some other sense or senses we can infer something about the world from the properties of language. Moreover, this is not a claim which he has put forward only once or in passing. For example, in *The Principles of Mathematics* he remarked that though grammatical distinctions cannot legitimately be assumed without more ado to indicate genuine philosophical distinctions, 'the study of grammar, in my opinion, is capable of throwing far more light on philosophical questions than is commonly supposed by philosophers'.[43] Again, even in *An Outline of Philosophy*, where he went as far as he could in a behaviourist interpretation of language, he suggested that 'quite important metaphysical conclusions, of a more or less sceptical kind',[44] can be derived from reflection on the relation between language and things. At a later date, in the *Inquiry*, he explicitly associated himself with those philosophers who 'infer properties of the world from properties of language'[45] and asserted his belief that 'partly by means of the study of syntax, we can arrive at considerable knowledge concerning the structure of the world'.[46] Moreover, in *My Philosophical Development* he quotes the paragraph in which this last assertion occurs with the endorsement 'I have nothing to add to what I said there'.[47]

Russell obviously does not mean that we can infer, without more ado, properties of the world from grammatical forms as they exist in ordinary language. If we could do this, we could infer the substance-accident metaphysics from the subject-predicate form of sentence, whereas we have seen that Russell eliminates the concept of substance by reductive analysis.[48] Nor does Russell mean that from the fact that a term can be eliminated, in the sense that sentences in which this term occurs can be translated into sentences of equivalent truth-value in which the term does not occur, we can infer that no entity exists corresponding to the term in question. As has already been noted, the fact that the term 'the golden mountain' can be eliminated does not prove that there is no golden mountain. It may show that we need not postulate such a mountain. But our grounds for thinking that there actually is no such mountain are empirical, not linguistic, grounds. Similarly, if 'similarity' can be eliminated, this does not by itself prove that there is no entity corresponding to 'similarity'. It may show that we cannot legitimately infer such an entity from language; but to show that language does not provide any adequate ground for inferring a subsistent entity 'similarity' is not the same thing as to prove that there is in fact no such entity. When referring to sentences in which the word 'similarity' cannot be replaced by 'similar' or some such word, Russell remarks that 'these latter need not be admitted'.[49] And it seems obvious that he has already decided, and rightly decided, but on grounds which were not purely linguistic, that it would be absurd to postulate an entity named 'similarity'. For this reason he says that if there are sentences in which 'similarity' cannot be replaced by 'similar', sentences of this class 'need not be admitted'.

The question can thus be formulated in this way. Can we infer properties of the world from the indispensable properties of a logically purified and reformed language? And the answer to this question seems to depend very largely on the sense which is given to the term 'infer' in this context. If it is suggested that a logically purified language can serve as an ultimate premiss from which we can deduce properties of the world, the validity of this idea appears to me questionable. For one thing it would have to be shown that no ontological decisions, made on grounds which could not reasonably be described as purely linguistic, had influenced the construction of the logically purified language. In other words, it would have to be shown that assessment of the indispensable features of language had not been influenced and guided by empirically-based convictions about features of extra-linguistic reality.

If, however, the claim that we can infer properties of the world from properties of language simply means that if we find that it is necessary to speak of things in certain ways, there is at least a strong presumption that there is some reason in things themselves for this necessity, the claim seems to be reasonable. Language has developed through the centuries in response to man's experience and needs. And if we find, for example, that we cannot get along without being able to say of two or more things that they are similar or alike, it is probable that some things are indeed of such a kind that they can be appropriately described as similar or alike, and that the world does not consist simply of entirely heterogeneous and unrelated particulars. But in the long run the question whether there actually are things which can appropriately be described in this way, is a question which has to be decided empirically.

It might perhaps be objected that we cannot talk of 'things' at all without implying similarity. For if there are things, they are necessarily similar in being things or beings. This is doubtless true. And in this sense we can infer from language that similarity is a feature of the world. But this does not alter the fact that it is ultimately through experience, and not from language, that we know that there are things. Reflection on language can doubtless serve to sharpen our awareness of features of extra-linguistic reality and to make us notice what we possibly had not noticed before. But that language can serve as an ultimate premiss for inferring properties of the world seems to be highly questionable.

Chapter Twenty-one

BERTRAND RUSSELL (3)

Introductory remarks – Russell's earlier moral philosophy and the influence of Moore – Instinct, mind and spirit – The relation of the judgment of value to desire – Social science and power – Russell's attitude towards religion – The nature of philosophy as conceived by Russell – Some brief critical comments.

1. We have been concerned so far with the more abstract aspects of Russell's philosophy. But we noted that his first book was on *German Social Democracy* (1896). And con-

comitantly with or in the intervals between his publications
on mathematics, logic, the theory of knowledge, the philosophy of science and so on he has produced a spate of books
and articles on ethical, social and political topics. At the 1948
International Philosophical Congress at Amsterdam a Communist professor from Prague took it upon himself to refer
to Russell as an example of an ivory-tower philosopher. But
whatever one's estimate may be of Russell's ideas in this or
that field of inquiry and reflection, this particular judgment
was patently absurd. For Russell has not only written on
matters of practical concern but also actively campaigned in
favour of his ideas. His imprisonment towards the close of
the First World War has already been mentioned. During
the Second World War he found himself in sympathy with
the struggle against the Nazis, and after the war, when the
Communists were staging take-overs in a number of countries, he vehemently criticized some of the more unpleasant
aspects of Communist policy and conduct. In other words,
his utterances were for once in tune with the official attitude
in his own country. And in 1949 he received the Order of
Merit from King George VI.[1] In more recent years he has not
only campaigned for the introduction of a system of world-
government but also sponsored the movement for nuclear
disarmament. In fact he carried his sponsorship to the extent
of taking a personal part in the movement of civil disobedi-
ence. And as he refused to pay the imposed fine, this activity
earned him a week or so in gaol.[2] Thus even at a very advanced age Russell has continued to battle on behalf of the
welfare of humanity, as he sees it. And the charge of 'ivory-
tower philosopher' is obviously singularly inappropriate.

In the following section, however, we shall be concerned
with the more theoretical aspects of Russell's ethical and political thought. To the general public he is, of course, best
known for his writing on concrete issues. But it would be
out of place in a history of philosophy to discuss Russell's
opinions about, say, sex[3] or nuclear disarmament, especially as
he himself does not regard discussion of such concrete issues
as pertaining to philosophy in a strict sense.

2. The first chapter in *Philosophical Essays* (1910) is entitled 'The Elements of Ethics' and represents a conflation

of an article on determinism and morals which appeared in the *Hibbert Journal* in 1908 and of two articles on ethics which appeared in 1910 in the February and May issues of the *New Quarterly*. At this period Russell maintained that ethics aims at discovering true propositions about virtuous and vicious conduct, and that it is a science. If we ask why we ought to perform certain actions, we eventually arrive at basic propositions which cannot themselves be proved. But this is not a feature peculiar to ethics, and it does not weaken its claim to be a science.

Now, if we ask for reasons why we ought to perform certain actions and not to perform others, the answer generally refers to consequences. And if we assume that an action is right because it produces good consequences or leads to the attainment of a good, it is clear that some things at any rate must be good in themselves. Not all things can be good. If they were, we could not distinguish between right and wrong actions. And some things may be considered good as means to something else. But we cannot do without the concept of things which are intrinsically good, possessing the property of goodness 'quite independently of our opinion on the subject, or of our wishes or other people's'.[4] True, people often have different opinions about what is good. And it may be difficult to decide between these opinions. But it does not follow from this that there is nothing which *is* good. Indeed, '*good* and *bad* are qualities which belong to objects independently of our opinions, just as much as *round* and *square* do'.[5]

Though goodness is an objective property of certain things, it is indefinable. It cannot therefore be identified with, say, the pleasant. That which gives pleasure may be good. But, if it is, this is because it possesses, over and above pleasantness, the indefinable quality of goodness. 'Good' no more means 'pleasant' than it means 'existent'.

Now if we assume that goodness is an intrinsic, indefinable property of certain things, it can be perceived only immediately. And the judgment in which this perception is expressed will be insusceptible of proof. The question arises, therefore, whether differences between such judgments do not weaken or even entirely undermine the thesis that there can be knowledge of what is good. Russell obviously does not deny that there have been and are different judgments about what things are good and bad. At the same time such differences, in his opinion, are neither so great nor so widespread as to compel us to relinquish the idea of moral knowledge. In fact, genuine differences between the judgments of different people in regard to intrinsic goodness and badness 'are, I believe, very rare indeed'.[6] Where they exist, the only remedy is to take a closer look.

In Russell's view genuine differences of opinion arise not so much in regard to intrinsic goodness and badness as in regard to the rightness and wrongness of actions. For an action is objectively right 'when, of all that are possible, it is the one which will probably have the best results'.[7] And it is obvious that people may come to different conclusions about means, even when they are in agreement about ends. In these circumstances the moral agent will act in accordance with the judgment at which he arrives after the amount of reflection which is appropriate in the given case.

The thesis that goodness is an intrinsic, indefinable property of certain things, together with the subordination of the concepts of right and obligation to the concept of the good, obviously show the influence of Russell's friend, G. E. Moore. And this influence persists, to some extent at least, in *Principles of Social Reconstruction* (1916). Russell is here mainly concerned with social and political themes; and he tells us that he did not write the book in his capacity as a philosopher. But when he says that 'I consider the best life that which is most built on creative impulses'[8] and explains that what he means by creative impulses are those which aim at bringing into existence good or valuable things such as knowledge, art and goodwill, his point of view is certainly in harmony with that of Moore.

3. At the same time, though there is certainly no explicit recantation in *Principles of Social Reconstruction* of the views which Russell took over from Moore, we can perhaps see in certain aspects of what he says the manifestation of a tendency to make good and bad relative to desire. In any case there is a marked tendency to interpret morality in the light of anthropology, of a certain doctrine about human na-

ture. I do not mean to imply that this is necessarily a bad thing. I mean rather that Russell is moving away from a purely Moorean point of view in ethics.

'All human activity', Russell agrees, 'springs from two sources: impulse and desire.'[9] As he goes on to say that the suppression of impulse by purposes, desires and will means the suppression of vitality, one's natural tendency is to think that he is talking about conscious desire. But the desire which lies at the basis of human activity is presumably in the first instance unconscious desire. And in *The Analysis of Mind* Russell insists, under the influence of psycho-analytic theory, that 'all primitive desire is unconscious'.[10]

The expression of natural impulse is in itself a good thing because men possess 'a central principle of growth, an instinctive urgency leading them in a certain direction, as trees seek the light'.[11] But this approval of natural impulse, which sometimes puts us in mind of Rousseau, stands in need of qualification. If we follow natural impulse alone, we remain in bondage to it, and we cannot control our environment in a constructive manner. It is mind, impersonal objective thought, which exercises a critical function in regard to impulse and instinct and enables us to decide what impulses need to be suppressed or diverted because they conflict with other impulses or because the environment makes it impossible or undesirable to satisfy them. It is also mind which enables us to control our environment to a certain extent in a constructive manner. So while he insists on the principles of 'vitality', Russell does not give a blanket approval to impulse.

We have seen that Russell attributes human activities to two sources, impulse and desire. Later on he attributes it to 'instinct, mind and spirit'.[12] Instinct is the source of vitality, while mind exercises a critical function in regard to instinct. Spirit is the principle of impersonal feelings and enables us to transcend the search for purely personal satisfaction by feeling the same interest in other people's joys and sorrows as in our own, by caring about the happiness of the human race as a whole and by serving ends which are in some sense supra-human, such as truth or beauty or, in the case of religious people, God.

Perhaps we can adopt the suggestion of Professor J. Buchler[13] that for Russell impulse and desire are the basic modes of initial stimulus, while instinct, mind and spirit are the categories under which human activities as we know them can be classified. In any case Russell obviously has in mind a progressive integration of desires and impulses under the control of mind, both in the individual and in society. At the same time he insists on the function of spirit, considered as the capacity for impersonal feeling. For 'if life is to be fully human it must serve some end which seems, in some sense, outside human life'.[14]

4. Even if in *Principles of Social Reconstruction* Russell retained, though with some misgiving, the Moorean idea that we can have intuitive knowledge of intrinsic goodness and badness, he did not retain the idea very long. For example, after having remarked in a popular essay, *What I Believe* (1925), that the good life is one inspired by love and guided by knowledge, he explains that he is not referring to ethical knowledge. For 'I do not think there is, strictly speaking, such a thing as ethical knowledge'.[15] Ethics is distinguished from science by desire rather than by any special form of knowledge. 'Certain ends are desired, and right conduct is what conduces to them.'[16] Similarly, in *An Outline of Philosophy* (1927) Russell explicitly says that he has abandoned Moore's theory of goodness as an indefinable intrinsic quality, and he refers to the influence on his mind in this respect of Santayana's *Winds of Doctrine* (1926). He now holds that good and bad are 'derivative from desire'.[17] Language is, of course, a social phenomenon, and, generally speaking, we learn to apply the word 'good' to the things desired by the social group to which we belong. But 'primarily, we call something "good" when we desire it, and "bad" when we have an aversion from it'.[18]

To say nothing more than this, however, would be to give an over-simplified account of Russell's ethical position. In the first place the utilitarian element in his earlier ethical ideas, an element common to him and to Moore, has remained unchanged. That is to say, he has continued to regard as right those actions which produce good consequences and as wrong those actions which produce bad consequences. And in this restricted field knowledge is possible. For example, if two men agree that a certain end X is desirable and so good, they can perfectly well argue about which possible action or series of actions is most likely to attain this end. And in principle they can come to an agreed conclusion representing probable knowledge.[19] But though the context would be ethical, the knowledge attained would not be in any way specifically different from knowledge of the appropriate means for attaining a certain end in a non-ethical context. In other words it would not be a case of a peculiar kind of knowledge called 'ethical' or 'moral'.

When we turn, however, from an examination of the appropriate means for attaining a certain end to value-judgments about ends themselves, the situation is different. We have seen that Russell once maintained that differences of opinion about values are not so great as to make it unreasonable to hold that we can and do have immediate knowledge of intrinsic goodness and badness, ethical intuition in other words. But he abandoned this view and came to the conclusion that a difference of opinion about values is basically 'one of tastes, not one as to any objective truth'.[20] If, for instance, a man tells me that cruelty is a good thing,[21] I can, of course, agree with him in the sense of pointing out the practical consequences of such a judgment. But if he still stands by his judgment, even when he realizes what it 'means', I can give him no theoretical proof that cruelty is wrong. Any 'argument' that I may employ is really a persuasive device designed to change the man's desires. And if it is unsuccessful there is no more to be said. Obviously, if someone professes to deduce a certain value-judgment from other value-judgments and one thinks that the alleged deduction is logically erroneous, one can point this out. And if a man meant by 'X is good' no more than that X has certain empirical consequences, we could argue about whether X does or does not tend in practice to produce these effects. For this would be a purely empirical matter. But the man would not be likely to say, even in this case, 'X is good' unless he approved of the consequences; and his approval would express a desire or taste. In the long run, therefore, we ultimately reach a point where theoretical proof and disproof no longer have a role to play.

The matter can be clarified in this way. Russell may have sometimes expressed himself in such a way as to imply that in his opinion judgments of value are a matter of purely personal taste, without involving other people in any way. But this is certainly not his considered opinion. In his view judgments of value are really in the optative mood. To say 'X is good' is to say 'would that everyone desired X', and to say 'y is bad' is to say 'would that everyone felt an aversion from y'.[22] And if this analysis is accepted, it is obvious that 'cruelty is bad', when taken as meaning 'would that everyone had an aversion from cruelty', is no more describable as true or false than 'would that everyone appreciated good claret'. Hence there can be no question of proving that the judgment 'cruelty is bad' is true or false.

Obviously, Russell is perfectly aware that there is a sense in which it is true to say that it does not matter much if a man appreciates good wine or not, whereas it may matter very much whether people approve of cruelty or not. But he would regard these practical considerations as irrelevant to the purely philosophical question of the correct analysis of the value-judgment. If I say 'cruelty is bad', I shall obviously do anything which lies in my power to see that education, for example, is not so conducted as to encourage the belief that cruelty is admirable. But if I accept Russell's analysis of the value-judgment, I must admit that my own evaluation of cruelty is not theoretically provable.

Now, Russell has sometimes been criticized for giving vehement expression to his own moral convictions, as though this were inconsistent with his analysis of the value-judgment. But he can make, and has made, the obvious retort that as in his opinion judgments of value express desires, and as he himself has strong desires, there is no inconsistency in giving them vehement expression. And this reply seems to be quite valid, as far as it goes. At the same time, when we remember that he is prepared to condemn certain lines of conduct, such as the treatment of the unfortunate prisoners at Auschwitz, even if it could be shown that such conduct would ultimately benefit the human race and increase the general happiness, it is very difficult to avoid the impression that he really does think after all that some things are intrinsically bad, whether other people think they are bad or not.

Indeed, Russell himself seems to have a suspicion that this is the case. For after having remarked that he sees no logical inconsistency between his ethical theory and the expression of strong moral preferences, he adds that he is still not quite satisfied. His own theory of ethics does not satisfy him, but then other people's theories he finds even less satisfactory.[23] Hence we can perhaps say that while Russell would like to be able to return to the idea of intrinsic goodness and badness, he is at the same time convinced that a truly empirical and scientific philosophy can neither discover Moore's indefinable property of goodness nor admit self-evident moral principles.

One possible line of objection against Russell's analysis of the value-judgment is that it does not at all represent what ordinary people think that they are saying when they make such judgments. But Russell has never been the man to worry much about what the non-philosopher thinks. Nor has he ever been a devotee of 'ordinary language'. It is understandable, however, if some younger moral philosophers[24] have tried to give an account of the judgment of values, which pays more attention to ordinary language and its implications and yet refrains from re-introducing Moore's indefinable non-natural property.

5. There is at least one part of ethics which Russell regards as belonging to philosophy in a strict sense, namely the analysis of the judgment of value, the doctrine that to exhibit the logical form of such judgments one has to express them in the optative rather than in the indicative mood. But social and political theory is regarded by Russell as lying wholly outside the sphere of philosophy in the proper sense. Hence, though it might be considered odd to say nothing at all about them, no apology is needed for treating them in a very brief and sketchy manner.

In a famous essay which he wrote in 1902 Russell spoke of 'the tyranny of non-human power',[25] Nature's triumphant indifference to human ideals and values, and he also condemned the worship of naked power, of force, and the creed

of militarism. He envisaged man turning his back on un-
thinking power and creating his own realm of ideal values,
even if this realm is doomed in the end to utter extinction.
It may therefore be somewhat surprising at first sight to find
Russell saying in 1938 that those economists are mistaken
who think that self-interest is the fundamental motive in social life, and that the basic concept in social science is that
of power.[26] For if the word 'power' were interpreted in the
same sense in which Russell condemned power in 1902, it
would seem to follow that in 1938 he has either radically
altered his opinions or is urging men to turn their backs on
social and political life, something which is very far from
being his intention.

In point of fact, however, Russell has never altered his dis-
like of 'naked power' and his condemnation of the love of
power for its own sake. When he says that power is the basic
concept in social science and that the laws of social dynamics
cannot be stated except in terms of it, he is using the term
to mean 'the production of intended effects'.[27] And when
he says that though the desire of commodities and material
comfort certainly operates in human life, the love of power is
more fundamental, he means by 'love of power' 'the desire
to be able to produce intended effects upon the outer world,
whether human or non-human'.[28] Whether the love of power
in this sense is a good or a bad thing depends on the nature of the effects which a man or group desires to produce.

The matter can be put in this way. In *Power* Russell assumes that energy is the basic concept in physics. He then
looks for a basic concept in social science and finds it in
power. And as power, like energy, is constantly passing from
one form to another, he assigns to social science the task of
discovering the laws of the transformation of power. But
though Russell rejects the economic theory of history as un-
realistic, that is, as minimizing the role of the fundamental
motive-force in social life, he does not attempt to classify all
human activities in terms of power. For example, it is possible to pursue knowledge for the sake of power, that is, of
control; and this impulse has become increasingly conspicuous in modern science. But it is also possible to pursue knowledge in a contemplative spirit, for love of the object itself.

Indeed, 'the lover, the poet and the mystic find a fuller satisfaction than the seeker after power can ever know, since they can rest in the object of their love'.[29]

If power is defined as the production of intended effects and love of power as the desire to produce such effects, it obviously follows that power is not an end in itself but a means to the attainment of ends other than itself. And in Russell's opinion 'the ultimate aim of those who have power (and we all have some) should be to promote social co-operation, not in one group as against another, but in the whole human race'.[30] Democracy is upheld as a safeguard against the arbitrary exercise of power.[31] And the ideal of social co-operation in the whole human race is represented as leading to the concept of a world-government possessing the authority and power to prevent the outbreak of hostility between nations.[32] Science has helped to unify the world on the technological plane. But politics has lagged behind science; and we have not yet achieved an effective world-organization capable of utilizing the benefits conferred by science and at the same time of preventing the evils which science has made possible.

It does not follow, of course, that social organization is for Russell the one worthwhile aim of life. In fact it is itself a means rather than an end, a means to the promotion of the good life. Man has acquisitive and predatory impulses; and it is an essential function of the State to control the expression of these impulses in individuals and groups, just as it would be the function of a world-government to control their expression as manifested by States. But man also has his creative impulses, 'impulses to put something into the world which is not taken away from anybody else'.[33] And it is the function of government and law to facilitate the expression of such impulses rather than to control them. Applied to world-government, this idea implies that different nations should remain free to develop their own cultures and ways of life.

Russell's analysis of social dynamics in terms of the idea of power is doubtless open to criticism on the ground of oversimplification. But the point to notice is that he has consistently subordinated fact to value, in the sense that he has always insisted on the primacy of ethical ends and on the need for organizing human society with a view to facilitating the harmonious development of the human personality. It scarcely needs to be added that Russell does not claim that his judgments about the ethical ends of social and political organization and about what constitutes a good life are exempt from his own analysis of the judgment of value. He would admit that they express personal desires, personal recommendations. And it is for this very reason, of course, that he does not regard them as pertaining to philosophy in a strict sense.

6. Except for noting that Russell abandoned belief in God at an early age, we have not yet said anything about his attitude to religion. To look for a profound philosophy of religion in his writings would be to look in vain. But as he has often referred to the subject, it seems appropriate to give a general indication of his views.

Though, like J. S. Mill before him, Russell evidently thinks that the evil and suffering in the world constitute an unanswerable objection to belief in a God who is described both as infinitely good and as omnipotent, he would not claim that the non-existence of a divine being transcending the world can be proved. Technically speaking, therefore, he is an agnostic. At the same time he does not believe that there is any real evidence for the existence of a God. And it is indeed clear from the whole character of his philosophy that the traditional arguments for God's existence are excluded. On a phenomenalistic analysis of causality no causal inference to a meta-phenomenal being can be valid. And if 'order, unity and continuity are human inventions just as truly as are catalogues and encyclopaedias',[34] we cannot get very far with an argument based on order and finality in the world. As for the arguments adduced by some modern scientists, there is, for example, nothing in evolution to warrant the hypothesis that it manifests a divine purpose. And even if a case can be made out for the thesis that the world had a beginning in time, we are not entitled to infer that it was created. For it might have begun spontaneously. It may seem odd that it should have done so; 'but there is no law of nature to the effect that things which seem odd to us must not happen'.[35]

Though, however, Russell does not think that there is any evidence for the existence of God, he has made it clear that belief in God, taken by itself, would no more arouse his hostility than belief in elves or fairies. It would simply be an example of a comforting but unsupported belief in a hypothetical entity, which does not necessarily make a man a worse citizen than he would otherwise be. Russell's attacks are directed primarily against the Christian religious bodies, which in his view have generally done more harm than good, and against theology only in so far as it has been invoked in support of persecution and religious wars and as a warrant for preventing the taking of means to certain ends which he considers desirable.

At the same time, though Russell often writes in a Voltairean manner, he is not simply a spiritual descendant of *les philosophes*. He attaches value to what we may call religious emotion and a religious attitude of serious concern about life. And in so far as he can be said to have a religion, it is the life of the 'spirit' as sketched in *Principles of Social Reconstruction*. True, this book appeared in 1916, but at a much later date he has remarked that the expression of his own personal religion which seems to him 'least unsatisfactory is the one in *Social Reconstruction*'.[36]

Russell's polemics against Christianity do not concern us here. It is sufficient to point out that though on occasion he pays tribute to, for example, the ideal of love and to the Christian idea of the value of the individual, attack is more prominent than commendation. And while Russell undoubtedly draws attention to some familiar black patches in Christian history, he tends to exaggerate and, sometimes, to sacrifice accuracy to wit and sarcasm. More relevant here, however, is the consideration that he has never tried systematically to dissociate what he regards as valuable in religion from theological belief. If he had, he might possibly have had second thoughts about his position, though it is probably too much to expect that he would ask himself seriously whether God is not in some sense an implicit presupposition of some of the problems which he himself has raised.

7. It is not possible to sum up Russell's view of the nature of philosophy in a concise statement. For he speaks in differ-

ent ways at different times.[37] And he has never been a man
for gathering together all the threads and showing in detail
how they fit together, how they form an intelligible pattern.
He has been too intent with getting on with the next matter
in hand. At the same time it is not, I think, very difficult
to understand how he came to express rather different views
about the nature and scope of philosophy. Nor is it very difficult to discover persistent elements in his concept of philosophy.

As far as its basic motive is concerned, philosophy has always been for Russell a pursuit of knowledge, of objective
truth. And he has expressed his conviction that one of the
main tasks of philosophy is to understand and interpret the
world, even to discover, as far as this is possible, the ultimate
nature of reality. True, Russell believes that in practice philosophers have often set out to prove preconceived beliefs;
and he has referred to Bradley's famous saying that metaphysics is the finding of bad reasons for what one believes by
instinct. He is also convinced that in practice some philosophers have employed thought and argument to establish comforting beliefs which have seemed to them to possess pragmatic value. Further, when comparing the aims and ambitions
of philosophy with the actual results achieved, he has
sometimes spoken as though science were the only means of
attaining anything which could properly be called knowledge.
But all this does not alter the fact that in regard to what
ought to be the attitude, motive and aims of the philosopher
Russell has maintained what can reasonably be described as
a traditional view. This is apparent in his earlier writings;
and it is also apparent in his later attack on 'linguistic' philosophy, that is, on philosophy as concerned exclusively with
mapping out so-called ordinary language, on the ground that
the philosophers who represent this tendency have abandoned
the important task of interpreting the world.[38]

As we have noted, however, the method on which Russell
lays the chief emphasis is analysis. In general philosophy this
means that the philosopher starts with a body of common
knowledge or what is assumed to be knowledge. This constitutes his data. He then reduces this complex body of knowledge, expressed in propositions which are somewhat vague

and often logically interdependent, to a number of propositions which he tries to make as simple and precise as possible. These are then arranged in deductive chains, depending logically on certain initial propositions which serve as premisses. 'The discovery of these premisses belongs to philosophy; but the work of deducing the body of common knowledge from them belongs to mathematics, if "mathematics" is interpreted in a somewhat liberal sense.'[39] In other words, philosophy proceeds by logical analysis from the complex and relatively concrete to what is simpler and more abstract. It thus differs from the special sciences, which proceed from the simpler to the more complex, and also from purely deductive mathematics.

The philosopher may find, however, that some of the logically implied premisses of a common body of assumed knowledge are themselves open to doubt. And the degree of probability of any consequence will depend on the degree of probability of the premiss which is most open to doubt. Thus logical analysis does not simply serve the purpose of discovering implied initial propositions or premisses. It also serves the purpose of helping us to estimate the degree of probability attaching to what commonly passes for knowledge, the consequences of the premisses.

Now, there can be little doubt that the method of analysis was suggested to Russell by his work in mathematical logic. And it is thus understandable that he has spoken of logic as the essence of philosophy and has declared that every philosophical problem, when properly analyzed, is found to be either not really a philosophical problem at all or else a logical problem, in the sense of being a problem of logical analysis.[40] This analysis is inspired by the principle of economy or Ockham's razor and leads to logical atomism.

We have noted, however, how Russell was converted to Wittgenstein's theory of the propositions of formal logic and pure mathematics as systems of 'tautologies'. And if we look at the matter from this point of view, it is perfectly understandable that he has emphasized the difference between logic and philosophy. For example, 'logic, I maintain, is not part of philosophy'.[41] But to say that formal logic, as a system of tautologies, falls outside philosophy is not, of course, incompatible with an insistence on the importance in philosophy of logical analysis, the reductive analysis which has been characteristic of Russell's thought. True, in proportion as his early work in mathematical logic has receded into the distance, Russell has become less and less inclined to speak of logic as the essence of philosophy. And the more he has come to emphasize the tentative character of philosophical hypotheses, so much the wider has he made the gap between philosophy and logic in the strict sense. Thus there is no question of maintaining that there has been no change in Russell's attitude. After all, having once said that logic is the essence of philosophy, he has declared at a later date that logic is not part of philosophy at all. At the same time we have to remember that when Russell made the first of these statements he meant, in part at any rate, that the method of philosophy is or ought to be the method of logical analysis. And he has never abandoned belief in the value of this method.

Though, however, Russell has retained his belief in the value of the reductive analysis which is a characteristic feature of his thought and has defended this sort of analysis against recent criticism, it is undeniable that his general conception of philosophy underwent a considerable change. We have seen that there was a time when he sharply distinguished between philosophical method on the one hand and scientific method on the other. Later on, however, we find him saying that the philosopher should learn from science 'principles and methods and general conceptions'.[42] In other words, Russell's reflections on the relation between philosophy and science, reflections which were posterior to his work in mathematical logic and to the first conception and employment of reductive analysis, had a considerable influence on his general idea of philosophy. Thus whereas at the time when he was saying that logic is the essence of philosophy, he tended to give the impression that if philosophical problems were properly analyzed and reduced to precise manageable questions they could be solved one by one, he later came to emphasize the need for bold and sweeping provisional hypotheses in philosophy. At the same time he has shown a marked tendency on occasion to question the philosopher's ability to find any real solutions to his problems. Perhaps the following remarks on Russell's ideas about the relation between philosophy and the empirical sciences may serve to make his different utterances more intelligible.

Philosophy, according to Russell, presupposes science, in the sense that it should be built upon a foundation of empirical knowledge.[43] It must therefore in some sense go beyond science. It is obvious that the philosopher is not in a better position than the scientist to solve problems which are recognized as pertaining to science. He must therefore have his own problems to solve, his own work to do. But what is this work?

Russell has said that the most important part of philosophy consists in criticism and clarification of notions which are apt to be regarded as ultimate and to be accepted in an uncritical manner.[44] This programme presumably covers the critical examination and 'justification' of scientific inference to which reference was made in the previous chapter. But it also includes criticism and clarification of supposedly basic concepts such as those of minds and physical objects. And the fulfilment of this task leads with Russell, as we have seen, to the interpretation of minds and physical objects as logical constructions out of events. But we have also seen that Russell does not consider reductive analysis in this context to be simply a linguistic affair, that is, simply a matter of finding an alternative language to that of minds and physical objects. In a real sense analysis is conceived as aiming at a knowledge of the ultimate constituents of the universe. And the entities of physical science, atoms, electrons and so on, are themselves interpreted as logical constructions. Philosophical analysis, therefore, does not go beyond science in the sense of trying to clarify confused concepts which science takes for granted. On the scientific level the concept of the atom is not confused. Or, if it is, it is hardly the philosopher's business to clarify it. Philosophy goes beyond science in the sense that it advances an ontological or metaphysical hypothesis.

It is in no way surprising, therefore, that Russell should have asserted that one of the jobs of philosophy is to suggest bold hypotheses about the universe. But a question at once arises. Are these hypotheses to be regarded exclusively as hypotheses which science is not yet in a position to confirm or refute, though it could in principle do so? Or is the philosopher entitled to propose hypotheses which are in principle unverifiable by science? In other words, has philosophy or has it not problems about the universe which are peculiarly its own?

Russell does indeed speak of the problems of philosophy as problems which 'do not, at least at present, belong to any of the special sciences',[45] and which science is thus not yet in a position to solve. Moreover, if the hypotheses of science are provisional, the hypotheses which philosophy advances as solutions to its problems are much more provisional and tentative. In fact, 'science is what you more or less know and philosophy is what you do not know'.[46] True, Russell has admitted that this particular statement was a jocular remark; but he considers that it is a justifiable joke provided that we add that 'philosophical speculation as to what we do not yet know has shown itself a valuable preliminary to exact scientific knowledge'.[47] If philosophical hypotheses are verified, they then become part of science and cease to be philosophical.

This point of view represents what we may call the positivist side of Russell. I do not mean to suggest that he has ever been a 'logical positivist'. For, as we have seen, he has always rejected the logical positivist criterion of meaning. When he says that unverified philosophical hypotheses do not constitute knowledge, he is not saying that they are meaningless. At the same time the statement that 'all *definite* knowledge —so I should contend—belongs to science'[48] can be described as positivist, if we mean by positivism the doctrine that it is only science which provides positive knowledge about the world. It is, however, worth remarking that when Russell makes statements of this nature, he seems to forget that on his theory of the unprovable postulates of scientific inference it is difficult to see how science can be asserted with confidence to provide definite knowledge, though, admittedly, we all believe that it is capable of doing so.

This positivist attitude, however, represents only one aspect of Russell's conception of the problems of philosophy. For he has also depicted the philosopher as considering problems which are not in principle capable of receiving scientific solutions. True, he seems generally to be referring to philosophy in the popular or in the historical sense. But he certainly remarks that 'almost all the questions of most interest to speculative minds are such as science cannot answer'.[49] Further, it is in the business of philosophy to study such questions, for example the problem of the end or ends of life, even if it cannot answer them. Obviously, such problems would be essentially philosophical problems. And even if Russell is sceptical about philosophy's capacity to answer them, he certainly does not regard them as meaningless. On the contrary, 'it is one of the functions of philosophy to keep alive interest in such questions'.[50]

There are indeed some perplexing juxtapositions of conflicting statements in Russell's writings. For example, in the very paragraph in which he says that 'philosophy should make us know the ends of life'[51] he also states that 'philosophy cannot itself determine the ends of life'.[52] Again, having said, as already mentioned, that philosophy should keep alive an interest in such problems as whether the universe has a purpose, and that 'some kind of philosophy is a necessity to all but the more thoughtless',[53] he proceeds to say that 'philosophy is a stage in intellectual development, and is not compatible with mental maturity'.[54]

It is, of course, possible that such apparent inconsistencies can be made to disappear by suitable distinctions in meaning and context. But it is unnecessary to embark here upon detailed exegesis of this sort. It is more to the point to suggest that in Russell's view of philosophy there are two main attitudes. On the one hand he feels strongly that through its impersonal pursuit of truth and its indifference to preconceived beliefs and to what one would like to be true science provides a model for theoretical thinking, and that metaphysical philosophy has a bad record in this respect. He is convinced too that though scientific hypotheses are always provisional and subject to possible revision, science gives us the nearest approach to definite knowledge about the world which we are capable of attaining. Hence such statements as 'whatever can be known, can be known by means of science'.[55] From this point of view the ideal situation would be that philosophy should give way altogether to science. And if in practice it cannot, as there will always be problems which science is not yet in a position to solve, philosophy should become as 'scientific' as possible. That is to say, the philosopher should resist the temptation to use philosophy to prove preconceived or comforting beliefs or to serve as a way of salvation.[56] And concrete judgments of value, as well as reflections depending on such judgments, should be excluded from 'scientific' philosophy.

On the other hand not only is Russell well aware that 'philosophy' in the popular and historical senses of the term covers a great deal more than would be admitted by the concept of 'scientific' philosophy, but he also feels that there are significant and important questions which science cannot answer but awareness of which broadens our mental horizons. He refuses to rule out such questions as meaningless. And even if he thinks that 'what science cannot discover, mankind cannot know',[57] he is also convinced that if such problems were to be forgotten 'human life would be impoverished',[58] if only because they show the limitations of scientific knowledge. In other words, a certain sympathy with positivism in a general sense is balanced by a feeling that the world has enigmatic aspects, and that to refuse to recognize them is the expression either of an unwarranted dogmatism or of a narrow-minded philistinism.

The matter can be expressed in this way. On his own confession one of the sources of Russell's original interest in philosophy was the desire to discover whether philosophy could provide any defence for some sort of religious belief.[59] He also looked to philosophy to provide him with certain knowledge. On both counts he was disappointed. He came to the conclusion that philosophy could not provide him either with a rational foundation for religious belief or with certainty in any field. There was, of course, mathematics; but mathematics is not philosophy. Russell thus came to the conclusion that science, however provisional its hypotheses may be and to whatever extent scientific inference may rest on unprovable postulates, is the only source of what can reasonably be called definite knowledge. Hence philosophy in a strict sense cannot be much more than philosophy of science and general theory of knowledge, together with an examination of problems which science is not yet in a position to solve but the raising and discussion of which can have a positive stimulative value for science by supplying the required element of anticipatory vision. At the same time Russell has always been passionately interested in the welfare of humanity, as he sees it. Hence he has never hesitated to go beyond the limits of 'scientific' philosophy and to treat of those subjects which involve explicit judgments of value and which are certainly covered by 'philosophy' in the popular sense of the term. A good many at any rate of the apparent inconsistencies in his thought are explicable in terms of these considerations. Some of the rest may be partly due to his reluctance to go back over his writings and to exclude differences in the use of the same term or, alternatively, to explain on each occasion in what precise sense he is using the term. It is also perhaps a relevant point that while Russell has recommended the piecemeal tackling of philosophical problems by logical analysis, he has always shown himself appreciative of the grandeur and attraction of sweeping hypotheses and theories.

8. In 1950 Russell received the Nobel Prize for Literature. And there is no doubt but that he is an elegant and, if one prescinds from a certain looseness in the use of terminology, clear writer. Obviously, his early work in mathematical logic is not for the general public. But apart from this, he has brought philosophical reflection to a wide circle of readers who would be unlikely to embark on Kant's first *Critique* or Hegel's *Phenomenology of Spirit*. In literary style he thus stands in the tradition of Locke and Hume and J. S. Mill, though his more popular writings remind one more of the French philosophers of the Enlightenment. In fact with the general public Russell has become the patron of rationalism and non-religious humanism.

Among philosophers nobody questions, of course, Russell's influence on modern British philosophy and similar currents of thought elsewhere. There has doubtless been a tendency in some countries, notably Germany, to dismiss him as an 'empiricist' who did some good work in mathematics in his early days. But he has discussed philosophical problems of interest and importance, such as the foundations of scientific inference and the nature of the judgment of value. And though some of the devotees of the cult of ordinary language may have criticized Russell's reductive analysis, in the opinion of the present writer such criticism is quite inadequate if it is framed entirely in linguistic terms. For example, if reductive analysis is taken to imply that in principle 'Russia invaded Finland' could be translated into a number of sentences in which the term 'Russia' would not occur but individuals only would be mentioned,[60] the relation between the original sentence and the translation being such that if the former is true (or false) the latter is true (or false) and *vice versa*, the ontological implication is that the State is not in any way an entity over and above its members. And it seems a quite inadequate criticism if it is simply pointed out that we cannot get along in ordinary language without using such terms as 'Russia'. It is true enough. But then we want to know what is the ontological implication of this point of view. Are we to say that the State *is* something over and above its members? If not, how is the concept of the State to be clarified? In terms of individuals related in certain ways? In what ways? It may be said that these questions can be answered by looking at the ways in which terms such as 'State' are actually used. But it seems obvious that in the process of looking we shall find ourselves referring to extra-linguistic factors. Similarly, it is not sufficient to criticize the statement, say, that the world is the class of things on the ground that we cannot get along without being able to refer to 'the world'. This is true. But then we can quite sensibly ask, 'Do you mean that the world cannot properly be regarded as the class of things? If so, how do you conceive it? Your way may be better; but we want to know what it is.'

These remarks are, however, not intended as a general apologia for Russell's use of reductive analysis. For it may very well be that on examining a particular case of such analysis we find that an essential feature is left out. And in the present writer's opinion this is verified, for example, in the case of Russell's analysis of the self. There was a time, as we have seen, when he thought that the phenomenology of consciousness or awareness implies that the I-subject is uneliminable. Later on, however, he depicted the self as a logical construction out of events, thus developing the phenomenalism of Hume. But it seems to me perfectly clear that when sentences beginning with the pronoun 'I' have been translated into sentences in which only 'events' are mentioned and the word 'I' does not appear, an essential feature of the original sentence has simply been omitted, with the result that the translation is inadequate. In a sense Wittgenstein saw this clearly when he spoke in the *Tractatus* about the metaphysical subject. True, he remarked that if I wrote a book about what I found in the world, I could not mention the metaphysical subject. But it could not be mentioned simply because it is subject and not object, not one of the objects which 'I' find in the world. Empirical psychology, therefore, can carry on without the concept of the metaphysical or transcendental ego or I-subject. But for the phenomenology of consciousness it is uneliminable, as Wittgenstein appears to have seen. Russell, however, attempted to eliminate it by eliminating consciousness. And the present writer does not consider his attempt to have been a success. This is not, of course, an argument against reductive analysis as such. What is genuinely superfluous should doubtless be dealt with by Ockham's razor. But it by no means follows that all that Russell thought superfluous *is* superfluous. The attempt, however, to eliminate the uneliminable may have a pragmatic value, in the sense that it can serve to show what cannot be eliminated by analysis.

This may perhaps sound as though the present writer looks on reductive analysis as *the* philosophical method but disagrees with some of Russell's applications of it. This would, however, be an erroneous impression. I think that reductive analysis has its uses. I do not see how exception can be taken to it as *a* possible method. But I certainly do not think that it is the only philosophical method. For one thing, we become aware of the I-subject, the transcendental ego, by the method of transcendental reflection, not by reductive analysis. True, I have suggested that the failure of reductive analysis to eliminate the I-subject may serve to draw attention to the subject. But in actual fact the failure serves this purpose only if it stimulates a transition to phenomenology, to transcendental reflection. The failure as such simply leaves us perplexed, as it did David Hume. For another thing, if reductive analysis is assumed to be *the* philosophical method, this seems to presuppose a metaphysics, an 'atomic' metaphysics opposed to the 'monistic' metaphysics of absolute idealism. And if one's choice of method presupposes a metaphysics, it is no good claiming that this metaphysics is the only 'scientific' one, unless it is uniformly successful in accounting for experience whereas other methods are not.

To turn to another point. We have seen that Russell set out to obtain certainty. And he has said that 'philosophy arises from an unusually obstinate attempt to arrive at real knowledge'.[61] This presupposes that reality, the universe, is intelligible.[62] But a few years later we are told that 'order, unity and continuity are human inventions'.[63] In other words, the intelligibility of the universe is imposed by man, by the human mind. And this enables Russell to dispose, for example, of the claim of Sir James Jeans, the astronomer, that the world should be conceived as the expressed thought of a divine mathematician. For the fact that the world can be interpreted in terms of mathematical physics is to be attributed to the skill of the physicist in imposing a network. It may be said, of course, that even if the original attempt to understand the world presupposes its intelligibility, this presupposition is simply an hypothesis, and that Russell afterwards comes to the conclusion that the hypothesis is not verified. But the refutation of the hypothesis is the result of an examination of the world, an analysis which itself presupposes the intelligibility of what is examined and analyzed. And in any case, if order, unity and continuity are human inventions, what becomes of the claim that science provides definite knowledge? It seems that what is provided is knowledge simply of the human mind and of its operations. And the very same thing might be said, of course, of the results of Russell's reductive analysis. But in any case can we really believe that science does not provide us with any objective knowledge of the extra-mental world? Nobody would deny that science 'works', that it has pragmatic value. In this case, however, the question immediately arises whether the world must not have certain intelligible characteristics for science to possess this pragmatic value. And if the intelligibility of reality is once admitted, the door is again opened to metaphysical questions which Russell is inclined to dismiss in a cavalier manner.

To conclude. Russell's total literary achievements, ranging from abstract mathematical logic to fiction,[64] is extremely impressive. In the history of mathematical logic his place is obviously assured. In general philosophy his development of empiricism with the aid of logical analysis, together with his recognition of the limitations of empiricism as a theory of knowledge, constitutes an important phase in modern British philosophical thought. As for his popular writings in the fields of ethics, politics and social theory, these obviously cannot be put on the same level as, say, *Human Knowledge*, much less *Principia Mathematica*. Yet they reveal, of course, a personality of interest, a humanist who has said, for example, that his intellect leads him to the conclusion that there is nothing in the universe which is higher than man, though his emotions violently rebel. He admits that he has always desired to find in philosophy some justification for the 'impersonal emotions'. And even if he has failed to find it, 'those who attempt to make a religion of humanism, which recognizes nothing greater than man, do not satisfy my emotions'.[65] Russell may be the great patron of non-religious humanism in Great Britain in the present century; but he has his reservations, at least on the emotive level.

It is thus difficult to classify Russell in an unambiguous manner, for example as an 'empiricist' or as a 'scientific humanist'. But why should we wish to do so? After all, he is Bertrand Russell, a distinct individual and not simply a member of a class. And if in his old age he has become, as it were, a national institution, this is due not simply to his philosophical writing but also to his complex and forceful personality, aristocrat, philosopher, democrat and campaigner for causes in one. It is indeed natural that those of us who hold firm beliefs which are very different from his and which he has attacked, should deplore certain aspects of his influence. But this should not blind one to the fact that Russell is one of the most remarkable Englishmen of the century.

EPILOGUE

We have seen that though Bertrand Russell has often expressed very sceptical views about the philosopher's ability to provide us with definite knowledge about the world and though he has certainly little sympathy with any philosopher who claims that his particular system represents final and definitive truth, he has always looked on philosophy as motivated by the desire to understand the world and man's relation to it. Even if in practice philosophy can provide only 'a way of looking at the results of empirical inquiry, a framework, as it were, to gather the findings of science into some sort of order',[1] this idea, as put forward by Russell, presupposes that science has given us new ways of seeing the world, new concepts which the philosopher has to take as a point of departure. The scope of his achievement may be limited, but it is the world with which he is ultimately concerned.

In an important sense G. E. Moore was much closer to being a revolutionary. He did not indeed lay down any restrictive dogmas about the nature and scope of philosophy. But, as we have seen, he devoted himself in practice exclusively to analysis as he understood it. And the effect of his example was to encourage the belief that philosophy is primarily concerned with analysis of meaning, that is, with language. True, Russell developed logical analysis and was often concerned with language; but he was concerned with much else besides. Both men, of course, directed attention, in their different ways, to analysis. But it was Moore rather than Russell who seems to us, on looking back, to be the herald, by force of example rather than by explicit theory, of the view that the primary task of the philosopher is the analysis of ordinary language.

For an explicit dogmatic statement about the nature and scope of philosophy we have, however, to turn to Ludwig Wittgenstein. We have noted that it was Wittgenstein who converted Russell to the view that the propositions of logic and pure mathematics are 'tautologies'. In the *Tractatus*

Logico-Philosophicus[2] Wittgenstein explained that what he meant by a tautology was a proposition which is true for all possible states of affairs and which therefore has as its opposite a contradiction, which is true for no possible state of affairs. A tautology, therefore, gives us no information about the world, in the sense of saying that things are one way when they could be another way. A 'proposition', however, as distinct from a tautology, is a picture or representation of a possible fact or state of affairs in the world. A proposition in this sense is either true or false; but we cannot know by inspecting its meaning (*Sinn*) whether it is true or false. To know this we have to compare it, as it were, with reality, with the empirical facts.[3] On the one hand therefore we have the tautologies of logic and pure mathematics which are necessarily true but give us no factual information about the world, while on the other hand there are propositions, empirical statements, which say something about how things are in the world but which are never necessarily true.

Now, propositions, in Wittgenstein's technical use of the term in the *Tractatus*, are identified by him with the propositions of the natural sciences.[4] This identification seems to be unduly restrictive. For there is no good reason, on Wittgenstein's premises that is to say, why an ordinary empirical statement, which would not normally be called a scientific statement, should be excluded from the class of propositions. But Wittgenstein would presumably admit this, in spite of the identification of the totality of propositions with the totality of the natural sciences. In any case the important point is that propositions are not philosophical. A scientific statement is not a philosophical proposition. Nor, of course, is a statement such as 'the dog is under the table'. Nor are tautologies philosophical propositions. Mathematics is no more philosophy than is natural science. It follows therefore that there is no room in Wittgenstein's scheme for philosophical propositions. In fact there are no such things.[5] And if there are no such things, it obviously cannot be the business of philosophy to enunciate them.[6]

What, then, is the function of philosophy? It is said to consist in the clarification of propositions.[7] And the propositions to be clarified are obviously not philosophical ones.

Indeed, if we take literally Wittgenstein's identification of propositions with those of the natural sciences, it follows logically that the business of philosophy is to clarify scientific propositions. But it is by no means immediately clear how and in what sense the philosopher can do this. Further, though the logical positivists of the Vienna Circle certainly attributed to philosophy a modest positive function as a kind of handmaid of science,[8] from what Wittgenstein says elsewhere in the *Tractatus*[9] he appears to be thinking primarily of a sort of linguistic therapeutic, designed to clear up logical confusion. For example, as Russell pointed out, in ordinary or colloquial language the grammatical form of a sentence often disguises the logical form. Hence there can arise for the philosopher the temptation to make 'metaphysical' statements (for instance, that 'the golden mountain' must have some peculiar kind of ontological status half-way between actual existence and nonentity) which are the result of not understanding the logic of our language. The philosopher who sees this can clear up the confusion in his colleague's mind by restating the misleading sentence so as to exhibit its logical form, on the lines of Russell's theory of descriptions. Again, if someone tries to say something 'metaphysical', it can be pointed out to him that he has failed to give any definite meaning (*Bedeutung*, reference) to one or more terms. An example actually given by Wittgenstein, who is extremely sparing of examples in the *Tractatus*, is 'Socrates is identical'. For the word 'identical' has no meaning when used in *this* way as an adjective. But what Wittgenstein has to say would doubtless apply, under certain conditions, to a question such as 'what is the cause of the world?' For if we assume that causality signifies a relation *between* phenomena, it makes no sense to ask for the cause of *all* phenomena. Further, on Wittgenstein's premises, we cannot talk about the world as a totality.[10]

Wittgenstein's *Tractatus* was one of the writings which exercised an influence on the Vienna Circle, the group of logical positivists who more or less recognized as their leader Moritz Schlick (1882–1936), professor of philosophy in the University of Vienna.[11] And there are certainly points of agreement between the doctrine of the *Tractatus* and logical positivism. Both are agreed, for example, about the logical status of the propositions of logic and pure mathematics and about the fact that no empirical statement is necessarily true.[12] Further, both the *Tractatus* and logical positivism exclude metaphysical propositions, that is, if considered as providing, or as capable of providing, information about the world, which is either true or false. But while in the *Tractatus* this exclusion follows from Wittgenstein's definition of the proposition and his identification of the totality of propositions with the totality of scientific propositions, in logical positivism it follows from a certain criterion of meaning, namely that the meaning of a 'proposition' or factually informative statement is identical with the mode of its verification, verification being understood in terms of possible sense-experiences. And it is at any rate disputable whether this criterion of meaning is necessarily implied by what Wittgenstein has to say in the *Tractatus*. To be sure, if a proposition asserts or denies a possible state of affairs, we cannot be said to know what it means unless we have sufficient knowledge of the state of affairs which would make it true to be able to distinguish between this state of affairs and the state of affairs which would make it false. In this sense we must know what would verify the proposition. But it by no means necessarily follows that the meaning of the proposition or factually informative statement is identical with the mode of its verification, if 'mode of verification' signifies what we or anyone else could *do* to verify the statement.

In any case, even if those are right who think that the logical positivist criterion of meaning is implicitly contained in the *Tractatus*, there seems to be a considerable difference of atmosphere between this work and the typical attitude of the logical positivists in the heyday of their early enthusiasm. The positivists admitted indeed that metaphysical statements could possess an emotive-evocative significance;[13] but some of them at least made it clear that in their opinion metaphysics was a pack of nonsense in the popular, and not simply in a technical, sense. If, however, we consider what Wittgenstein has to say about the metaphysical subject,[14] we can discern a certain seriousness and profundity of thought. To attempt to say something about the metaphysical subject, the

I-subject as a pole of consciousness, is inevitably to reduce it to the status of an object. All statements about the metaphysical subject are thus attempts to say what cannot be said. At the same time in a real sense the metaphysical subject shows itself as the limit of 'my world', as the correlative of the object. Strictly speaking, not even this can be said. None the less attempts to do so can facilitate our in some sense 'seeing' what cannot be *said*. But the 'mysticism' which makes an occasional appearance in the *Tractatus* was not congenial to the logical positivists.

To all intents and purposes logical positivism was introduced into England by the publication in 1936 of *Language, Truth and Logic*[15] by A. J. Ayer (b. 1910). This book, with its drastic and lively attack on metaphysics and theology, enjoyed a *succès de scandale*; and it remains as probably the clearest exposition of dogmatic logical positivism. But though logical positivism, as mediated by this work, certainly attracted a great deal of attention, it can hardly be said to have won a notable degree of acceptance among professional philosophers in Great Britain.[16] For the matter of that, Professor Ayer himself has considerably modified his views, as can be seen from his later writings.[17] And it is now generally recognized that logical positivism constituted an interlude in the development of modern British philosophy.[18]

Meanwhile Wittgenstein was engaged in changing his views.[19] In the *Tractatus* he had tried to exhibit the 'essence' of the proposition. And the effect of his definition had been to place descriptive language in a privileged position. For it was only descriptive statements which were recognized as possessing meaning (*Sinn*). He came, however, to see more clearly the complexity of language, the fact that there are many kinds of propositions, descriptive statements forming only one class. In other words, Wittgenstein came to have a clearer view of actual language as a complex vital phenomenon, as something which in the context of human life has many functions or uses. And this understanding was accompanied by a radical change in Wittgenstein's conception of meaning. Meaning became use or function and was no longer identical with 'picturing'.

If we apply these ideas to logical positivism, the result is the dethronement of the language of science from the position of a uniquely privileged language. For logical positivism meant in effect the selection of the language of science as the model language. Its criterion of meaning, as applied to synthetic propositions in general, was the result of an extension or extrapolation of a certain analysis of the scientific statement, namely as a prediction of certain possible sensible experiences. And, apart from the question whether or not this analysis of the scientific statement is tenable, the dethronement of scientific language as the model language involved the abandonment of the logical positivist criterion of meaning, if considered as a general criterion. Hence, whatever one may think of the precise relation between the *Tractatus* and logical positivism, Wittgenstein's later ideas about language were certainly incompatible with dogmatic logical positivism.

At the same time Wittgenstein had no intention of resuscitating the idea of the philosopher which was excluded by the *Tractatus*, the idea, that is to say, of the philosopher as capable of extending our factual knowledge of the world by pure thought or philosophical reflection. The difference between the concept of the function of philosophy offered in the *Tractatus* and that offered in *Philosophical Investigations* is not one between a revolutionary concept and a traditional concept. Wittgenstein sees himself as having attempted in the *Tractatus* to reform language, to interfere with its actual use, by, for example, equating the proposition with the descriptive statement, and indeed, if we take literally his identification of the totality of propositions with the totality of the natural sciences, with the scientific statement. In *Philosophical Investigations*, however, we are told that 'philosophy may in no way interfere with the actual use of language; it can in the end only describe it'.[20] Negatively, philosophy uncovers examples of nonsense resulting from our not understanding the limits of language;[21] positively, it has the function of describing the actual use of language.

The sort of thing that Wittgenstein has in mind can be explained with the aid of his own analogy of games.[22] Suppose that someone asks me what a game is. And suppose that I reply in this way: 'Well, tennis, football, cricket, chess, bridge, golf, racquets, baseball are all games. And then there are others too, playing at Red Indians, for example, or hide-and-seek.' The other man might retort impatiently: 'I am perfectly well aware of all this. But I did not ask you what activities are customarily called "games": I asked you what a game is, that is to say, I wanted to know the definition of a game, what is the essence of "game". You are as bad as Socrates' young friends who, when asked what beauty is, started mentioning beautiful things or people.' To this I might reply: 'Oh, I see. You imagine that because we use one word "game", it must signify one meaning, one single essence. But this is a mistake. There are only games. There are indeed resemblances, of various sorts. Some games are played with a ball, for example. But chess is not. And even in the case of games which are played with a ball the balls are of different kinds. Consider football, cricket, golf, tennis. True games have some sort of rules, explicit or implicit. But the rules differ with different games. And in any case a definition of "game" in terms of rules would hardly be adequate. There are rules of conduct in criminal courts, but the processes of law are not generally recognized as games. In other words, the only proper answer to your original question is to remind you how the word "game" is used in actual language. You may not be satisfied. But in this case you are evidently still labouring under the mistaken idea that there must be a single meaning, a single essence, corresponding to each common word. If you insist that we must find such a meaning or essence, you are really insisting on a reform of or interference with language.'

In using this sort of analogy Wittgenstein is clearly thinking primarily of his own attempt in the *Tractatus* to give the essence of the proposition, whereas in point of fact there are many kinds of propositions, many kinds of sentences, descriptive statements, commands, prayers, and so on.[23] But his point of view possesses a wider field of application. Suppose, for example, that a philosopher identifies the 'I' or self with the pure subject or, alternatively, with the body in the sense in which we commonly use the term 'body'. Has he given the essence of 'I', of the self or ego? Wittgenstein might point out that neither interpretation of the pronoun

'I' is compatible with the actual use of language. For example, the identification of the 'I' with the metaphysical subject is not compatible with such a sentence as 'I go for a walk'. Nor is the identification of the 'I' with the body in the ordinary sense compatible with such a sentence as 'I consider Tolstoy a greater writer than Ethel M. Dell'.

This way of disposing of exaggerated philosophical theories, interpreted as attempts to 'reform' language, is described by Wittgenstein as bringing words 'back from their metaphysical to their everyday usage'.[24] And it obviously presupposes that actual language is all right as it is. Consequently, it is all the more necessary to understand that Wittgenstein is not excluding, for example, the technical language which has been developed in order to express man's growing scientific knowledge and new scientific concepts and hypotheses. What he is opposed to is the belief that the philosopher is capable of digging out, as it were, or revealing hidden meanings, hidden essences. And the only reform of language which he allows the philosopher is the restatement which may be required in order to clear up those confusions and misunderstandings which give rise to what Wittgenstein considers to be bogus philosophical problems and theories. Reform of this kind, however, is simply designed to bring out the real logic of actual language. Philosophy can thus be said to aim at the elimination of difficulties, perplexities, problems, which arise from our not understanding the actual use of language. In spite, therefore, of the change in Wittgenstein's view of language, his general idea of philosophy as a kind of linguistic therapeutic remains the same in broad outline.

Though, however, Wittgenstein himself did not hesitate to dogmatize about the nature and function of philosophy, those philosophers who either have been influenced by his post-*Tractatus* line of reflection or have thought much the same thoughts for themselves, have, generally speaking, refrained from dogmatic pronouncements of this sort. For example, in his 1931 paper on 'Systematically Misleading Expressions'[25] Professor Gilbert Ryle of Oxford (b. 1900), while announcing that he had come to the conclusion that the business of philosophy was at least, and might be no more than, the detection in linguistic idioms of recurrent misconstructions and absurd theories, added that his conversion to this view was reluctant and that he would like to be able to think that philosophy had a more sublime task. In any case if one looks at the writings of those British philosophers who sympathize with Wittgenstein's later ideas, one can see that they have devoted themselves to the implementation of the positive programme of 'describing' the actual use of language rather than simply to the rather negative task of eliminating puzzles or difficulties.

The implementation of the positive programme can take various forms. That is to say, the emphasis can be differently placed. It is possible, for example, to concentrate on exhibiting the peculiar characteristics of different types of language in the sense in which the language of science, the language of morals, the language of the religious consciousness and aesthetic language constitute different types; and one can compare one type of language with another. When the logical positivists turned scientific language into a model language, they tended to lump together a number of other different kinds of propositions as possessing only emotive-evocative significance. The dethronement, however, of scientific language from the position of the model language, except, of course, for specific purposes, naturally encouraged a more careful examination of other types of language, taken separately. And a great deal of work has been done on the language of morals.[26] Again, there has been an appreciable amount of discussion of the language of religion. If, for instance, we wish to determine the range of meaning of the term 'God', it is not of much use to say that it is 'meaningless' because it is not a scientific term. We have to examine its uses and functions in the language which, as Wittgenstein puts it, is 'its native home'.[27] Further, one can compare the use of images and analogies in religious language with their use in, say, the language of poetry. It is indeed probably true to say that in the discussion of religious language in recent British philosophy the factor which has attracted the most public attention has been the contention of some philosophers that this or that religious statement really says nothing because it excludes nothing.[28] But it must be remembered that the discussion as a whole brought once more into prominence the subject of analogical language, a theme which was treated by a number of medieval thinkers but which, with some exceptions, was little treated by later philosophers.[29]

It is also possible to concentrate not so much on different general types of language in the sense mentioned above as on the different kinds of sentences in ordinary colloquial language and on the distinctions made in or implied by such language. This kind of mapping-out of ordinary language was characteristic of the late Professor J. L. Austin (1911–60) of Oxford, who distinguished himself by his meticulous care in differentiating between types of 'speech-acts'[30] and showed by actual analysis how inadequate was the logical positivist classification of propositions, and how much more complex and subtle ordinary language is than one might think.

Not unnaturally a good deal of criticism has been levelled against this concentration on ordinary language. For at first sight it looks as though philosophy were being reduced to a trivial occupation or a practically useless game played for its own sake by a number of university professors and lecturers. But though the practitioners of the analysis of ordinary language, notably Austin, have deliberately chosen examples of sentences which make those who are accustomed to talk about Being raise their eyebrows, in the opinion of the present writer such analysis is by no means useless. For example, in the development of language in response to experience human beings have expressed in a concrete way a multitude of distinctions between varying degrees of responsibility. And the activity of reflecting on and mapping out these distinctions can be of considerable use. On the one hand it serves the purpose of drawing our attention to factors which have to be taken into account in any adequate discussion of moral responsibility. On the other hand it sets us on our guard when confronted with philosophical theories which ride roughshod, in one direction or another, over the distinctions which human experience has found it necessary to express. It may indeed be objected that ordinary language is not an infallible criterion by which to judge philosophical theories. But Austin did not say that it was. He may have tended to act as though he thought this. But in word at least he dis-

claimed any such dogmatism, simply observing that in a conflict between theory and ordinary language the latter was
more likely to be right than the former, and that in any
case philosophers, when constructing their theories, neglected
ordinary language at their peril.[31] In any case, even if we
consider that the importance of ordinary language has been
exaggerated, it does not necessarily follow that we have to
consider examination of such language useless or irrelevant
to philosophy.

The point can be made clearer perhaps by reference to
Professor G. Ryle's celebrated book, *The Concept of Mind*
(London, 1949). From one point of view it is a dissolution
of the theory of 'the ghost in the machine', the dualistic
theory attributed to Descartes, by means of an examination
of what we are accustomed to say about man and his mental
activities in ordinary language. But from another point of
view it might be considered as an attempt to exhibit the concept of mind, and indeed of the nature of man, which finds
concrete expression in the sentences of ordinary language.
And such an attempt is undoubtedly useful and relevant to
philosophy.[32] Obviously, if one works backwards, as it were,
from a philosophical theory to a view implicit in ordinary
language, one is returning to a point antecedent to the raising of philosophical problems. And the only valid reason for
stopping there would be the belief that any real problems
which then arise are not philosophical in character but psychological or physiological or both, belonging, that is to say,
to science and not to philosophy. At the same time it is useful to remind oneself and obtain a clear view of what we
ordinarily say about man. For ordinary language certainly
favours a view of man as a unity; and in so far as this view
can be considered as expressing man's experience of himself,
it has to be taken into account.

And yet, of course, it is a great mistake to oppose ordinary
language to theory, as though the former were entirely free
of the latter. Apart from the fact that theories and beliefs of
one kind or another leave their deposits, as it were, in ordinary language, our language is not in any case a simple photo-
graph of bare facts. It expresses interpretation. Hence it cannot be used as a touchstone of truth. And philosophy cannot

be simply uncritical of so-called ordinary language. Nor can it be critical without indulging in theory.

Needless to say, this is not a discovery of the present writer. It is a matter of common recognition.[33] Hence it is only to be expected that in recent years the concept of philosophy should have tended to broaden, even within the analytic movement itself. One expression of this process, in certain circles at least, has been the displacement of the dogmatic restriction of the nature and scope of philosophy, which was characteristic of Wittgenstein, by an attitude of tolerance which is willing to give a hearing even to the avowed metaphysician, provided, of course, that he is prepared to explain why he says what he does. But it is not simply a matter of toleration, of the growth of a more 'ecumenical' spirit. There have also been signs of a developing conviction that analysis is not enough. For example, in *Thought and Action*,[34] Professor Stuart Hampshire observed that the language of ethics cannot be adequately treated unless it is examined in the light of the function of such language in human life. Hence the need for a philosophical anthropology.

The concentration on ordinary language, however, which is in harmony with the ideas expounded by Wittgenstein in *Philosophical Investigations*, represents only one tendency, even if a prominent one, in the analytic movement as a whole. For it has long been recognized that a great deal of what was popularly called 'linguistic analysis' would be far better described as 'conceptual analysis'. And the idea of conceptual analysis can open up wide vistas. For instance, in his well-known book *Individuals: An Essay in Descriptive Metaphysics*[35] Mr. P. F. Strawson of Oxford spoke of descriptive metaphysics as exploring and describing the actual structure of our thought about the world, that is, as describing the most general features of our conceptual structure, whereas revisionary metaphysics is concerned with changing our conceptual structure, with making us see the world in a new light. Revisionary metaphysics was not condemned, but descriptive metaphysics, in the sense explained, was said to need no further justification than that of inquiry in general.

In so far as generalization in this matter is legitimate, it seems safe to say that the following remarks represent an attitude towards metaphysics which is not uncommonly adopted by contemporary British philosophers. To describe metaphysics as meaningless, as the logical positivists did, is to pass over the obvious fact that the great metaphysical systems of the past often expressed visions of the world which can be stimulating and, in their several ways, illuminating. Further, in the context of logical positivism to say that metaphysical propositions are meaningless is really to say that they are different from scientific propositions.[36] This is true enough; but it contributes little to an understanding of metaphysics as an historical phenomenon. To obtain this understanding we have to examine actual metaphysical systems with a view to sorting out the various types of metaphysics and the different kinds of arguments employed.[37] For it is a mistake to suppose that they all conform to one invariable pattern. Again, we cannot legitimately take it for granted that metaphysics is simply an attempt to answer questions which arise out of 'the bewitchment of our intelligence by means of language'.[38] This is a matter for detailed examination. Moreover, it is clear that the impulse to develop a unified interpretation of the world in terms of a set of concepts and categories is not something intrinsically improper or blameworthy. True, since the time of Kant we cannot accept the idea that the philosopher is capable of deducing the existence of any entity in an *a priori* manner. Further, before attempting to construct large-scale syntheses it would be wiser to do more spade-work by tackling precise questions separately. At the same time philosophical problems tend to interlock; and in any case it would be absurd to attempt to ban metaphysical synthesis. The construction of a world-view or *Weltanschauung* is indeed a somewhat different activity from that of trying to answer particular questions to which, in principle, quite definite answers can be given. But while the demand that philosophers who are interested in pursuing the second sort of activity should devote themselves to synthesis instead is unjustified, a wholesale condemnation of metaphysical synthesis is also unreasonable.

As far as it goes, this growth of a more tolerant attitude towards forms of philosophy other than the microscopic analysis which has been a conspicuous feature of recent British

thought is something to be welcomed. Taken by itself, however, it leaves a good many questions unanswered. Suppose,
for the sake of argument, that we accept the restriction of
philosophy to the clarification of propositions which are not
philosophical propositions, the restriction which is made in
the *Tractatus.* The presupposition is clear enough, namely
that philosophy is not a discipline with a special subject-
matter of its own, alongside the particular sciences.[39] The
philosopher cannot enunciate philosophical propositions
which increase our knowledge of the world. If, however, we
drop the dogmatic restriction of the nature and scope of
philosophy and show ourselves prepared to regard metaphysics, at least in some recognizable form, as a legitimate philosophical activity, we can reasonably be expected to explain
what change in the concept of philosophy is implied by this
concession. It is really not sufficient to say that we do not
undertake to reform language, and that the word 'philosophy', as actually used, certainly covers metaphysics, whereas
it no longer covers physics or biology. For the following question can always be asked: 'When you say that you have no
wish to prohibit metaphysics, do you mean simply that if
some people feel the urge to develop theories which are akin
to poetic and imaginative visions of reality, and which cannot
legitimately lay claim to represent or increase knowledge,
you have no desire to interfere with them? Or are you seriously prepared to admit the possibility that metaphysics is
capable in some sense of increasing our knowledge? If so, in
what sense? And what do you think that metaphysical knowledge is or could be about or of?'

The analytic philosophers might, of course, reply that it is
simply a question of their being prepared to give the metaphysician a hearing instead of barring the way in advance to
all dialogue and mutual understanding. It is the metaphysician's business to explain what he is about. When he has
done so, his own account of his activities can be examined.

Though, however, this line of reply is reasonable up to a
point, it seems to neglect two facts. First, if we repudiate a
dogmatic restrictive definition of philosophy, this repudia-
tion has implications. And it is not unreasonable if we are
invited to make them explicit. Secondly, as the analytic phi-

losophers like to point out, they do not constitute a completely 'homogeneous' school. On the contrary, several rather different tendencies are discernible; and it is obvious enough from an examination of their writings that a number of philosophers who would popularly be classed as 'analysts' are doing something very different from what could accurately be described as 'linguistic analysis'. It is all very well for them to say that they are doing 'philosophy'. No doubt they are. But what is philosophy in this wide sense? What precisely is its nature, function and scope? It is in regard to their British colleagues' view on such general issues that the continental philosopher of a different tradition is apt to find himself hopelessly at sea.

The conclusion to be drawn is perhaps that the so-called revolution in philosophy has lost any clearly defined shape, and that no clear concept of the nature of philosophy has yet taken the place of the various restrictive definitions proposed by the logical positivists, by the *Tractatus* and then again by *Philosophical Investigations*. This obviously does not prevent British philosophers from doing valuable work on particular themes. But it means that the external observer may well be left wondering what particular game is being played, and why. What is the relevance of philosophy to life? And why is it thought necessary to have chairs of philosophy in universities? Such questions may be naïve, but they require an answer.

APPENDIX

JOHN HENRY NEWMAN

Introductory remarks – Newman's approach to the problem of religious belief in his university sermons – The approach in The Grammar of Assent *– Conscience and God – The convergence of probabilities and the illative sense – Final remarks.*

1. To say that we are concerned here with John Henry Newman (1801–90) simply as a philosopher is perhaps somewhat misleading. For it might be understood as suggesting that in addition to his many other interests and activities Newman devoted himself to philosophical problems for their own sake, for their intrinsic interest as theoretical puzzles. And this would be far from the truth. Newman's approach to the philosophical topics which he discussed was that of a Christian apologist. That is to say, he wrote from the point of view of a Christian believer who asks himself to what extent, and in what way, his faith can be shown to be reasonable. Newman made no pretence of temporarily discarding his faith, as it were, in order to give the impression of starting all over again from scratch. He tried, of course, to understand other people's points of view. But his discussion of religious belief was conducted, as it might be expressed, within the area of faith. That is to say, it was a question of faith seeking understanding of itself rather than of an unbelieving mind wondering whether there was any rational justification for making an act of faith. At the same time the attempt to show that Christian belief is in fact reasonable led Newman to develop philosophical ideas. To put the matter in another way, his attempt to exhibit the insufficiency of contemporary rationalism and to convey a sense of the Christian vision of human existence led him to delineate lines of thought which, while certainly not intended to present the content of Chris-

tian belief as a set of conclusions logically deduced from self-evident principles, were meant to show to those who had eyes to see that religious faith was not the expression of an irrational attitude or a purely arbitrary assumption. And even if it involves a certain mutilation of his thought as a whole, we can pick out for brief consideration here some of the lines of thought which can reasonably be described as philosophical.

Now there have been apologists who concerned themselves not so much with the reasons people actually have for believing as with developing arguments which, in their opinion, should convince the minds of any unbelievers capable of understanding the terms used, though the ordinary believer may never have thought of these arguments at all and might even be incapable of understanding and appreciating them if they were presented to him. Newman, however, is more concerned with showing the reasonableness of faith as it actually exists in the great mass of believers, most of whom know nothing of abstract philosophical arguments. And he tries to make explicit what seems to him to be the chief ground which he himself and other people have for a living belief in God.[1] In other words, he tries to outline a phenomenological analysis of the spontaneous movement of the mind culminating in assent to the existence of God as a present reality. At the same time he obviously does not intend to write simply as a psychologist who may describe various reasons why people believe in God, even if some or all these reasons appear to him unable to justify assent to God's existence. On the contrary, Newman argues that the main empirical ground on which belief rests is a sufficient ground.

An analogy may clarify the point. We all have a practical belief in the objective existence of external objects independently of their being perceived by us. And there is clearly a difference between making explicit the grounds which people actually have for this belief and trying, as some philosophers have done, to justify the belief by excogitating philosophical arguments which are thought to provide better and sounder grounds for belief than those which people actually have, even if they are not reflectively aware of them. Indeed, it is arguable that the philosopher is not in a position to provide better grounds for the belief in question than those on which our belief actually, if implicitly, rests. Analogously, Newman is very conscious of the difference between showing that religious belief, as it actually exists, is reasonable and showing that it would be reasonable if people had other grounds for believing than those which they in fact have.

There is a further point which is worth noticing. When Newman talks about belief in God, he is thinking of what we might call a living belief, a belief which involves an element of personal commitment to a personal being apprehended as a present reality and which tends to influence conduct, not about a mere notional assent to an abstract proposition. Hence when he is reflecting on grounds for belief in God, he tends to neglect impersonal metaphysical arguments addressed simply to the intellect and to concentrate on the movement of the mind which, in his opinion, brings a man up against God as a present reality, as manifested in the voice of conscience. His line of thought is therefore addressed to the man who has a lively sense of moral obligation. Similarly, when dealing with the evidences for the truth of Christianity he is speaking primarily to the genuine and open-minded inquirer, particularly to the man who already believes in God, and who has, as Newman puts it, a presentiment of the possibility of revelation. In both cases he presupposes certain subjective conditions, including moral conditions, in his reader. He does not profess to provide demonstrations modelled on those of mathematics.

Given this approach, it is not surprising that the name of Newman has often been linked with that of Pascal. Both men were concerned with Christian apologetics, and both fixed their attention on effective belief and on the way in which people actually think and reason in concrete issues rather than on a mathematical model of demonstration. The 'spirit of geometry' was alien to both minds. And both emphasized the moral conditions for appreciating the force of arguments in favour of Christianity. If therefore someone excludes Pascal from the class of philosophers on the ground that he was a special pleader, he is likely to treat Newman in the same way. Conversely, if someone recognizes Pascal as a philosopher, he is likely to accord a similar recognition to Newman.[2]

Newman's philosophical background was, however, very different from that of Pascal. For it was constituted to a large extent by British philosophy. As a student Newman acquired some knowledge of Aristotle. And though nobody would call him an Aristotelian, the Greek philosopher certainly exercised some influence on his mind. As for Platonism, which in certain respects he found congenial, Newman's knowledge of it seems to have been obtained mainly from certain early Christian writers and the Fathers. Of British philosophers he certainly studied Francis Bacon, and he knew something of Hume, whom he considered acute but dangerous; but in the *Apologia* he states that he never studied Berkeley. For Locke, however, he felt a profound respect. He tells us explicitly that he felt this respect 'both for the character and the ability of Locke, for his manly simplicity of mind and his outspoken candour';[3] and he adds that 'there is so much in his remarks upon reasoning and proof in which I fully concur, that I feel no pleasure in considering him in the light of an opponent to views which I myself have ever cherished as true'.[4] Besides Locke we must mention Bishop Butler,[5] who exercised an obvious and admitted influence on Newman's mind.

Later on Newman studied the writings of Dean Mansel (1820–71), of some of the Scottish philosophers and the *Logic* of J. S. Mill. Further, in spite of a disclaimer on his part, it can be shown that he had some acquaintance with Coleridge. Of German thought, however, Newman appears to have known little, particularly at first-hand. If therefore we leave the early study of Aristotle out of account, we can say that his philosophical ideas were formed in the climate of British empiricism and of the influence of Butler. Newman's varied interests and activities left him indeed little time and energy for serious philosophical reading, even if he had had the inclination to read widely in this field. But in any case what he did read was simply a stimulus for forming his own ideas. He was never what would be called a disciple of any philosopher.

As for Scholastic philosophy, Newman knew little about it. In later years he at any rate possessed some writings by pioneers in the revival of Scholasticism. And when Leo XIII published his Encyclical *Aeterni Patris* in 1879, urging the study of St. Thomas, Newman composed, even if he did not send, an appreciative letter to the Pope. But it is fairly evident from the letter that what he had in mind was a revival of intellectual life in the Church, in continuity with the thought of the Fathers and Doctors, rather than of Thomism in particular. And in any case the old-fashioned textbook Thomism would hardly have been congenial to Newman's mind. It is true that since his death a number of Scholastic philosophers have adopted or adapted lines of thought suggested by his writings and have used them to supplement traditional arguments. But it scarcely needs saying that this fact provides no adequate reason for making out that Newman was 'really' a Scholastic. His approach was quite different, though he was quite willing to admit that other approaches might have their uses.

2. In a university sermon which he preached at Oxford in 1839 Newman insists that faith 'is certainly an exercise of Reason'[6]. For the exercise of reason lies 'in asserting one thing, because of some other thing.'[7] It can be seen in the extension of our knowledge beyond the immediate objects of sense-perception and of introspection;[8] and it can be seen also in religious belief or faith, inasmuch as this is 'an acceptance of things as real, which the senses do not convey, upon certain previous grounds'.[9] In other words, as Newman does not postulate any faculty of intuiting God (or indeed any external immaterial being), he must admit that in some sense at least the existence of God is inferred.

Reasoning, however, is not necessarily correct: there can be faulty reasoning. And Newman is well aware that for the rationalist any process of reasoning or inference presupposed by religious faith is invalid. According to the popular or common idea of reason and its exercise we should exclude the influence of all prejudices, preconceptions and temperamental differences and proceed simply according to 'certain scientific rules and fixed standards for weighing testimony and examining facts'[10], admitting only such conclusions 'as can produce their reasons'.[11] It is evident, however, that most believers are unable to produce reasons for their belief. And even when they are, it by no means follows that they began to believe for this reason or that they will cease believing if the reasons are challenged or placed in doubt. Further, 'faith is a principle of action, and action does not allow time for minute and finished investigations'.[12] Faith does not demand unquestionable demonstration; and it is influenced by antecedent probabilities and presumptions. True, this is frequently verified in the case of non-religious belief. For example, we frequently believe what we read in the newspapers, without any examination of the evidence. But though this behaviour is undoubtedly necessary for life, the fact remains that what appears probable or credible to one man may appear in quite a different light to someone else. 'It is scarcely necessary to point out how much our inclinations have to do with our belief.'[13] It is thus easy to understand the rationalist depreciation of faith as the expression of wishful thinking.

In a real sense, of course, unbelief or scepticism is in the same boat as faith. For unbelief 'really goes upon presumptions and prejudices as much as Faith does, only presumptions of an opposite nature. . . . It considers a religious system so improbable, that it will not listen to the evidence of it; or, if it listens, it employs itself in doing what a believer could do, if he chose, quite as well . . . ; viz., in showing that the evidence might be more complete and unexceptionable than it is.'[14] Sceptics do not really decide according to the evidence; for they make up their minds first and then admit or reject evidence according to their initial assumption. Hume provides a signal example of this when he suggests that the impossibility of miracles is sufficient refutation of the testimony of witnesses. 'That is, the antecedent improbability is a sufficient refutation of the evidence.'[15]

Newman seems to be quite justified in suggesting that unbelievers often proceed according to assumptions, and that they are as open as anyone else to the influence of inclination and temperament. But though this is a polemical point of some value, it obviously does not show that faith, considered as what Newman calls an exercise of reason, measures up to the standard demanded by the rationalist, if this standard is understood as that of strict logical demonstration from self-evident principles. Newman, however, has no intention of pretending that it does. He argues instead that the rationalist conception of reasoning is far too narrow and does not square with the way in which people actually, and legitimately, think and reason in concrete issues. It must be remembered that his contention is that faith is reasonable, not that its content is logically deducible according to the model of mathematical demonstration.

It is no valid argument against the reasonableness of religious faith to say that it assumes what are judged to be antecedent probabilities. For we all find ourselves under the necessity of making assumptions, if we are to live at all. We cannot live simply by what is logically demonstrable. For example, we cannot demonstrate that our senses are trustworthy, and that there is an objective external world with which they put us in contact. Nor can we demonstrate the validity of memory. Yet in spite of our being sometimes deceived, to express the matter in a popular way, we assume and cannot help assuming that our senses are fundamentally trustworthy, and that there is an objective external world. Indeed, nobody but the sceptic questions scientific inference as such, though the scientist does not prove the existence of a public physical world but assumes it. Again, we do not allow our mistakes and slips to destroy all belief in the validity of memory. Further, unless we try to adopt a position of complete scepticism, a position which we cannot maintain in practice, we necessarily assume the possibility of valid reasoning. We cannot demonstrate it *a priori*; for any attempt at demonstration presupposes what we are trying to demonstrate. In fine, 'whether we consider processes of Faith or other exercise of Reason, men advance forward on grounds which they do not, or cannot produce, or if they could, yet could not prove to be true, on latent or antecedent grounds which they take for granted'[16].

We can note in passing that in Newman's readiness to say that the existence of a public external world is an unprovable assumption we can perhaps discern an echo of his impression at an early age, an impression recorded in the first chapter of the *Apologia*, that there were only two luminously self-evident beings, himself and his Creator. But we are also reminded of Hume's contention that though we cannot prove the existence of bodies apart from our perceptions, Nature has placed us under the necessity of believing in it. A philosopher can indulge in sceptical reflections in his study; but in ordinary life he, like the rest of mankind, has a natural belief in the continued objective existence of bodies even when they are not perceived. Reason cannot demonstrate the truth of this belief. But the belief is none the less reasonable. The unreasonable man would be the one who tried to live as a sceptic and not to act on any assumption which could not be proved.

It is indeed obviously true that men cannot help believing in the existence of an external, public world,[17] and that it would be unreasonable to attempt to act on any other assumption. If we refused to act on anything but logically demonstrated conclusions, we could not live at all. As Locke aptly remarked, if we refused to eat until it had been demonstrated that the food would nourish us, we should not eat at all. But it can be objected that belief in God is not a natural belief comparable to that in the existence of an external world. We cannot help believing in practice that bodies exist independently of our perception; but there does not seem to be any such practical necessity to believe in God.

Newman's line of argument is that there is something, namely conscience, which belongs to human nature as much as do the powers of perceiving and of reasoning, and which predisposes to belief in God, in the sense that it carries with it a 'presentiment' of the divine existence. A belief in God which is based on conscience is thus not grounded simply on the temperamental idiosyncrasy of certain individuals, but rather on a factor in human nature as such or at least on a factor in every human nature which is not morally stunted or maimed. The voice of conscience does not indeed carry with it any proof of its own credentials. In this sense it is an 'assumption'. But it manifests the presence of a transcendent God; and assent to the existence of the God so manifested is reasonable.

Before, however, we consider Newman's argument from conscience to the existence of God a little more closely, we can turn our attention to his approach to the problem of religious belief as outlined in his much later work, *The Grammar of Assent*, which was published in 1870.[18]

3. Assent, as Newman uses the term, is given to a proposition and is expressed by assertion. But I cannot properly be said to assent to a proposition unless I understand its meaning. This understanding is called by Newman apprehension. Hence we can say that assent presupposes apprehension.

There are, however, two types of apprehension, corresponding to two types of propositions. 'The terms of a proposition do or do not stand for things. If they do, then they are singular terms, for all things that are, are units. But if they do not stand for things they must stand for notions, and are common terms. Singular nouns come from experience, common from abstraction. The apprehension of the former I call real, and of the latter notional.'[19]

Exception might be taken to some of the expressions and statements in this quotation. But the general thesis seems to be reasonably clear. Apprehension or understanding of a term which stands for a thing or person is called real, while apprehension of an abstract idea or universal concept is called notional. If we apply this distinction to propositions, apprehension of, for example, a proposition in geometry would be notional, while the apprehension of the statement 'William is the father of James' would be real.

It follows from this that we must also distinguish between two types of assent. Assent given to a proposition apprehended as notional, as concerned with abstract ideas or universal terms, is notional assent, while that which is given to propositions apprehended as real, as concerned directly with things or persons, is real assent.

Now Newman takes it that things and persons, whether objects of actual experience or presented imaginatively in memory, strike the mind much more forcibly and vividly than do abstract notions. Real apprehension therefore is 'stronger than notional, because things, which are its objects, are confessedly more impressive and effective than notions, which are the object of notional [apprehension]. Experiences and their images strike and occupy the mind, as abstractions and their combinations do not.'[20] Similarly, although, according to Newman, all assent is alike in being unconditional,[21] acts of assent 'are elicited more heartily and forcibly, when they are made upon real apprehension which has things for its objects, than when they are made in favour of notions and with a notional apprehension'.[22] Further, real assent, though it does not necessarily affect conduct, tends to do so in a way in which purely notional assent does not.[23]

Real assent is also called belief by Newman. And it is obvious that the belief in God with which he is primarily concerned as a Christian apologist is a real assent to God as a present reality, and an assent which influences life or conduct, not simply a notional assent to a proposition about the idea of God. True, if assent is given to propositions, real assent will in this case be given to the proposition 'God exists' or 'there is a God'. But it will be given to the proposition apprehended as real, the term 'God' being understood as signifying a present reality, a present personal being. And from this it follows that Newman is not, and cannot be, primarily interested in a formal demonstrative inference to God's existence. For in his view, which recalls that of Hume, demonstration exhibits the logical relations between notions or ideas. That is to say, it derives conclusions from premisses, the terms of which stand for abstract or general ideas. Thus the assent given to the conclusion is notional and lacks that element of personal commitment which Newman associates with real assent to the existence of God.

As has already been mentioned, however, Newman does not postulate in man any power of intuiting God directly. Hence some sort of inference is required, some movement of the mind from what is given in experience to what transcends immediate experience or perception. At the same time it must not be the type of inference which leads to notional rather than to real assent. Thus the following questions arise: 'Can I attain to any more vivid assent to the Being of a God, than that which is given merely to notions of the intellect? . . . Can I believe as if I saw? Since such a high assent requires a present experience or memory of the fact, at first sight it would seem as if the answer must be in the negative; for how can I assent as if I saw, unless I have seen? But no one in this life can see God. Yet I conceive a real assent is possible, and I proceed to show how.'[24] Newman's attempt to show how this real assent is possible will be considered in the next section.

4. We have seen that according to Newman even our non-religious beliefs rest on at any rate latent assumptions.[25] Something is taken for granted, whether explicitly or implicitly. There is some point of departure which is taken as given, without proof. In the case of belief in God this point of departure, the given basis of the movement of the mind, is conscience. Conscience is as much a factor in human nature, in the complex of mental acts, 'as the action of memory, of reasoning, of imagination, or as the sense of the beautiful'.[26] And it is 'the essential principle and sanction of Religion in the mind'.[27]

Conscience, however, can be considered under two aspects which, though not separate in fact, are none the less distinguishable. In the first place we can consider it as a rule of right conduct, as judging about the rightness or wrongness of particular actions. And it is an empirical fact that different people have made different ethical judgments. Some societies, for example, have approved conduct which other societies have condemned. In the second place we can consider conscience simply as the voice of authority, that is, as imposing obligation. And the sense of obligation is essentially the same in all who possess a conscience. Even if A thinks that he ought to act in one way while B thinks that he ought to act in another way, the consciousness of obligation, considered in itself, is similar in both men.

Considered under this second aspect, as the voice of internal authority, conscience 'vaguely reaches forward to something beyond self, and dimly discerns a sanction higher than self for its decisions, as evidenced in that keen sense of obligation and responsibility which informs them'.[28] The inward law of conscience does not indeed carry with it any proof of its own validity, but it 'commands attention to it on its own authority'.[29] The more this inward law is respected and followed, the clearer become its dictates, and at the same time the clearer becomes the presentiment or vague awareness of a transcendent God, 'a supreme Power, claiming our habitual obedience'.[30]

A lively sense of obligation thus carries the mind forward

to the thought of something beyond the human self. Further, conscience possesses an emotive aspect, on which Newman lays considerable emphasis. Conscience produces 'reverence and awe, hope and fear, especially fear, a feeling which is foreign for the most part, not only to Taste, but even to the Moral Sense, except in consequence of accidental associations'.[31] And Newman argues that there is an intimate connection between affections and emotions on the one hand and persons on the other. 'Inanimate things cannot stir our affections; these are correlative with persons.'[32] Hence 'the phenomena of Conscience, as a dictate, avail to impress the imagination with the picture of a Supreme Governor, a Judge, holy, just, powerful, all-seeing, retributive'.[33] In other words, conscience can produce that 'imaginative' awareness of God which is required for the vivid assent to which reference has already been made.

What Newman says on this matter was doubtless verified in his own case. When he spoke of the mind of a child who recognizes obligation and who has been preserved from influences destructive of his 'religious instincts'[34] as reaching forward 'with a strong presentiment of the thought of a Moral Governor, sovereign over him, mindful and just',[35] we may well discern a generalization from his own experience. Further, if we consider what he has to say as a descriptive account of the basis of real assent to God, it is doubtless verified in many other cases. For it is certainly arguable that with many believers respect for the dictates of conscience is a powerful influence in keeping alive the consciousness of God as a present reality. True, it is possible to neglect and disobey the dictates of conscience and still believe in God. But it is also probably true that if one habitually turns a deaf ear to the voice of conscience, so that it becomes dim or obscured, belief in God, if retained, tends to degenerate into what Newman would call a purely notional assent. In other words, from the phenomenological point of view Newman's account of the relation between conscience and belief in or real assent to God has an indubitable value. There are indeed other factors which have to be considered in a phenomenological analysis of belief in God. But Newman certainly illustrates one aspect of the matter.

At the same time Newman is not concerned simply with describing the way in which, in his opinion, people come to believe in God, as though the belief were or could be on the same level as a belief, say, in the existence of elves and fairies. He wishes to show that belief in God is reasonable, and in some sense or other he intends to indicate the outlines of a 'proof' of God's existence. For instance, he says explicitly that the argument from conscience is 'my own chosen proof of that fundamental doctrine [God's existence] for thirty years past'.[36] And elsewhere he remarks that while he does not intend to prove 'here' the existence of a God, 'yet I have found it impossible to avoid saying where I look for the proof of it'.[37]

But what sort of a proof is it? In a sermon preached in 1830 Newman says that 'Conscience implies a relation between the soul and a something exterior, and that, moreover, superior to itself; a relation to an excellence which it does not possess, and to a tribunal over which it has no power'.[38] In spite, however, of the use of the word 'imply', he can hardly mean that the idea of conscience implies the idea of God in such a way that to assert the existence of conscience and deny the existence of God constitutes a logical contradiction. Moreover, elsewhere Newman uses phrases which suggest a causal inference. For instance, he says of conscience that 'from the nature of the case, its very existence carries on our minds to a Being exterior to ourselves; for else whence did it come?'[39] And we have already noted his remark, when speaking of the emotive aspect of conscience, that 'inanimate things cannot stir our affections; these are correlative with persons'.[40] But Newman is, of course, aware that by no means all philosophers would agree that we can legitimately infer the existence of God from the sense of obligation. And if he skates lightly over views different from his own, it is fairly evident that he is really concerned not so much with a causal inference to an explanatory hypothesis, analogous to causal inference in science, as with inviting his hearers or readers to enter into themselves and to reflect on the question whether they are not in some sense aware of God as manifested in the voice of conscience.

In other words, Newman seems to be primarily concerned

with personal insight into the 'significance' or 'implications' of the awareness of obligation in a sense of these terms which it is difficult to define. And his line of thought appears to bear more resemblance to the phenomenological analyses performed in our own day by Gabriel Marcel than to metaphysical arguments of the traditional type. Newman admits indeed that a generalized inductive argument is possible. Just as from sense-impressions 'we go on to draw the general conclusion that there is a vast external world',[41] so by induction from particular instances of awareness of an inner imperative, an awareness which opens the mind to the thought of God, we can conclude to 'the Ubiquitous Presence of One Supreme Master'.[42] But assent to the conclusion of a generalized inductive argument will be, for Newman, a notional assent. Hence an argument of this kind appears to fall into the same class as arguments from Nature to God, of which he says in one place that while he has no intention of questioning their beauty and cogency, he certainly does question 'whether in matter of fact they make or keep men Christians'.[43] For such an argument to be 'effective', yielding real assent, we have to 'apply our general knowledge to a particular instance of that knowledge'.[44] That is to say, for assent to the conclusion of a generalized moral argument to become a living belief and the basis of religion, I have to enter within myself and hear the voice of God manifesting itself in the voice of conscience.[45] It is the personal appropriation of the truth which counts for Newman, not a mere intellectual assent to an abstract proposition.

In other words, Newman really wants to make us 'see' something for ourselves in the context of our personal experience rather than to argue that one proposition follows logically from another. After all, he says himself that he does not intend to deal 'with controversialists'.[46] In a real sense he wishes to make us see what we are. Without conscience a man is not really a man. And unless conscience leads us to belief in God by bringing us, so to speak, up against God as a present reality manifested in the sense of obligation, it remains stunted. Human nature expands, as it were, in faith. It is from the start open to God. And in Newman's view this potential openness is realized, basically, through personal insight into the 'phenomenon' of conscience. It is thus probably a mistake to interpret his argument from conscience to God as a public proof of the existence of God. True, the phenomenological analysis is public in the sense that it is a written explicitation of what Newman regards as the spontaneous movement of the unspoiled mind. But the public analysis cannot possibly do what Newman wishes it to do, to facilitate real assent, unless it is interiorized, applied, as he puts it, to the particular instance.

5. We cannot examine here Newman's discussion of the evidences for the truth of Christianity. But there is a logical point connected with the discussion which is worth mentioning.

Formal demonstrative inference can, of course, be employed within theology, to exhibit the implications of statements. But when we are considering the evidences for Christianity in the first place, we are largely concerned, Newman takes it, with historical matters, with matters of fact. And at once a difficulty arises. On the one hand in reasoning about matters of fact rather than about the relations between abstract ideas our conclusions enjoy some degree of probability, perhaps a very high degree, but still only probability. On the other hand all assent, Newman insists, is unconditional. How then can we be justified in giving unconditional assent, such as is demanded of the Christian, to a proposition which is only probably true?

To answer this objection Newman makes use of ideas found in Pascal, Locke and Butler and argues that an accumulation of independent probabilities, converging towards a common conclusion, can render this conclusion certain. In his own words, where there is a 'cumulation of probabilities, independent of each other, arising out of the nature and circumstances of the case which is under review; probabilities too fine to avail separately, too subtle and circuitous to be convertible into syllogisms, too numerous and various for such conversion, even were they convertible',[47] but which all, taken together, converge on a certain conclusion, this conclusion can be certain.

It can doubtless be admitted that we do in fact often take a convergence of probabilities as sufficient proof of the truth of a proposition. But it can still be objected against Newman that no definite rule can be given for determining when the truth of a certain conclusion is the only possible rational explanation of a given convergence. Hence though we may be perfectly justified in assuming the truth of the conclusion for all practical purposes, an unconditional or unqualified assent is unjustified. For any hypothesis remains revisible in principle. It is all very well for Newman to say that in the case of religious inquiry we are 'bound in conscience to seek truth and to look for certainty by modes of proof, which, when reduced to the shape of formal propositions, fail to satisfy the severe requisitions of science'.[48] The fact remains that if unconditional assent to a proposition is taken to exclude the possibility of the proposition turning out to be false, it cannot legitimately be given to a conclusion drawn from a convergence unless we are able to show that at some point probability is transferred into certainty.

Obviously, Newman can hardly mean by unconditional assent one which excludes all possibility of the relevant proposition turning out to be false. For if all assent is unconditional, it must include assent to propositions which we very well know might turn out to be false. In its most general form the statement that all assent is unconditional can hardly mean more than that assent is assent. However, in the case of adherence to Christianity Newman clearly has in mind an absolute self-commitment, an unqualified assent in the fullest sense. And though he would doubtless admit that there is no infallible abstract rule for determining when a convergence of possibilities is such that the conclusion is certain, he argues that man possesses a 'faculty' of the mind, analogous to the Aristotelian *phronesis*, which is susceptible of different degrees of development and which is in principle capable of discerning the point at which the convergence of probabilities amounts to conclusive proof. This is the illative sense. 'In no class of concrete reasonings, whether in experimental science, historical research, or theology, is there any ultimate test of truth and error in our inferences besides the trustworthiness of the Illative Sense that gives them its sanction.'[49] We either 'see' or we do not see that a given inference is valid. Similarly, we either see or we do not see that the only rational explanation of a given accumulation of converging independent probabilities is the truth of the conclusion on which they converge. By the nature of the case there can be no further criterion of judgment than the mind's estimate of the evidence in a particular case.

It may seem that Newman places the emphasis on subjective or psychological states. He says, for example, that 'certitude is a mental state: certainty is a quality of propositions. Those propositions I call certain, which are such that I am certain of them.'[50] And this may give the impression that in his opinion any proposition is certainly true if it causes the feeling of being certain in a human being. But he goes on to say that in concrete questions certitude is not a 'passive impression made upon the mind from without . . . but . . . an active recognition of propositions as true. . . .'[51] And as 'everyone who reasons is his own centre',[52] there can be no further criterion of evidence or of the validity of inference in concrete matters of fact than seeing that the evidence is sufficient or that the inference is valid. Newman has no intention of denying the objectivity of truth. He means rather that if we think that a man's reasoning in questions of fact is faulty, we can only ask him to look again at the evidence and at his process of reasoning. If it is objected that there can be a 'logic of words',[53] the sort of deduction which can be performed by a machine, Newman does not deny this. But he insists that a distinction must be made between the logic of words and reasoning about matters of fact. The former leads to purely notional assent; and this does not interest him when he is writing as a Christian apologist who wishes to justify real assent. He does not set out to argue that reasoning about Christian evidences can be reduced to the logic of words, to formal demonstrative inference. What he wishes to show is rather that in all concrete issues of fact we have to employ inference which is not so reducible, and that the believer's assent to the conclusion of reasoning about the evidences for Christianity cannot therefore be justifiably described as a mere leap or as the result of wishful thinking because it does not conform to a pattern of demonstration which certainly has its uses but which is inappropriate outside a certain limited field.

6. We have already had occasion to refer to a certain affinity between Newman's reflections on conscience and Gabriel Marcel's phenomenological analyses. But the intellectual antecedents and formations of the two men were, needless to say, very different; and whereas Newman was out to prove something, to show that Christian belief is reasonable, the apologetic motive is much less obvious with Marcel. Indeed, Marcel's philosophical reflections helped to bring him to Christianity, whereas Newman's philosophical reflections presuppose the Christian faith, in the sense that it is a case of faith reflecting on itself. At the same time there are certain limited affinities.

Similarly, in spite of the great differences between the two men Newman's preoccupation with the personal appropriation of truth as a basis for life and with personal self-commitment may put us in mind of Kierkegaard,[54] whose span of life (1813–55) fell entirely within that of Newman. This is not to suggest, of course, that Newman knew anything at all about the Danish thinker, or even of his existence. But though Newman certainly did not go so far as Kierkegaard in describing truth as subjectivity, there is none the less a certain degree of spiritual affinity between the two men.

As for Newman's insistence on the moral conditions for the fruitful pursuit of truth in religious inquiry, this has become a commonplace of the newer apologetics, as has indeed Newman's approach from within the soul rather than from external Nature. In other words, there is at any rate some affinity between Newman's approach to apologetics and that associated in modern times with the name of Maurice Blondel (1861–1949).

The point of these remarks is this. If we take Newman simply as he stands, there are a good many questions which modern British logicians and philosophers would wish to ask, and objections which they would feel inclined to make. But it seems safe to say that Newman is not now regarded, except possibly by a few devotees, as a philosopher whose thought one either accepts or rejects, as the case may be. By saying that he is not 'now' regarded I do not mean to imply that he was ever looked on in this light. I mean rather that the growth of interest in his philosophical thought and in his style of apologetics has coincided with the spread of movements in philosophy and in apologetics which, on our looking back, are seen to have certain affinities with elements in Newman's reflections. Hence those who take an interest in his philosophical reflections tend to look on them as a source of stimulus and inspiration rather than as a rigid, systematic doctrine, which, of course, Newman himself never intended them to be. And in this case detailed criticism of particular points necessarily seems pedantic and appears, to those who value Newman's general approach, as more or less irrelevant.

APPENDIX

A SHORT BIBLIOGRAPHY

Part III: Chapters XI–XIII

1. GENERAL WORKS RELATING TO IDEALISM IN AMERICA

Abbagnano, N. *L'idealismo inglese e americano*. Naples, 1926.

Adams, G. P. *Idealism and the Modern Age*. New Haven, 1919.

Barrett, C. and Others. *Contemporary Idealism in America*. New York, 1932.

Cunningham, G. W. *The Idealistic Argument in Recent British and American Philosophy*. New York, 1933.

Frothingham, O. B. *Transcendentalism in New England*. New York, 1876.

Jones, A. L. *Early American Philosophers*. New York, 1898.

Miller, P. *The New England Mind: The Seventeenth Century*. New York, 1939.

Parrington, V. L. *Main Currents of American Thought*. New York, 1927.

Riley, I. W. *American Philosophy: The Early Schools*. New York, 1907.

Rogers, A. K. *English and American Philosophy Since 1800*. New York, 1922.

Royce, J. *Lectures on Modern Idealism*. New Haven, 1919.

Schneider, H. W. *The Puritan Mind*. New York, 1930.

  A History of American Philosophy. New York, 1946.

Stovall, F. *American Idealism*. Oklahoma, 1943.

2. EMERSON

Texts

The Complete Works of Ralph Waldo Emerson, edited by E. W. Emerson. 12 vols. Boston, 1903–4. (Fireside edition, Boston, 1909.)

Works, 5 vols. London, 1882–3.

    6 vols., edited by J. Morley. London, 1883–4.

The Journals of Ralph Waldo Emerson, edited by E. W. Emerson and W. F. Forbes. 10 vols. Boston, 1909–14.

The Letters of Ralph Waldo Emerson, edited by R. L. Rusk. New York, 1939.

Studies

Alcott, A. B. *R. W. Emerson, Philosopher and Seer*. Boston, 1882.

Bishop, J. *Emerson on the Soul*. Cambridge (Mass.), and London, 1965.

Cabot, J. E. *A Memoir of R. W. Emerson*. 2 vols. London, 1887.

Cameron, K. W. *Emerson the Essayist: An Outline of His Philosophical Development through 1836*. 2 vols. Raleigh (N.C.), 1945.

Carpenter, F. I. *Emerson and Asia*. Cambridge (Mass.), 1930.

    Emerson Handbook. New York, 1953.

Christy, A. *The Orient in American Transcendentalism*. New York, 1932.

Firkins, O. W. *R. W. Emerson*. Boston, 1915.

Garnett, R. *Life of Emerson*. London, 1888.

Gray, H. D. *Emerson: A Statement of New England Transcendentalism as Expressed in the Philosophy of Its Chief Exponent*. Palo Alto (Calif.), 1917.

Hopkins, V. C. *Spires of Form: A Study of Emerson's Aesthetic Theory*. Cambridge (Mass.), 1951.

James, W. *Memories and Studies*. New York, 1911. (Includes an address on Emerson.)

Masters, E. L. *The Living Thoughts of Emerson*. London, 1948.

Matthiessen, F. O. *American Renaissance: Art and Expression in the Age of Emerson and Whitman*. London and New York, 1941.

Michaud, R. *Autour d'Emerson*. Paris, 1924.

    La vie inspirée d'Emerson. Paris, 1930.

Mohrdieck, M. *Demokratie bei Emerson*. Berlin, 1943.

Paul, S. *Emerson's Angle of Vision*. Cambridge (Mass.), 1952.

Perry, B. *Emerson Today*. New York, 1931.

Reaver, J. R. *Emerson as Myth-Maker*. Gainesville (Fla.), 1954.

Rusk, R. L. *The Life of Ralph Waldo Emerson*. New York, 1949.

Sahmann, P. *Emersons Geisteswelt*. Stuttgart, 1927.

Sanborn, F. B. (editor). *The Genius and Character of Emerson*. Boston, 1885.

Simon, J. R. *W. Emerson in Deutschland*. Berlin, 1937.

Whicher, S. B. *Freedom and Fate: An Inner Life of Ralph Waldo Emerson*. Philadelphia, 1953.

3. ROYCE

Texts

The Religious Aspect of Philosophy. Boston, 1885.

California: A Study of American Character. Boston, 1886.

The Spirit of Modern Philosophy. Boston, 1892.

The Conception of God: A Philosophical Discussion concerning the Nature of the Divine Idea as a Demonstrable Reality. New York, 1897. (This work, by several authors, includes Royce's intervention at a philosophical discussion in 1895.)

Studies of Good and Evil. New York, 1898.

The World and the Individual. 2 vols. New York, 1900–1.

The Conception of Immortality. Boston, 1900.

The Philosophy of Loyalty. New York, 1908.

Race Questions, Provincialisms and Other American Problems. New York and London, 1908.

William James and Other Essays on the Philosophy of Life. New York, 1911.

The Sources of Religious Insight. Edinburgh, 1912.

The Problem of Christianity. 2 vols. New York, 1913.

War and Insurance. New York, 1914.

Lectures on Modern Idealism. New Haven, 1919. (Edition by J. E. Smith. New York and London, 1964.)

Royce's Logical Essays, edited by D. S. Robinson. Dubuque (Iowa), 1951.

Josiah Royce's Seminar 1913–14, as recorded in the notebooks of H. Costello, edited by G. Smith. New Brunswick, 1963.

Studies

Albeggiani, F. *Il sistema filosofico di Josiah Royce*. Palermo, 1930.

Amoroso, M. L. *La filosofia morale di Josiah Royce*. Naples, 1929.

Aronson, M. J. *La philosophie morale de Josiah Royce*. Paris, 1927.

Cotton, J. H. *Royce on the Human Self*. Cambridge (Mass.), 1954.

Creighton, J. E. (editor). *Papers in Honor of Josiah Royce on His Sixtieth Birthday*. New York, 1916.

De Nier, M. *Royce*. Brescia, 1950.

Dykhuizen, G. *The Conception of God in the Philosophy of Josiah Royce*. Chicago, 1936.

Fuss, P. *The Moral Philosophy of Josiah Royce*. Cambridge (Mass.), 1965.

Galgano, M. *Il pensiero filosofico di Josiah Royce*. Rome, 1921.

Humbach, K. T. *Einzelperson und Gemeinschaft nach Josiah Royce*. Heidelberg, 1962.

Loewenberg, J. *Royce's Synoptic Vision*. Baltimore, 1955.

Marcel, G. *La métaphysique de Royce*. Paris, 1945.

Olgiati, F. *Un pensatore americano: Josiah Royce*. Milan, 1917.

Smith, J. E. *Royce's Social Infinite*. New York, 1950.

Part IV: Chapters XIV–XVI

1. GENERAL WORKS RELATING TO PRAGMATISM

Baumgarten, E. *Der Pragmatismus: R. W. Emerson, W. James, J. Dewey*. Frankfurt, 1938.

Bawden, H. H. *Pragmatism*. New York, 1909.

Berthelot, R. *Un romantisme utilitaire*. 3 vols. Paris, 1911–13.

Childs, J. L. *American Pragmatism and Education: An Interpretation and Analysis*. New York, 1956.

Chiocchetti, E. *Il pragmatismo*. Milan, 1926.

Hook, S. *The Metaphysics of Pragmatism*. Chicago, 1927.

Kennedy, G. (editor). *Pragmatism and American Culture*. Boston, 1950.

Lamanna, E. P. *Il pragmatismo anglo-americano*. Florence, 1952.

Leroux, E. *Le pragmatisme américain et anglais*. Paris, 1922.

Mead, G. H. *The Philosophy of the Present*. Chicago, 1932.

Moore, A. W. *Pragmatism and Its Critics*. Chicago, 1910.

Moore, E. C. *American Pragmatism: Peirce, James and Dewey*. New York, 1961.

Morris, C. W. *Six Theories of Mind*. Chicago, 1932.

Murray, D. L. *Pragmatism*. London, 1912.

Perry, R. B. *Present Philosophical Tendencies*. New York, 1912.

Pratt, J. B. *What is Pragmatism?* New York, 1909.

Simon, P. *Der Pragmatismus in der modernen französischen Philosophie*. Paderborn, 1920.

Spirito, U. *Il pragmatismo nella filosofia contemporanea*. Florence, 1921.

Stebbing, L. S. *Pragmatism and French Voluntarism*. Cambridge, 1914.

Sturt, H. (editor). *Personal Idealism*. London, 1902.

Van Wessep, H. B. *Seven Sages: The Story of American Philosophy*. New York, 1960. (Includes Chapters on James, Dewey and Peirce.)

Wahl, J. A. *Les philosophies pluralistes d'Angleterre et d'Amérique*. Paris, 1920.

Wiener, P. P. *Evolution and the Founders of Pragmatism*. Cambridge (Mass.), 1949.

2. PEIRCE

Texts

Collected Papers of Charles Sanders Peirce. 8 vols. Cambridge, Mass. Volumes I–VI, edited by C. Hartshorne and P. Weiss and first published 1931–5, have been reissued in 1960 as three volumes. Volumes VII–VIII, edited by A. W. Burke, were published in 1958.

There are also some books of selections, such as:

Chance, Love and Logic, edited by M. R. Cohen, with a supplementary essay by J. Dewey. New York, 1923.

The Philosophy of Peirce. Selected Writings, edited by J. Buchler. London, 1940 (reprint, New York, 1955).

Essays in the Philosophy of Science, edited by V. Tomas. New York, 1957.

Values in a Universe of Chance, edited by P. P. Wiener. Stanford and London, 1958.

Studies

Boler, J. F. *Charles Peirce and Scholastic Realism. A Study of Peirce's Relation to John Duns Scotus.* Seattle, 1963.

Buchler, J. *Charles Peirce's Empiricism.* London, 1939.

Carpenter, F. I. *American Literature and the Dream.* New York, 1955. (Includes a chapter on Peirce.)

Feibleman, J. K. *An Introduction to Peirce's Philosophy Interpreted as a System.* New York, 1946; London, 1960.

Freeman, E. *The Categories of Charles Peirce.* La Salle (Ill.), 1934.

Gallie, W. B. *Peirce and Pragmatism.* Penguin Books, 1952.

Goudge, T. A. *The Thought of C. S. Peirce.* Toronto and London, 1950.

Guccione Monroy, A. *Peirce e il pragmatismo americano.* Palermo, 1959.

Kempski, J. V. *C. A. Peirce und der Pragmatismus.* Stuttgart and Cologne, 1952.

Mullin, A. A. *Philosophical Comments on the Philosophies of C. S. Peirce and L. Wittgenstein.* Urbana (Ill.), 1961.

Murphey, M. G. *The Development of Peirce's Philosophy.* Cambridge (Mass.), 1961.

Thompson, M. *The Pragmatic Philosophy of C. S. Peirce.* Chicago and London, 1953.

Wennerberg, H. *The Pragmatism of C. S. Peirce.* Lund, 1963.

Wiener, P. P. and Young, F. H. (editors). *Studies in the Philosophy of Charles Sanders Peirce.* Cambridge (Mass.), 1952.

3. JAMES

Texts

The Principles of Psychology. New York, 1890.

The Will to Believe and Other Essays. New York and London, 1897 (reprint, New York, 1956).

The Varieties of Religious Experience. New York and London, 1902.

Pragmatism. New York and London, 1907.

The Meaning of Truth. New York and London, 1909.

A Pluralistic Universe. New York and London, 1909.

Some Problems of Philosophy. New York and London, 1911.

Memories and Studies. New York and London, 1911.

Essays in Radical Empiricism. New York and London, 1912.

Collected Essays and Reviews. New York and London, 1920.

The Letters of William James, edited by H. James. 2 vols. Boston, 1926.

Annotated Bibliography of the Writings of William James, edited by R. B. Perry. New York, 1920.

Studies

Bixler, J. S. *Religion in the Philosophy of William James*. Boston, 1926.

Blau, T. *William James: sa théorie de la connaissance et de la verité*. Paris, 1933.

Boutroux, E. *William James*. Paris, 1911. (English translation by A. and B. Henderson. London, 1912.)

Bovet, P. *William James psychologue: l'intérêt de son oeuvre pour les éducateurs*. Saint Blaise, 1911.

Busch, K. A. *William James als Religionsphilosoph*. Göttingen, 1911.

Carpio, A. P. *Origen y desarrollo de la filosofia norteamericana. William James y el pragmatismo*. Buenos Aires, 1951.

Castiglioni, G. *William James*. Brescia, 1946.

Compton, C. H. (compiler). *William James: Philosopher and Man*. New York, 1957. (Quotations and References in 652 books.)

Cugini, U. *L'empirismo radicale di W. James*. Naples, 1925.

Kallen, H. M. *William James and Henri Bergson*. Chicago, 1914.

Knight, M. *William James*. Penguin Books, 1950.

Knox, H. V. *The·Philosophy of William James*. London, 1914.

Le Breton, M. *La personnalité de William James*. Paris, 1929.

Maire, G. *William James et le pragmatisme religieux*. Paris, 1934.

Menard, A. *Analyse et critique des 'Principes de la Psychologie' de William James*. Paris, 1911.

Morris, L. *William James*. New York, 1950.

Nassauer, K. *Die Rechtsphilosophie von William James*. Bremen, 1943.

Perry, R. B. *The Thought and Character of William James*. 2 vols. Boston, 1935. (This is the standard biography.)
The Thought and Character of William James. Briefer Version. New York, 1954.
In the Spirit of William James. New Haven, 1938.

Reverdin, H. *La notion d'expérience d'après William James*. Geneva, 1913.

Roback, A. A. *William James, His Marginalia, Personality and Contribution*. Cambridge (Mass.), 1942.

Royce, J. *William James and Other Essays on the Philosophy of Life*. New York, 1911.

Sabin, E. E. *William James and Pragmatism*. Lancaster (Pa.), 1916.

Schmidt, H. *Der Begriff der Erfahrungskontinuität bei William James und seine Bedeutung für den amerikanischen Pragmatismus*. Heidelberg, 1959.

Switalski, W. *Der Wahrheitsbegriff des Pragmatismus nach William James*. Braunsberg, 1910.

Turner, J. E. *Examination of William James' Philosophy*. New York, 1919.

There are several collections of essays by various authors such as:

Essays Philosophical and Psychological in Honor of William James. New York, 1908.

In Commemoration of William James, 1842–1942. New York, 1942.

William James, the Man and the Thinker. Madison (Wis.), 1942.

4. SCHILLER

Texts

Riddles of the Sphinx. First published anonymously (by 'a Troglodyte') at London in 1891, then with the author's name at New York in 1894.

New edition, with sub-title *A Study in the Philosophy of Humanism.* London, 1910.

Axioms as Postulates, in *Personal Idealism,* edited by H. Sturt. London, 1902.

Humanism, Philosophical Essays. London, 1903 (2nd edition, 1912).

Studies in Humanism. London, 1907 (2nd edition, 1912).

Plato or Protagoras? London, 1908.

Formal Logic: A Scientific and Social Problem. London, 1912 (2nd edition, 1931).

Problems of Belief. London, 1924.

Why Humanism?, in *Contemporary British Philosophy,* First Series, edited by J. H. Muirhead. London, 1924.

Tantalus, or The Future of Man. London, 1924.

Eugenics and Politics. London, 1926.

Pragmatism, in *Encyclopædia Britannica,* 14th edition, 1929.

Logic for Use: An Introduction to the Voluntarist Theory of Knowledge. London, 1929.

Social Decay and Eugenical Reform. London, 1932.

Must Philosophers Disagree? and Other Essays in Popular Philosophy. London, 1934.

Studies

Abel, R. *The Pragmatic Humanism of F. C. S. Schiller.* New York and London, 1955.

Marett, R. *Ferdinand Canning Scott Schiller.* London, 1938. (British Academy lecture.)

White, S. S. *A Comparison of the Philosophies of F. C. S. Schiller and John Dewey.* Chicago, 1940.

5. DEWEY

Texts

Psychology. New York, 1887 (3rd revised edition, 1891).

Leibniz's New Essays Concerning the Human Understanding. A Critical Exposition. Chicago, 1888.

The Ethics of Democracy. Ann Arbor, 1888.

Applied Psychology. Boston, 1889.

Outlines of a Critical Theory of Ethics. Ann Arbor, 1891.

The Study of Ethics: A Syllabus. Ann Arbor, 1894.

The Psychology of Number and Its Applications to Methods of Teaching Arithmetic (with J. A. McLellan). New York, 1895.

The Significance of the Problem of Knowledge. Chicago, 1897.

My Pedagogic Creed. New York, 1897.

Psychology and Philosophic Method. Berkeley, 1899.

The School of Society. Chicago, 1900 (revised edition, 1915).

The Child and the Curriculum. Chicago, 1902.

The Educational Situation. Chicago, 1902.

Studies in Logical Theory (with Others). Chicago, 1903.

Logical Conditions of a Scientific Treatment of Morality. Chicago, 1903.

Ethics (with J. H. Tufts). New York, 1908.

How We Think. New York, 1910.

The Influence of Darwin on Philosophy and Other Essays in Contemporary Thought. New York, 1910.

Educational Essays, edited by J. J. Findlay. London, 1910.

Interest and Effort in Education. Boston, 1913.

German Philosophy and Politics. New York, 1915 (revised edition, 1942).

Schools of Tomorrow (with E. Dewey). New York, 1915.

Democracy and Education. New York, 1916.

Essays in Experimental Logic. Chicago, 1916.

Reconstruction in Philosophy. New York, 1920 (enlarged edition, 1948).

Letters from China and Japan (with A. C. Dewey, edited by E. Dewey. New York, 1920).

Human Nature and Conduct: An Introduction to Social Psychology. New York, 1922.

Experience and Nature. Chicago, 1925 (revised edition, 1929).

The Public and Its Problems. New York, 1927 (2nd edition, 1946).

Characters and Events. Popular Essays in Social and Political Philosophy, edited by J. Ratner. 2 vols. New York, 1929.

Impressions of Soviet Russia and the Revolutionary World, Mexico, China, Turkey. New York, 1929.

The Quest for Certainty. New York, 1929.

Individualism, Old and New (reprinted articles), New York, 1930.

Philosophy and Civilization. New York, 1931.

Art as Experience. New York, 1934.

A Common Faith. New Haven, 1934.

Education and The Social Order. New York, 1934.

Liberalism and Social Action. New York, 1935.

The Teacher and Society (with Others). New York, 1937.

Experience and Education. New York, 1938.

Logic: The Theory of Inquiry. New York, 1938.

Intelligence in the Modern World: John Dewey's Philosophy, edited by J. Ratner. New York, 1939. (Mostly selections from published writings.)

Theory of Valuation. Chicago, 1939.

Freedom and Culture. New York, 1939.

Education Today, edited by J. Ratner. New York, 1940.

Knowing and the Known (with A. F. Bentley). Boston, 1949.

There are several books of selections and compilations based on Dewey's writings, such as:

Intelligence in the Modern World: John Dewey's Philosophy, edited by J. Ratner. New York, 1939.

Dictionary of Education, edited by R. B. Winn. New York, 1959.

Dewey on Education, selected with an introduction and notes by M. S. Dworkin. New York, 1959.

For fuller bibliographies see:

A Bibliography of John Dewey, 1882–1939, by M. H. Thomas

and H. W. Schneider, with an introduction by H. W. Schneider. New York, 1939.

The Philosophy of John Dewey, edited by P. A. Schilpp. New York, 1951 (2nd edition).

Studies

Baker, M. *Foundation of John Dewey's Educational Theory*. New York, 1955.

Baumgarten, E. *Der Pragmatismus: R. W. Emerson, W. James, J. Dewey*. Frankfurt, 1938.

Bausola, A. *L'etica di John Dewey*. Milan, 1960.

Brancatisano, F. *La posizione di John Dewey nella filosofia moderna*. Turin, 1953.

Buswell, J. O. *The Philosophies of F. R. Tennant and J. Dewey*. New York, 1950.

Child, A. *Making and Knowing in Hobbes, Vico and Dewey*. Berkeley, 1953.

Corallo, G. *La pedagogia di Giovanni Dewey*. Turin, 1950.

Crosser, P. K. *The Nihilism of John Dewey*. New York, 1955.

Edman, I. *John Dewey, His Contribution to the American Tradition*. Indianapolis (Ind.), 1955.

Feldman, W. T. *The Philosophy of John Dewey. A Critical Analysis*. Baltimore, 1934.

Fleckenstein, N. J. *A Critique of John Dewey's Theory of the Nature and the Knowledge of Reality in the Light of the Principles of Thomism*. Washington, 1954.

Geiger, G. R. *John Dewey in Perspective*. London and New York, 1938.

Gillio-Tos, M. T. *Il pensiero di John Dewey*. Naples, 1938.

Grana, G. *John Dewey e la metodologia americana*. Rome, 1955.

Gutzke, M. G. *John Dewey's Thought and Its Implications for Christian Education*. New York, 1956.

Handlin, O. *John Dewey's Challenge to Education: Historical Perspectives on the Cultural Context*. New York, 1959.

Hook, S. *John Dewey: An Intellectual Portrait*. New York, 1939.

Leander, F. *The Philosophy of John Dewey. A Critical Study*. Göteborg, 1939.

Levitt, M. *Freud and Dewey on the Nature of Man*. New York, 1960.

Mack, R. D. *The Appeal to Immediate Experience. Philosophic Method in Bradley, Whitehead and Dewey*. New York, 1945.

Mataix, A., (S.J.). *La norma moral en John Dewey*. Madrid, 1964.

Nathanson, J. *John Dewey*. New York, 1951.

Roth, R. J., (S.J.). *John Dewey and Self-Realization*. Englewood Cliffs (N.J.), 1963.

Thayer, H. S. *The Logic of Pragmatism: An Examination of John Dewey's Logic*. New York and London, 1952.

White, M. G. *The Origin of Dewey's Instrumentalism*. New York, 1943.

White, S. S. *A Comparison of the Philosophies of F. C. S. Schiller and John Dewey*. Chicago, 1940.

Symposia on Dewey:

John Dewey, The Man and His Philosophy, edited by S. S. White. Cambridge (Mass.), 1930. (Discourses in honour of Dewey's seventieth birthday.)

The Philosopher of the Common Man, edited by S. S. White. New York, 1940. (Essays in celebration of Dewey's eightieth birthday.)

The Philosophy of John Dewey, edited by P. A. Schilpp. New York, 1951 (2nd edition).

John Dewey: Philosopher of Science and Freedom, edited by S. Hook. New York, 1950.

John Dewey and the Experimental Spirit in Philosophy, edited by C. W. Hendel. New York, 1959.

John Dewey: Master Educator, edited by W. W. Brickman and S. Lehrer. New York, 1959.

Dialogue on John Dewey, edited by C. Lamont. New York, 1959.

John Dewey: His Thought and Influence, edited by J. Blewett. New York, 1960.

Part V: Chapters XVII–XXI[1]

1. SOME GENERAL WORKS DESCRIBING OR ILLUSTRATING RE-
CENT PHILOSOPHY, ESPECIALLY IN GREAT BRITAIN.

Adams, G. P. and Montague, W. P. (editors). *Contemporary American Philosophy.* 2 vols. New York, 1930.

Ayer, A. J. and Others. *The Revolution in Philosophy.* London, 1956. (Broadcast Talks.)

Black, M. *Language and Philosophy.* Ithaca and London, 1949.
  Problems of Analysis: Philosophical Essays. Ithaca and London, 1954.

Blanshard, B. *Reason and Analysis.* London and New York, 1962. (A critical discussion of linguistic philosophy.)

Boman, L. *Criticism and Construction in the Philosophy of the American New Realism.* Stockholm, 1955.

Charlesworth, M. *Philosophy and Linguistic Analysis.* Pittsburgh and Louvain, 1959. (Critical as well as historical.)

Drake, D. and Others. *Essays in Critical Realism.* New York and London, 1921.

Flew, A. G. N. (editor). *Logic and Language* (first series). Oxford, 1951.
  Logic and Language (second series). Oxford, 1955.
  Essays in Conceptual Analysis. Oxford, 1953.
  New Essays in Philosophical Theology. London, 1955.

Gellner, E. *Words and Things.* London, 1959. (A very critical treatment of linguistic philosophy in England.)

Ginestier, P. *La pensée anglo-saxonne depuis 1900.* Paris, 1956.

Holt, E. B. and Others. *The New Realism.* New York, 1912.

Kremer, R. P. *Le néo-realisme américain.* Louvain, 1920.
  La théorie de la connaissance chez les néo-realistes anglais. Louvain, 1928.

Lewis, H. D. (editor). *Contemporary British Philosophy* (third series). London, 1956.

Linsky, L. (editor). *Semantics and the Philosophy of Language.* Urbana (Ill.), 1952.

Mace, C. A. (editor). *British Philosophy in the Mid-Century.* London, 1957.

MacIntyre, A. (editor). *Metaphysical Beliefs.* London, 1957.

Muirhead, J. H. *Rule and End in Morals.* London, 1932. (Discusses the ethical issues treated by Prichard, Carritt, Ross, Joseph, and others.)

Pears, D. F. (editor). *The Nature of Metaphysics.* London, 1957. (Broadcast Talks.)

Sellars, R. W. and Others. *Essays in Critical Realism.* New York and London, 1920.

Urmson, J. O. *Philosophical Analysis. Its Development between the Two World Wars.* Oxford, 1956.

Warnock, G. J. *English Philosophy Since 1900.* (A clear account of the development of the analytic movement.)

Warnock, M. *Ethics Since 1900.* London, 1960. (Mainly on the development of English ethical theory from Bradley. But discusses the ideas of the American philosopher C. L. Stevenson and contains a chapter on Sartre.)

2. G. E. MOORE

Texts

Principia Ethica. Cambridge, 1903 (2nd edition, 1922; new edition, 1960).

Ethics. London, 1912 (and reprints).

Philosophical Studies. London, 1922 (new edition, 1960). (This work includes 'The Refutation of Idealism' from *Mind*, 1903.)

Some Main Problems of Philosophy. London, 1953. (This volume includes some hitherto unpublished lectures delivered in the winter of 1910–11.)

Philosophical Papers. London, 1959. (This volume includes 'A Defence of Common Sense' from *Contemporary British Philosophy*, Second Series, 1925.)

Commonplace Book, 1919–1953, edited by C. Lewy. London, 1962.

Studies

Braithwaite, R. B. *George Edward Moore, 1873–1958.* London, 1963. (British Academy lecture.)

Schilpp, P. A. (editor). *The Philosophy of G. E. Moore.* New York, 1952.

White, A. R. *G. E. Moore: A Critical Exposition.* Oxford, 1958.

3. RUSSELL

Texts

German Social Democracy. London and New York, 1896.

An Essay on the Foundations of Geometry. Cambridge, 1897.

A Critical Exposition of the Philosophy of Leibniz. Cambridge, 1900.

The Principles of Mathematics. Cambridge, 1903.

Principia Mathematica (with A. N. Whitehead). 3 vols. Cambridge, 1910–13 (2nd edition, 1927–35).

Philosophical Essays (reprinted articles). London and New York, 1910.

The Problems of Philosophy. London and New York, 1912.

Our Knowledge of the External World as a Field for Scientific Method in Philosophy. London and Chicago, 1914 (revised edition, 1929).

The Philosophy of Bergson (controversy with Professor H. W. Carr). London, Glasgow and Cambridge, 1914.

Scientific Method in Philosophy. Oxford, 1914.

War, the Offspring of Fear (pamphlet). London, 1915.

Principles of Social Reconstruction. London, 1916 (2nd edition, 1920).

Policy of the Entente, 1904–1914: A Reply to Professor Gilbert Murray (booklet). Manchester and London, 1916.

Justice in War-Time. London and Chicago, 1916 (2nd edition, 1924).

Political Ideals. New York, 1917.

Mysticism and Logic and Other Essays (reprinted essays). London and New York, 1918.

Roads to Freedom: Socialism, Anarchism and Syndicalism. London, 1918.

Introduction to Mathematical Philosophy. London and New York, 1919.

The Practice and Theory of Bolshevism. London and New York, 1920 (2nd edition, 1949).

The Analysis of Mind. London, 1921, New York, 1924.

The Problem of China. London and New York, 1922.

Free Thought and Official Propaganda (lecture). London and New York, 1922.

The Prospects of Industrial Civilization (with D. Russell). London and New York, 1923.

The ABC of Atoms. London and New York, 1923.

Icarus, or the Future of Science (booklet). London and New York, 1924.

How To Be Free and Happy (lecture). New York, 1924.

The ABC of Relativity. London and New York, 1925 (revised edition, 1958).

On Education, Especially in Early Childhood. London and New York, 1926. (In America with the title *Education and the Good Life.*)

The Analysis of Matter. London and New York, 1927 (reprint, 1954).

An Outline of Philosophy. London and New York, 1927. (In America with the title *Philosophy.*)

Selected Papers of Bertrand Russell (selected and introduced by Russell). New York, 1927.

Sceptical Essays (largely reprints). London and New York, 1928.

Marriage and Morals. London and New York, 1929.

The Conquest of Happiness. London and New York, 1930.

The Scientific Outlook. New York, 1931.

Education and the Social Order. London and New York, 1932. (In America with the title *Education and the Modern World.*)

Freedom and Organization, 1814–1914. London and New York, 1934. (In America with the title *Freedom versus Organization.*)

In Praise of Idleness and Other Essays. New York, 1935.

Religion and Science. London and New York, 1935.

Which Way to Peace? London, 1936.

The Amberley Papers (with P. Russell.) 2 vols. London and New York, 1937.

Power: A New Social Analysis. London and New York, 1938.

An Inquiry into Meaning and Truth. London and New York, 1940.

Let the People Think (essays). London, 1941.

A History of Western Philosophy: Its Connection with Political and Social Circumstances from the Earliest Times to the Present Day. London and New York, 1945 (2nd edition, 1961).

Human Knowledge: Its Scope and Limits. London and New York, 1948.

Authority and the Individual. London and New York, 1949.

Unpopular Essays (largely reprints). London and New York, 1950.

The Impact of Science on Society (lectures). New York, 1951.

New Hopes for a Changing World. London, 1951.

Human Society in Ethics and Politics. London and New York, 1954.

Logic and Knowledge: Essays, 1901–1950, edited by R. C. Marsh. London and New York, 1956. (This volume includes Russell's 1918 lectures on the philosophy of logical atomism, also the article on logical atomism written for *Contemporary British Philosophy*, First Series, 1924.)

Why I am not a Christian, and Other Essays. London and New York, 1957.

My Philosophical Development. London and New York, 1959.

Wisdom of the West. London, 1959.

Has Man a Future? Penguin Books, 1961.

Fact and Fiction. London, 1961.

Studies

Clark, C. H. D. *Christianity and Bertrand Russell.* London, 1958.

Dorward, A. *Bertrand Russell.* London, 1951. (A booklet written for the British Council and the National Book League.)

Feibleman, J. K. *Inside the Great Mirror. A Critical Examination of the Philosophy of Russell, Wittgenstein and their Followers.* The Hague, 1958.

Fritz, C. A. *Bertrand Russell's Construction of the External World.* New York and London, 1952.

Götlind, E. *Bertrand Russell's Theories of Causation.* Upsala, 1952.

Jourdain, P. E. B. *The Philosophy of Mr. Bertrand Russell* (satire). London and Chicago, 1918.

Leggett, H. W. *Bertrand Russell* (pictorial biography). London, 1949.

Lovejoy, A. O. *The Revolt Against Dualism.* Chicago, 1930. (Chapters 6–7 treat of Russell's theory of mind.)

McCarthy, D. G. *Bertrand Russell's Informal Freedom.* Louvain, 1960 (doctorate dissertation).

Riveroso, E. *Il pensiero di Bertrand Russell.* Naples, 1958.

Santayana, G. *Winds of Doctrine.* London, 1913. (Includes a study of Russell's philosophy.)

Schilpp, P. A. (editor). *The Philosophy of Bertrand Russell.* New York, 1946 (2nd edition).

Urmson, J. O. *Philosophical Analysis. Its Development between the Two World Wars.* Oxford, 1956. (Includes a critical discussion of Russell's reductive analysis. Russell's reply, together with replies to criticisms by G. J. Warnock and P. F. Strawson, is reprinted in chapter 18 of *My Philosophical Development.*)

Wood, A. *Bertrand Russell, The Passionate Sceptic* (biographical). London, 1957.

Russell's Philosophy: A Study of Its Development (an unfinished essay printed at the end of Russell's *My Philosophical Development*).

Wood, H. G. *Why Mr. Bertrand Russell is not a Christian.* London, 1928.

There are, of course, many articles on particular points or aspects of Russell's thought in *Mind, Analysis, The Proceedings of the Aristotelian Society, The Philosophical Review,* and other periodicals. But they cannot possibly be listed here.

NOTES

CHAPTER ELEVEN

1 Johnson's philosophical correspondence with Berkeley can be found in the second volume of the critical edition of the bishop's *Works* edited by Professor T. E. Jessop.

2 Obviously if by prevailing inclination or strongest motive we mean the motive which actually 'prevails', it *would* be absurd to claim that we can resist it. But then the statement that we always follow it becomes tautological.

3 Benjamin Franklin, it may be noted, emphasized the virtues and values which proved to be of advantage in the frontier societies.

4 Part I, 1791; Part II, 1792. Paine was also the author of the *Age of Reason*, the two parts of which appeared respectively in 1794 and 1796.

5 In using the distinction in this way Henry was not simply following Cousin. For Cousin insisted that the existence of God is known by inductive reasoning from the existence of finite substances, though he tried to combine this thesis with an idea of God inspired by German metaphysical idealism, an idea which led to accusations of pantheism by clerical critics. Henry was interested chiefly in the redemptive power of Christianity in history, and while accepting Cousin's idea of reason, he transposed it into the setting of Christian theology.

6 *Complete Works*, II, p. 279 (London, 1866). References are given according to volume and page of this edition.

7 *Ibid.*, II, p. 280.

8 *Ibid.*, II, pp. 280–1.

9 *Ibid.*, I, p. 112.

10 *Ibid.*, II, p. 167.

11 *Ibid.*, I, p. 117.

12 *Ibid.*

13 *Ibid.*

14 *Ibid.*, I, p. 59.

15 *Ibid.*, I, p. 35.

16 *Ibid.*, I, p. 20.

17 *Ibid.*, I, p. 244.

18 *Ibid.*, I, p. 24.

19 *Ibid.*

CHAPTER TWELVE

1 The exaltation of the State, which is even described as 'divine', reappears in Royce's essay, *California: A Study of American Character* (1886).

2 *The Religious Aspect of Philosophy*, p. 433.

3 In *The Spirit of Modern Philosophy* (1892), Royce speaks of the one infinite Self of which all finite selves are moments or organic parts.

4 The sub-title of *The Conception of God* is *A Philosophical Discussion Concerning the Nature of the Divine Idea as a Demonstrable Reality*. Howison, the personal idealist, was one of the participants in the original discussion of 1895.

5 *The World and the Individual*, I, p. 12 (1920 edition).

This work will be referred to simply as *The World*.

6 *Ibid.*, I, p. 12.

7 *Ibid.*, I, pp. 16–17.

8 *Ibid.*, I, p. 19.

9 *Ibid.*, I, p. 25.

10 It is certainly not the intention of the present writer to suggest that the artist or poet necessarily first forms a clear idea of the work to be done and then gives concrete embodiment to this idea. If, for example, the poet had a clear idea of the poem, the poem would already have been composed. And all that remained would be to write down a poem already existing in the poet's mind. At the same time the poet would not start working without some sort of conceived purpose, some sort of 'idea' which could reasonably be regarded as the beginning of a total action.

11 *Ibid.*, I, p. 36.

12 *Ibid.*, I, p. 36.

13 *Ibid.*, I, p. 32.

14 *Ibid.*

15 *Ibid.*, I, p. 93.

16 The argument might perhaps be summed up in this way. If things are completely independent of ideas, ideas are completely independent of things. And in this case truth, considered as a relation between idea and things, is unattainable.

17 *Ibid.*, I, pp. 226–7.

18 *Ibid.*, I, p. 260.

19 *Ibid.*, I, p. 348. For example, 'my world' is the embodiment of my will, the fulfilment of my purpose, the expression of my interests. And it is thus unique. But, as is explained in the following paragraphs, we cannot remain simply with the concept of 'my world'.

20 We must remember that for Royce 'internal meaning' is primary.

21 *The World*, I, p. 355.

22 *Ibid.*, II, pp. 170–1.

23 *Ibid.*, II, p. 172.

24 *Ibid.*, II, p. 170.

25 *Ibid.*, II, p. 264. Royce expresses his general agreement with the theory of the origins of self-consciousness given in the second volume of *Mental Development in the Child and the Race* (1896), by James Mark Baldwin (1861–1934), of Princeton University.

26 *Ibid.*, II, p. 177.

27 *Ibid.*, I, p. 397.

28 *Ibid.*, I, p. 396.

29 That is to say, if we are looking for a metaphysical concept of the self rather than for an empirical account of, say, the origins and development of self-consciousness.

30 *Ibid.*, II, p. 276.

31 Needless to say, for the atheist existentialist, such as Sartre, the idea of a God-given vocation is devoid of validity.

32 Here again one is put in mind of modern existentialism.

33 *Ibid.*, I, p. 469.

34 *Ibid.*, II, p. 293.

35 *Ibid.*, II, p. 347.

36 *Ibid.*, II, p. 351.

37 *Ibid.*, II, p. 359.

38 *Ibid.*, II, p. 360.

39 'By the Ought you mean, at any temporal instant, a rule that, if followed, would guide you so to express, at that instant, your will, that you should be thereby made nearer to union with the divine, nearer to a consciousness of the oneness of your will and the Absolute Will, than you would if you acted counter to this Ought', *The World*, II,

pp. 347–8. Here the emphasis is placed on 'the instant', not on the universal.

40 In 1908 Royce published *The Philosophy of Loyalty* and in 1916 *The Hope of the Great Community*.

41 *The Problem of Christianity*, 1, p. 68.

42 Cf. *War and Insurance* (1914), and *The Hope of the Great Community* (1916).

43 *The World*, 1, pp. 444–5.

44 *The Conception of Immortality*, p. 80.

45 *The World*, 1, p. 475.

46 Royce's interest in mathematical logic found expression in *The Relation of the Principles of Logic to the Foundation of Geometry* (1905).

47 *The World*, 1, p. 507.

48 *Ibid.*, 1, p. 515.

49 *Ibid.*, 1, p. 513.

50 *Ibid.*, 11, p. 143.

51 *Ibid.*, 11, p. 331.

52 The term 'universal' is used here, needless to say, in the sense of the concrete universal.

53 *Ibid.*, 1, p. 588.

54 Cf., the Appendix to *The Moral Philosophy of Josiah Royce* by Peter Fuss (Cambridge, Mass., 1965).

CHAPTER THIRTEEN

1 Le Conte's writings include *Religion and Science* (1874), and *Evolution: Its Nature, Its Evidence and Its Relation to Religious Thought* (1888).

2 See Vol. VII, Pt. II, of this *History*, p. 150. For Lotze, to recognize the fact of the unity of consciousness is *eo ipso* to recognize the existence of the soul. He thus tries to avoid phenomenalism on the one hand and postulating an occult soul-substance on the other. For Bowne, the self is an immediate datum of consciousness, not a hidden entity which has to be inferred from the existence of faculties and their acts.

3 *The Immanence of God*, p. 19.

4 *Ibid.*, p. 18.

5 *Ibid.*, p. 32.

6 Obviously, what really needs to be shown is that metaphysical explanation is required at all. That empirical science cannot provide it is clear enough.

7 Jack Gould Schurman (1854–1942), who became President of Cornell University in 1892, the same year in which he founded *The Philosophical Review*, believed that American culture was destined to prove the great mediator between East and West, and that idealism was peculiarly suited both to America and to the fulfilment of this task. Just as Kant mediated between rationalism and empiricism, so can speculative idealism mediate between the sciences and the arts. It has a synthesizing function in cultural life.

8 Though not a prolific writer, Creighton's influence as a teacher was considerable. And he and his colleagues at Cornell were responsible for the philosophical education of a good many future American professors.

9 Another representative of this form of idealism at Michigan was the author of *Dynamic Idealism* (1898), Alfred Henry Lloyd.

10 See Vol. VII, Pt. II, of this *History*, pp. 160–1.

[11] For Morris philosophy is as much a science as other sciences.

[12] That is to say, if we regard the object of knowledge as phenomena, in the sense of appearances of what does not itself appear, we are led inevitably to postulate unknowable things-in-themselves.

[13] Among Flewelling's publications are *Personalism and The Problems of Philosophy* (1915), *The Reason in Faith* (1924), *Creative Personality* (1925) and *Personalism in Theology* (1943).

[14] Knudson is the author of *The Philosophy of Personalism* (1927), *The Doctrine of God* (1930), and *The Validity of Religious Experience* (1937).

[15] Brightman published among other writings, *Religious Values* (1925), *A Philosophy of Ideals* (1928), *The Problem of God* (1930), *Is God a Person?* (1932), *Moral Laws* (1933), *Personality and Religion* (1934), *A Philosophy of Religion* (1940), and *The Spiritual Life* (1942).

[16] Brightman argues, for instance, that the 'waste' involved in the process of evolution suggests the idea of a finite God who meets with opposition. Again, the divine reason sets limits to the divine will and power. Further, there is in God a 'given' element which he progressively masters. But where this 'given' element comes from is left obscure.

[17] Author of *Time and Reality* (1904), *Truth and Reality* (1911), *A Realistic Universe* (1916), *Cosmic Evolution* (1925), *God and Creation* (2 volumes, 1934), and *Religion of Tomorrow* (1943).

[18] In distinguishing between 'lower' and 'higher' judgments of value obviously play an important part.

[19] It would, however, be a mistake to suppose that all philosophers who believe in creative evolution have postulated a fixed, preconceived goal or *telos* of the evolutionary process. Indeed, unless the creative agent is conceived in a recognizably theistic manner, such a postulate is inappropriate.

[20] *God and Creation*, II, p. 34. According to Boodin, God, as conceived according to his intrinsic essence, is eternal; but from another point of view, namely when he is considered as the creative activity comprising the whole history of the cosmos, he is temporal.

[21] The personal idealist is not, of course, committed to denying the hypothesis of evolution. But he takes the idea of personality as his point of departure and as the fixed point, as one might put it, in his reflections, whereas the evolutionary idealist emphasizes the aspect of the person as a product of a general creative activity immanent in the whole cosmos.

[22] Hocking's writings include *The Meaning of God in Human Experience* (1912), *Human Nature and Its Remaking* (1918), *Man and the State* (1926), *The Self, Its Body and Freedom* (1928), *Lasting Elements of Individualism* (1937), *Thoughts on Life and Death* (1937), *Living Religions and a World Faith* (1940), *Science and the Idea of*

God (1944) and *Experiment in Education* (1954).

23 *The Meaning of God in Human Experience*, p. 314.

24 *Types of Philosophy*, p. 441.

25 *Human Nature and Its Remaking*, p. 329.

26 The line of thought of Royce and Hocking is sometimes described as absolutistic personalism in distinction from the pluralistic personalism of Bowne and other 'personal idealists'.

27 Blanshard studied at Oxford, and he is regarded as carrying on the tradition of Oxford idealism.

28 The second volume has not appeared at the time of writing.

29 Urban is the author of, among other writings, *Valuation: Its Nature and Laws* (1909), *The Intelligible World: Metaphysics and Value* (1929), *Language and Reality* (1939) and *Beyond Realism and Idealism* (1949). In the present context the relevant work is the last-named one.

CHAPTER FOURTEEN

1 See, for example, *Chauncey Wright and the Foundations of Pragmatism* by E. H. Madden (Seattle, 1963).

2 In 1868 Peirce published some articles in *The Journal of Speculative Philosophy* on certain alleged faculties of the human mind, such as that of recognizing intuitively, without the need of any previous knowledge, the premisses which constitute the absolute points of departure for reasoning.

3 The fact that in 1883 Peirce divorced his first wife and subsequently remarried probably contributed to the termination of his appointment at Johns Hopkins. But there appear to have been other factors too, such as the offence which he sometimes gave by intemperate expressions of moral indignation and his lack of conformity on some points with the requirements of academic life.

4 Peirce refers in this context to the Scholastic maxim that every being is one, true and good.

5 5.569. References are given in the customary way to volume and numbered paragraph of the *Collected Papers of Charles Sanders Peirce*.

6 2.327.

7 5.567.

8 *Ibid*.

9 The question whether it concerns a realm of possibility, as contrasted with actuality, is a question for the metaphysician.

10 Peirce remarks that an entirely meaningless proposition is to be classed with true propositions, because it cannot be refuted. But he adds the saving provision, 'if it be called a proposition at all' (2.327).

11 When asked whether his principle of fallibilism, as it is called, the assertion that all assertions are uncertain, is itself fallible or infallible, uncertain or certain, Peirce answers that he does not intend to claim that his assertion is absolutely certain. This may be logical, but it involves a certain weakening of his position.

12 5.211.

13 5.153.

14 5.506.

15 5.565.

16 6.498.

17 1.55.

18 5.13, note.

19 Under the general heading of speculative grammar Peirce also considers terms, propositions and the fundamental principles of logic, those of identity, non-contradiction and excluded middle.

20 2.93.

21 5.175.

22 Strictly speaking, the theory of ideas belongs to epistemology. But Peirce insists that it is grounded on the logic of relations. And he emphasizes the relevance of the theory to pragmatism.

23 As in human experience acting involves an act of the will, Peirce tends to speak of this type of idea as the idea of a volition. In any case he insists that an idea of a 'secondness' cannot be simply reduced to ideas of 'firstness'. If, for example, we try to reduce the idea of the wind moving the blind to ·simpler ideas of sense-data, taken separately, the whole idea of acting disappears.

24 In theory at least Peirce distinguishes between 'idea' and 'concept', a universal idea being subjectively apprehended in an intellectual concept.

25 5.9.

26 Peirce's realism was not derived from Scotus, but it was to a great extent developed through reflection on and a transformation of the doctrine of the mediaeval Franciscan, or of what Peirce believed to be his doctrine. Indeed, on occasion Peirce even called himself a 'Scotistic realist'. On this subject see *Charles Peirce and Scholastic Realism: A Study of Peirce's Relation to John Duns Scotus*, by John F. Boler (Seattle, 1963).

27 The 'essence' of whiteness is embodied in an idea through the power of attention, which is said to 'abstract' it.

28 What Peirce calls 'realism' is not what everyone would understand by the term. But we are concerned here with his use of the word.

29 P. 67.

30 Obviously, when a prediction is fulfilled, the result may be directly observable. But Peirce's point is that a scientific hypothesis states what *would* be the case *if* a condition were fulfilled, and that a 'would be' is not, *as such*, directly observable.

31 5.398.

32 The term 'Protestant' in this context is ambiguous. For there is no one belief about the Eucharist which can be called *the* Protestant belief. But Peirce obviously has in mind those who deny the real presence of Christ in the Sacrament, and, more particularly, those who deny a change which justifies the statement that the consecrated bread and wine *are* the Body and Blood of Christ.

33 5.401.

34 *Ibid.*

35 2.198.

36 *Ibid.*

37 *Ibid.*

38 4.243.

39 5.433.

40 4.540.

41 2.654.

42 2.198.

43 5.35.

44 *Ibid.*

45 2.151.

46 The upholder of the emotive theory of ethics would claim that this analysis fails to do justice to the peculiar character of moral utterances. But to say this is, of course, to recognize the difference between Peirce's theory of ethics and the emotive theory.

47 5.423.

48 *Ibid.*

49 *Ibid.* Elsewhere (6.3) Peirce says that the chief cause of the backwardness of metaphysics is that it has been so often in the hands of theologians, who have an axe to grind.

50 1.487.

51 6.2.

52 5.21.

53 5.66.

54 1.303.

55 *Ibid.*

56 6.32.

57 4.457.

58 1.482.

59 According to Peirce laws of fact can be divided into logically necessary and logically contingent laws, while logically contingent laws can be subdivided into metaphysically necessary and metaphysically contingent laws (1.483).

60 Cf. 4.319.

61 6.201.

62 Cf. 1.409.

63 The actual world, it will be remembered, is for Peirce part of the wider sphere of real possibility. It consists of actualized possibilities and of possibilities in the process of actualization.

64 1.409.

65 1.447.

66 *Ibid.*

67 'Tychism' or 'chance-ism', coined by Peirce from the Greek word *tyche*.

68 6.33.

69 1.204.

70 1.172.

71 6.158.

72 6.102. Tychism is mentioned because Peirce connects mind with firstness, and so, rather surprisingly, with chance, while matter is connected with secondness, and with agapism, and evolution with thirdness, synechism (6.32).

73 6.25.

74 Peirce believed that God's existence is from one point of view evident enough. 'Where would such an idea, say as that of God, come from if not from direct experience?' (6.493).

75 6.483.

76 6.157.

77 6.489–490.

78 6.502.

79 6.503.

80 1.453.

81 *Ibid.*

82 One can compare Peirce's different ways of alluding to Hegelianism with the different ways in which he speaks of metaphysics. Needless to say, the different statements must in both cases be interpreted in the light of their immediate contexts.

83 1.524.

84 *Ibid.*

85 1.362.

86 *Ibid.* The 'third' would be every state of the universe at an assignable point of time, mediating between God as First and God as Second.

CHAPTER FIFTEEN

1 Henry James, junior, the

novelist, was a younger brother of William.

2 The copyright date is 1896, but the volume appeared in 1897.

3 This work represents Gifford Lectures given at Edinburgh in 1901–2.

4 This work represents the Hibbert Lectures given at Oxford in 1908–9.

5 *The Will to Believe*, p. vii (1903 edition).

6 We shall mention presently another sense of the word 'monism'.

7 *Some Problems of Philosophy*, p. 35.

8 *The Meaning of Truth*, p. xii.

9 *Essays in Radical Empiricism*, p. 107.

10 *Treatise of Human Nature*, Appendix, p. 636 (Selby-Bigge edition).

11 *Essays in Radical Empiricism*, p. 117.

12 *Ibid.*, p. 93.

13 *Ibid.*, p. 94.

14 *Ibid.*

15 *A Pluralistic Universe*, p. 314.

16 *Pragmatism*, p. 51.

17 *Ibid.*, p. 45.

18 *The Will to Believe*, p. 124.

19 *Pragmatism*, p. 47.

20 *The Will to Believe*, p. 124, note 1.

21 *Collected Essays and Reviews*, p. 410.

22 *Pragmatism*, p. 47.

23 *The Meaning of Truth*, p. v.

24 *Ibid.*, p. 196.

25 *Ibid.*, p. 202.

26 *Pragmatism*, p. 201.

27 *Ibid.*, p. 206.

28 *Ibid.*, p. 207.

29 *The Meaning of Truth*, p. 205.

30 *Pragmatism*, pp. 216–17.

31 *Ibid.*, p. 217.

32 *The Will to Believe*, p. 11.

33 *Ibid.*, p. 3.

34 One might, however, object against James's thesis that if a question is in principle unanswerable on intellectual grounds, it cannot, on the pragmatist analysis of meaning, be a meaningful question, and that in this case the issue of belief or unbelief does not arise.

35 *The Meaning of Truth*, p. 221.

36 For James such propositions are truths *in posse*, which are made (actually) true by successful application, by their 'working'. But this implies that they are empirical hypotheses, a view which is not favoured by most modern logicians.

37 *Pragmatism*, p. 198.

38 *Ibid.*, p. ix.

39 *The Meaning of Truth*, p. xii.

40 *Ibid.*, p. xiv.

41 *Pragmatism*, p. 54.

42 *Essays in Radical Empiricism*, p. 253.

43 *Ibid.*, p. 255.

44 *The Meaning of Truth*, p. 124.

45 *Ibid.*, p. 85.

46 See, for example, *The Meaning of Truth*, p. 90.

47 *Pragmatism*, p. 259.

48 *Ibid.*, p. 262.

49 James relates rival theories of the universe to different types of temperament.

50 *The Meaning of Truth*, p. 125.

51 James's talk about cash-value is apt to create an unfor-

tunate impression. But he is referring, of course, to analyzing ideas on beliefs in terms of their 'practical consequences'.

[52] *Pragmatism*, p. 92.

[53] *Ibid.*, p. 99.

[54] James quotes a well-known passage from A. J. Balfour's *The Foundations of Belief* (p. 30).

[55] *Pragmatism*, p. 106.

[56] *Ibid.*, p. 109.

[57] *A Pluralistic Universe*, p. 307.

[58] *Ibid.*

[59] *Ibid.*, p. 311.

[60] James applied the pragmatist method to the issue between the theories of free will and determinism, as also to that between pluralism and monism.

[61] *Pragmatism*, p. 47.

[62] Vol. VII, p. 139.

[63] *Ibid.*, pp. 139–40.

[64] *Ibid.*, pp. 182–4.

[65] *Ibid.*, pp. 148–9. James refers frequently to Fechner in his writings.

[66] It is worth mentioning that Maurice Blondel once used the term *pragmatism* for his philosophy of action. But when he became acquainted with American pragmatism, he dropped the term, as he did not agree with the interpretation given to it by William James.

[67] Strictly speaking, Bradley did not hold that personality is an 'unreal appearance' of the Absolute. It is a real appearance; but, being appearance, it cannot be fully real.

[68] *Personal Idealism*, p. vi.

[69] A second edition, with the authors' name, appeared in 1894 and a new edition in 1910.

[70] *Humanism*, p. xiii (2nd edition, 1912). Schiller's reference is to an essay, *Reality and Idealism*, which he published in 1892. It is reprinted in *Humanism*, pp. 110–27.

[71] *Ibid.*, p. xxv.

[72] *Contemporary British Philosophy*, First Series, p. 401.

[73] See *Axioms as Postulates* in *Personal Idealism*, p. 64.

[74] *Formal Logic*, p. 382.

[75] *Ibid.*, p. ix.

[76] *Axioms as Postulates* in *Personal Idealism*, p. 124.

[77] *Humanism*, p. 59.

[78] *Ibid.*, p. 58.

[79] *Contemporary British Philosophy*, First Series, p. 405.

[80] *Ibid.*, p. 406.

[81] *Humanism*, p. 59.

[82] See especially *Logic in Use*, also *Problems of Belief*, chapters XI–XII.

[83] *Contemporary British Philosophy*, First Series, p. 406.

[84] *Axioms as Postulates* in *Personal Idealism*, p. 61.

[85] *Contemporary British Philosophy*, First Series, p. 409.

CHAPTER SIXTEEN

[1] The article was published in the issue of April, 1882.

[2] In this connection Dewey notes the influence exercised on his mind by William James's *Principles of Psychology*.

[3] An experimental school, commonly known as The Dewey School.

[4] During this period Dewey made several journeys abroad, to Europe, the Far East, Mexico and, in 1928, to Russia.

[5] Written in collaboration with J. H. Tufts.

[6] *The Quest for Certainty*, p. 225.

7 Ibid.

8 Logic, I, p. 42.

9 Ibid., p. 42.

10 The Quest for Certainty, p. 3.

11 Ibid., p. 166.

12 Logic, p. 49.

13 Ibid., p. 43.

14 Experience and Nature, p. 8 (Dover Publications edition 1958).

15 Dewey remarks, for example, that 'I should think it fairly obvious that we experience most things as temporally prior to our experiencing of them', The Influence of Darwin, p. 240.

16 Experience and Nature, p. 381.

17 The Quest for Certainty, p. 23.

18 Experience and Nature, p. 42.

19 Dewey is, of course, aware of the practical aspects of the thought of Plato and Aristotle. But he is opposed to the whole idea of a sphere of immutable Being and Truth, and the dichotomy between the sphere of Being and the sphere of Becoming is the aspect of Plato's philosophy which he emphasizes.

20 The Quest for Certainty, p. 103.

21 Ibid., p. 41.

22 Ibid., p. 42.

23 Ibid.

24 Ibid., p. 299.

25 Reconstruction in Philosophy, p. 26.

26 Ibid., p. 188.

27 Ibid., p. 188.

28 Ibid., p. 193.

29 The Quest for Certainty, p. 273.

30 Ibid.

31 Creative Intelligence, p. 55.

32 The Quest for Certainty, p. 255.

33 Logic, pp. 104–5. Bertrand Russell objects that this definition would apply to the activity of a drill sergeant in transforming a collection of new recruits into a regiment, though this activity could hardly be described as a process of inquiry. Cf. The Philosophy of John Dewey, edited by P. A. Schilpp, p. 143.

34 Ibid., p. 94.

35 Ibid.

36 Ibid.

37 Ibid., p. 98.

38 Reconstruction in Philosophy, p. 138.

39 Logic, p. 283.

40 Ibid., p. 264.

41 Studies in Logical Theory, p. 3. Dewey often depicts the term of inquiry as an enrichment and deepening of experience.

42 Twentieth Century Philosophy, edited by D. D. Runes, pp. 463–4 (New York, 1943).

43 Logic, p. 345, note 6.

44 Reconstruction in Philosophy, p. 156.

45 Ibid., p. 157.

46 Ibid., p. 160.

47 Cf., for example, Outlines of a Critical Theory of Ethics, p. 3.

48 Human Nature and Conduct, p. 30.

49 Ibid., p. 32.

50 Ibid., p. 25.

51 Ibid., p. 38.

52 Ibid., p. 319.

53 Ibid., p. 58.

54 Ibid., p. 75.

55 Ibid., p. 126.

56 Ibid., p. 170.

57 Ibid., p. 225.

58 Reconstruction in Philosophy, p. 177.

59 *Ibid.*, p. 184.

60 *Democracy and Education*, p. 61.

61 *Human Nature and Conduct*, p. 210.

62 Cf. *The Quest for Certainty*, p. 260.

63 *Ibid.*, p. 260.

64 'A judgment about what is *to be* desired and enjoyed is therefore a claim on future action; it possesses *de jure* and not merely *de facto* quality', *Ibid.*, p. 263.

65 *Ibid.*, p. 265.

66 *Theory of Valuation*, p. 17.

67 *Ibid.*, p. 22.

68 *Human Nature and Conduct*, p. 317.

69 *Reconstruction in Philosophy*, p. 186.

70 *Problems of Men*, p. 59.

71 *The Public and Its Problems*, p. 166. It is in this work that Dewey's most detailed discussion of the State is to be found.

72 *Reconstruction in Philosophy*, p. 183.

73 *Ibid.*, pp. 184–5.

74 This point of view is expanded in, for example, *My Pedagogic Creed*.

75 *Democracy and Education*, p. 59.

76 *Human Nature and Conduct*, p. 331.

77 *Ibid.*, p. 264.

78 Cf. *The Quest for Certainty*, pp. 288–91.

79 *A Common Faith*, p. 33.

80 *Ibid.*, pp. 50–1.

81 *Ibid.*, p. 19.

82 *Experience and Nature*, pp. 414–15. The reference to an infinite self-representative series is to the doctrine of Royce.

83 Dewey himself deals, for example, with the category of causality.

84 There is, of course, a big difference between the attitudes of Hegel and Dewey. For Dewey is concerned with the active transformation of a situation, and not simply with the dialectical overcoming of a contradiction. But both men assume that contradiction *is* something to be overcome.

CHAPTER SEVENTEEN

1 It must be noted, however, that though for Case independent physical things are knowable, their existence and nature is known mediately, being inferred from sense-data, which are caused modifications of the nervous system.

2 It is significant that Case was the author of the article on Aristotle in the eleventh edition of the *Encyclopædia Britannica*.

3 *Statement and Inference*, I, p. 87.

4 According to G. E. Moore, *esse est percipi* is the basic tenet of idealism. But he understands the thesis in a wide sense.

5 *Statement and Inference*, II, p. 777. Cook Wilson prefers the example of heat to that of colour. For people who are innocent of theory are accustomed to speak of themselves as 'feeling hot', whereas nobody speaks of 'feeling coloured'. To see the relation between colour and the subject, a greater degree of reflection is required.

6 *Ibid.*, II, p. 567.

7 *Kant's Theory of Knowledge* (1909), p. 118.

[8] *Kant's Theory of Knowledge*, p. 124.

[9] *Ibid.*, p. 86.

[10] According to Prichard, we could judge or infer that the direct objects of perception are physical bodies which are entirely independent of the perceiving subject, if we could be said to 'know' the former. But perception, for Prichard, is never knowledge.

[11] *Essays in Ancient and Modern Philosophy*, p. 231.

[12] *Ibid.*

[13] This book, published in 1932, shows the influence of Cambridge thinkers, such as Moore and Russell, whereas Cook Wilson had shown little respect for Cambridge thought.

[14] Reprinted in *Moral Obligation: Essays and Lectures* (1949).

[15] This does not mean that we cannot say what things possess this quality or have intrinsic value. Moore was convinced that we can.

[16] See, for example, *Ethics Since 1900* by M. Warnock (London, 1960).

[17] Professor Stuart Hampshire's *Thought and Action* (London, 1959) is an example of this tendency.

[18] This programme was reprinted as an Appendix in *The New Realism*.

[19] *The New Realism*, p. 24. As far as care for language and breaking up vague and complex problems into manageable and quite definite questions were concerned, the new realists' idea of proper philosophical procedure was similar to that of G. E. Moore in England.

[20] *Ibid.*, p. 477.

[21] *Ibid.*, p. 478.

[22] *Ibid.*, p. 358.

[23] *Ibid.*, p. 366. The unreal object must be distinguished from the unthinkable, such as a round square.

[24] *Ibid.*, p. 360.

[25] *Ibid.*, p. 366.

[26] *Ibid.*

[27] *Ibid.*, p. 367.

[28] *Ibid.*, p. 372.

[29] *Ibid.*, p. 482.

[30] *Ways of Knowing* (1925), p. 396.

[31] *The New Realism*, p. 475.

[32] In an essay on the development of American realism Montague attributes to the critical realists in general the doctrine that we know directly only 'mental states or ideas'. Cf. *Twentieth Century Philosophy* (1943). Edited by D. D. Runes, p. 441.

[33] He published his *General Theory of Value* in 1926.

[34] Santayana's *Realms of Being* comprises four volumes: *The Realm of Essence* (1927), *The Realm of Matter* (1930), *The Realm of Truth* (1938), and *The Realm of Spirit* (1940).

[35] According to Strong, introspection is the one case in which we are directly aware of 'stuff' as distinct from structure. But neither Strong nor Drake meant to imply that stones, for instance, are conscious. Their panpsychism was linked with the idea of emergent evolution. Even those things which we call 'material' possess a potential energy which at a certain level of evolution manifests itself in consciousness.

[36] As in *The Philosophy of Physical Realism* (1932).

37 Lovejoy published, for instance, *The Great Chain of Being* in 1936 and *Essays in the History of Ideas* in 1948.

38 Bradley was interested in psychology. But it is notorious that for many years psychology was frowned on at Oxford and regarded as not qualifying for recognition as a science.

39 The best known of Alexander's articles illustrating his realist theory of knowledge is 'The Basis of Realism', which appeared in the *Proceedings of the British Academy* for 1914.

40 In other words, the mind does not create the materials of an illusion but derives them from sensible experience. But it can be said to constitute the illusion *as* an illusion by an erroneous judgment in regard to context.

41 *Space, Time and Deity,* 1, p. 2.

42 *Ibid.,* 1, p. 4.

43 *Ibid.,* 1, p. 4.

44 *Ibid.,* 1, p. 38.

45 *Ibid.,* 1, p. 60.

46 *Ibid.,* 1, p. 66.

47 *Ibid.,* 11, p. 237.

48 *Ibid.,* 11, p. 238.

49 *Ibid.*

50 *Ibid.,* 11, p. 240.

51 *Ibid.,* 11, p. 309.

52 *Ibid.,* 11, p. 345.

53 *Ibid.*

54 *Ibid.,* 11, p. 353.

55 *Ibid.,* 11, p. 365.

56 *Ibid.,* 11, p. 429.

57 In Mr. G. J. Warnock's excellent little book, *English Philosophy Since 1900,* Alexander is passed over in silence.

58 The increase not only in tolerance of but also in sympathy with 'descriptive metaphysics' has, of course, contributed to this revival of interest in Whitehead.

59 *Process and Reality,* p. vii (1959 edition).

60 *Ibid.,* p. viii.

61 *Ibid.,* p. 4.

62 *Ibid.,* p. 17.

63 *Ibid.,* p. 529.

64 'Creativity', as described by Whitehead, is not an actual entity, like God, but 'the universal of univerals' (*Process and Reality,* p. 31).

CHAPTER EIGHTEEN

1 In other words, Moore approves of Bradley's protest against the psychologizing of logic.

2 *Mind,* Vol. 8 (1899), p. 180.

3 *Ibid.*

4 *Ibid.,* p. 182.

5 *Ibid.,* Vol. 8, p. 182.

6 *Ibid.,* p. 183.

7 *Ibid.,* p. 179.

8 *Ibid.*

9 In Baldwin's *Dictionary of Philosophy and Psychology.*

10 Article 'Relative' in Baldwin's *Dictionary of Philosophy and Psychology.*

11 *Mind,* Vol. 12 (1903), reprinted in *Philosophical Studies.*

12 *Philosophical Studies,* p. 7.

13 *Ibid.,* p. 17.

14 *Ibid.,* p. 25.

15 *Ibid.,* p. 27.

16 *Ibid.,* p. 30.

17 *Contemporary British Philosophy,* Second Series, edited by J. H. Muirhead (1925) and reprinted in *Philosophical Papers* (1959).

18 *Principia Ethica,* p. 2, s.2 (1959 reprint). In reference to this work the letter 's' signifies the section.

19 *Principia Ethica*, p. 6, s.6.

20 *Ibid.*, p. 9, s.10.

21 *Ibid.*, p. 10, s.10.

22 *Ibid.*, p. 59, s.36.

23 *Ibid.*, p. 41, s.27.

24 *Ibid.*, p. 41, s.26.

25 *Ibid.*, p. 41, s.26.

26 In 'A Reply to my Critics' contained in *The Philosophy of G. E. Moore*, edited by P. A. Schilpp, p. 582 (New York, 1952, 2nd edition).

27 In *Principia Ethica* Moore laid most stress on the values of personal affection and aesthetic enjoyment, that is, the appreciation of the beautiful in art and Nature. And this attitude exercised a considerable influence at the time on what was known as the Bloomsbury Circle.

28 *Ibid.*, p. 148, s.89.

29 *The Philosophy of G. E. Moore*, edited by P. A. Schilpp, pp. 546–7.

30 *Ibid.*, p. 554.

31 It is not, of course, my intention to suggest that Moore's ethics must pass into the emotive theory. What I suggest is simply that it is understandable if to some minds the emotive theory appears more intelligible and tenable. But this theory in its original form was very soon seen to constitute a gross oversimplification of complex issues. And subsequent ethical discussion became much more sophisticated and also, in a real sense, more ecumenical.

32 In a well-known essay on 'Moore and Ordinary Language' (*The Philosophy of G. E. Moore*, edited by P. A. Schilpp, Chapter 13), Professor N. Malcolm maintained that Moore's way of proving the denials of common sense propositions to be false was to appeal to ordinary language. Moore himself (*ibid.*, pp. 668–9) admitted that he considered the sort of argument referred to by Malcolm as a good argument, and that he himself had said that this sort of argument amounted to a disproof of the proposition 'there are no material things'. He added, however, that in the case of such a proposition as 'we do not know for certain that there are material things', something more is required if the proposition is to be proved to be false. For in point of fact many more philosophers have held that we do not *know* that there are material things than have held that there are actually no material things.

33 I say 'normally at any rate', because if a man was convinced that all statements made by a certain authority were necessarily true, he might wish to claim that he knew that any such statement was true, even if he was not at all sure of what it meant.

34 *Proceedings of the British Academy*, Vol. 25, 1939.

35 *Philosophical Papers*, p. 53.

36 *Philosophical Studies*, p. 68.

37 These lectures form the text of *Some Main Problems of Philosophy*, which will be referred to in notes as *Main Problems*.

38 *Philosophical Studies*, p. 171.

39 *Philosophical Papers*, p. 54.

40 *The Philosophy of G. E. Moore*, edited by P. A. Schilpp, p. 658.

41 *Philosophical Papers*, p. 45.
42 *Ibid.*, p. 226.
43 *Ibid.*
44 *Main Problems*, p. 29.
45 *Ibid.*
46 We have only to think, for example, of the late J. L. Austin's attack on the theory.
47 *A Hundred Years of British Philosophy*, p. 547 (London, 1938).

CHAPTER NINETEEN

1 In *Contemporary British Philosophy*, First Series, edited by J. H. Muirhead, p. 79.
2 In 1937 Russell published, together with Patricia Russell, *The Amberley Papers* in two volumes, containing the letters and diaries of his parents.
3 Bertrand Russell succeeded to the earldom in 1931.
4 Russell abandoned belief in God at the age of eighteen. But he continued to believe for some years that metaphysics could provide a theoretical justification of emotive attitudes of awe and reverence towards the universe.
5 Whether Russell ever had a profound knowledge of Hegel's general system is, of course, another question.
6 *My Philosophical Development*, p. 40.
7 *Ibid.*
8 For some brief comments on Russell's view of Leibniz see Vol. IV of this *History*, pp. 276-8.
9 *The Principles of Mathematics*, p. 115 (2nd edition, 1937). Two classes are said to be 'similar' when they 'have the same number' (*ibid.*, p. 113).
10 *Ibid.*, p. 523.
11 *Ibid.*, p. 524.

12 *The Principles of Mathematics*, p. x (Introduction to 2nd edition).
13 *Principia Mathematica*, I, p. 72.
14 *The Philosophy of Bertrand Russell*, edited by P. A. Schilpp, p. 692. As Russell notes in the introduction to the second edition of *The Principles of Mathematics*, he had been convinced by F. P. Ramsey's *The Foundations of Mathematics* (1931), that there are two classes of paradoxes. Some are purely logical or mathematical and can be cleared up by the simple (original) theory of types. Others are linguistic or semantic, such as the paradox arising out of the statement 'I am lying'. These can be cleared up by linguistic considerations.
15 *Ibid.*
16 It seems to the present writer that in the *Tractatus* Wittgenstein so defines the essence of the proposition that it follows logically that any proposition *about* propositions is a pseudo-proposition, devoid of 'sense' (*Sinn*). In this case to avoid the conclusion one has to reject the definition.
17 That is, there can no more be a totality of languages than there can be a class of all classes. The latter notion was for Russell self-contradictory. A class of *all* classes would be additional to *all* classes. It would also be a member of itself which is ruled out by the theory of types.
18 *Principia Mathematica*, I, p. 71.
19 *Ibid.*
20 The theory found a preliminary expression in Russell's

article *On Denoting* in *Mind* for 1905.

21 'An indefinite description is a phrase of the form "a so-and-so" and a definite description is a phrase of the form "the so-and-so" (in the singular)', *Introduction to Mathematical Philosophy*, p. 167.

22 *My Philosophical Development*, p. 84.

23 *Introduction to Mathematical Philosophy*, p. 177.

24 *The Philosophy of Bertrand Russell*, edited by P. A. Schilpp, ch. 5.

25 Some analytic philosophers might wish to say that Russell was trying to 'reform' language, to create an ideal language. But he did not intend, of course, to prohibit people from saying what they are accustomed to say.

26 This is understood nowadays. But in the past statements have sometimes been made which said or implied that Russell was the discoverer of this distinction between grammatical and logical form.

27 Russell has expressed his disappointment that comparatively little attention was paid to the mathematical techniques developed in the course of the work.

28 Author of *The Mathematical Analysis of Logic* (1847), and *An Investigation of the Laws of Thought* (1854).

29 Author of *Pure Logic* (1864) and other logical studies. Whereas Boole was a professor of mathematics, Jevons occupied a chair of political economy and did not possess Boole's 'mathematizing' turn of mind, though he invented a calculating machine to carry out the processes of inference.

30 Author of *The Logic of Chance* (1866), *Symbolic Logic* (1881), and *The Principles of Empirical or Inductive Logic* (1889).

31 *Appendix A* in *The Principles of Mathematics* is devoted to 'the logical and arithmetical doctrines of Frege'.

32 It was rejected both by the 'Formalists', such as David Hilbert (1862–1943) and by the 'Intuitionists' who followed Luitzen Brouwer (b. 1881).

33 It is a notorious fact that since the publication of *Principia Mathematica* comparatively little attention has been paid in England to symbolic logic. This is not to say that no good work has subsequently been done in England on logical theory. But, generally speaking, the attention of philosophers has been concentrated rather on 'ordinary language'. It is Polish and American logicians who have been most prominent in the field of symbolic logic.

34 From *The Study of Mathematics*, written in 1902 and first published in the *New Quarterly* in 1907. See *Philosophical Essays*, p. 82, and *Mysticism and Logic*, p. 69.

35 *My Philosophical Development*, p. 208.

36 See *My Philosophical Development*, p. 103 and *The Principles of Mathematics*, p. xi (in the Introduction to the second edition).

37 *Mysticism and Logic*, p. 155.

38 It will be noted that Russell and Moore are at one on this matter.

[39] *Mysticism and Logic*, p. 157.

[40] *Our Knowledge of the External World*, pp. 88–9.

[41] *Mysticism and Logic*, p. 128.

[42] *Ibid.*, p. 143.

[43] *My Philosophical Development*, p. 134.

[44] *Logic and Knowledge*, p. 127.

[45] *Mysticism and Logic*, pp. 131–2.

[46] So far as the present writer is aware, Russell has never given a systematic account of the methods of analysis practised by himself, comparing them with one another and noting both their common and their differentiating features. On this subject the reader can profitably consult *The Unity of Russell's Philosophy* by Morris Weitz in *The Philosophy of Bertrand Russell*, edited by P. A. Schilpp.

[47] *The Problems of Philosophy*, p. 156.

[48] P. 128.

[49] The lectures on logical atomism which Russell delivered in 1918 and which were published in *The Monist*, 1918–19, have been reprinted in *Logic and Knowledge*, edited by R. Marsh (London, 1956).

[50] This was the result of a second prosecution, arising, like the first, out of Russell's outspoken opposition to the First World War.

[51] Wittgenstein, then still an Austrian citizen, joined the Austrian army and was subsequently a prisoner-of-war of the Italians.

[52] *Logic and Knowledge*, p. 179.

[53] Russell notes that it was Wittgenstein who first drew his attention to the truth that propositions are not names for facts. For to every proposition there 'correspond' at least two propositions, one true, the other false. The false proposition 'corresponds with' the fact in the sense that it is its relation to the fact which makes it false.

[54] *Logic and Knowledge*, p. 197.

[55] When the truth or falsity of a molecular proposition depends simply on the truth or falsity of its constituent propositions it is said to be a truth-function of these constituents.

[56] *Logic and Knowledge*, p. 202.

[57] *Ibid.*, p. 232.

[58] Later on Russell came to doubt this theory and to believe that, even if it is true in some sense, Wittgenstein exaggerated its importance.

[59] Needless to say, neither Wittgenstein nor Russell questioned the fact that logic and mathematics can be applied.

[60] Russell discusses the impact of Wittgenstein on his thought in ch. X of *My Philosophical Development*.

[61] In the opinion of the present writer the theory of the world which is found at the beginning of the *Tractatus* has nothing to do with inductive metaphysics. For Wittgenstein, the world exists for us only in so far as it is describable, in so far as we can speak meaningfully about states of affairs in the world. And the theory of atomic facts and simple objects is really an answer to the question, what

must the world (any world) be like as a necessary condition for meaningful descriptive language? The approach, in other words, is *a priori*. The theory of the world is not an induction from observation of simple objects and atomic facts.

62 *Logic and Knowledge*, p. 277.

63 Cf. *My Philosophical Development*, pp. 165–6.

64 This was followed by *The Analysis of Matter* in 1927, the same year in which *An Outline of Philosophy* appeared. Needless to say, the intervening period between 1921 and 1927 was punctuated not only by articles but also by books, such as *The Prospects of Industrial Civilization* (1923), *The ABC of Atoms* (1923), *The ABC of Relativity* (1925), and *On Education* (1926).

65 As Russell notes, this was much the same view as that held by Ernst Mach. See Vol. VII, Pt. II, of this *History*, p. 132.

66 *Logic and Knowledge*, p. 279.

67 It should hardly be necessary to point out that neutral monism is not the opposite of pluralism. It is 'monistic' in the sense that it admits no ultimate specific difference between the natures of mental and physical particulars or events. In themselves these particulars are neither specifically mental nor specifically physical or material. Hence the term 'neutral'.

68 *The Analysis of Mind*, p. 307.

69 For some brief remarks about Brentano see Vol. VII, Pt. II, of this *History*, pp. 205–6.

70 *The Analysis of Mind*, pp. 17–18.

71 *Ibid.*, p. 25.

72 *Ibid.*, p. 143.

73 *Ibid.*

74 *Ibid.*, p. 105.

75 *Ibid.*, p. 25.

76 *Ibid.*, p. 156.

77 *Ibid.*, p. 139.

78 *Ibid.*, p. 308.

79 In *An Outline of Philosophy* an event is said to be 'something occupying a small finite amount of space-time' (p. 287), and each minimal event is said to be a 'logically self-subsistent entity' (p. 293).

80 *Contemporary British Philosophy*, First Series, p. 382.

81 P. 300.

82 On unperceived events see *The Analysis of Matter*, pp. 215–16.

83 *My Philosophical Development*, p. 135.

84 In this work 'acquaintance' is replaced by 'noticing'. Cf. pp. 49f.

85 Cf. *The Analysis of Matter*, p. 197, and *The Scientific Outlook* (1931), pp. 74–5.

86 *My Philosophical Development*, p. 104.

87 *The Scientific Outlook*, p. 98.

88 *My Philosophical Development*, p. 195.

89 *Ibid.*

90 *Human Knowledge, Its Scope and Limits* (1948), p. 197.

91 Obviously, the problem of solipsism presupposes the epistemological theses which give rise to it. And one's natural comment is that these theses might well be re-examined. But this is not the path which Russell chooses.

CHAPTER TWENTY

[1] Cf. *My Philosophical Development*, p. 128.

[2] It will be referred to simply as *Human Knowledge*.

[3] *Human Knowledge*, p. 11.

[4] Russell calls them 'postulates'. The reason for this will be discussed presently.

[5] *Human Knowledge*, p. 10.

[6] Russell thus presupposes that what is generally regarded as scientific knowledge really is knowledge. If we start with undiluted scepticism, we shall get nowhere. After all, the problem of justifying scientific inference only arises because we are convinced that there is such a thing but at the same time see no adequate basis for it in pure empiricism.

[7] For Russell's actual formulation of the five principles the reader is referred to *Human Knowledge*, pp. 506 ff.

[8] Obviously, the ordinary man would comment: 'I don't need any postulate to know this'. But it must be remembered that for Russell it is *logically* possible that the similarity of experiences should be causally independent, and that in pure empiricism there is nothing which makes it objectively more probable that the similar experiences have a common causal origin than that they do not.

[9] Cf. *My Philosophical Development*, pp. 200 f.

[10] *Human Knowledge*, p. 526.

[11] The postulates are *a priori* in the sense of being logically antecedent to the inferences made in accordance with them; but they exist first of all in the form of an empirical propensity and are recognized as postulates only through an examination of examples of non-demonstrative inferences. They are not absolutely *a priori* eternal truths.

[12] *Human Knowledge*, p. 527.

[13] *My Philosophical Development*, p. 204.

[14] *Human Knowledge*, p. 526.

[15] Cf. *My Philosophical Development*, p. 204.

[16] Some discussion of language can also be found in *The Analysis of Mind* and *The Outline of Philosophy*.

[17] *Human Knowledge*, p. 71.

[18] Russell refuses to commit himself to the general statement that there can be no thought without language. But in his opinion complicated, elaborate thought at any rate requires language.

[19] Russell's well-known reference to the type of linguistic analysis which 'is, at best, a slight help to lexicographers, and, at worst, an idle tea-table amusement' (*My Philosophical Development*, p. 217), is obviously polemical and constitutes an exaggeration if considered as a description of 'Oxford philosophy' as a whole; but at the same time it illustrates, by way of contrast, the direction of his own interest, namely in language as an instrument in understanding the world.

[20] *An Inquiry into Meaning and Truth*, p. 77. This work will be referred to henceforth as *Inquiry*.

[21] Reference has already been made to the special case of Witt-

genstein's contention in the *Tractatus*.

22 This follows in any case from Russell's view of object-words as meaningful in isolation. 'Hard' by itself, for example, is neither true nor false.

23 *Inquiry*, p. 30.

24 *Human Knowledge*, p. 127.

25 *Inquiry*, p. 193.

26 *Ibid.*, p. 29.

27 *Human Knowledge*, p. 85.

28 *Ibid.*, p. 86.

29 *Inquiry*, p. 171.

30 Russell uses the term 'belief' in such a wide sense that even animals can be said to have beliefs. Cf. *Inquiry*, p. 171 and *Human Knowledge*, p. 329. But we are here concerned with language, and so with human beings.

31 'Ineffable knowledge' is not identical with knowledge of what goes beyond our experience.

32 *Human Knowledge*, p. 465.

33 *Inquiry*, p. 308.

34 Cf. *Inquiry*, pp. 175 and 309.

35 *Human Knowledge*, p. 129.

36 Cf. *Philosophical Essays*, p. 156.

37 *Inquiry*, p. 305.

38 *My Philosophical Development*, p. 189. Cf. *Human Knowledge*, pp. 164–5.

39 *Human Knowledge*, p. 169. Some further specification of these 'general circumstances' seems to be required.

40 *Ibid.*, p. 128.

41 It is not necessary that the facts should be extra-linguistic. For we can, of course, make statements about *words*, which are made true or false by their relation to linguistic facts. Obviously, this would not apply, for example, to stipulative definitions. But these would in any case be excluded by Russell's custom of predicating truth or falsity of *beliefs*. For a mere declaration that one intends to use a given word in a certain sense cannot be described as a belief.

42 *Human Knowledge*, p. 170.

43 P. 42.

44 P. 275.

45 P. 341.

46 P. 347.

47 P. 173.

48 According to Russell, if Aristotle had thought and written in Chinese instead of in Greek, he would have evolved a somewhat different philosophy.

49 *Inquiry*, p. 347.

CHAPTER TWENTY-ONE

1 I do not mean to imply, of course, that this high honour was not a tribute to Russell's eminence as a philosopher.

2 The short period was passed in the prison infirmary, it is only fair to add, not in the usual conditions of prison life.

3 We may remark in passing that in 1940 Russell's appointment to the College of the City of New York was cancelled because of his views on marriage and sexual conduct. True, he was given a chair at the Barnes Foundation, Philadelphia, but this appointment lasted only until 1943. The New York episode led to a good deal of acrid controversy, on which the present writer does not feel called upon to pass any comment.

4 *Philosophical Essays*, p. 10.

5 *Ibid.*, p. 11.

6 *Ibid.*, p. 53.

7 *Ibid.*, p. 30.

8 *Principles of Social Reconstruction*, p. 5.

9 *Ibid.*, p. 12.

10 P. 76.

11 *Principles of Social Reconstruction*, p. 24.

12 *Ibid.*, p. 205.

13 In *The Philosophy of Bertrand Russell*, edited by P. A. Schilpp, p. 524.

14 *Principles of Social Reconstruction*, p. 245.

15 P. 37.

16 P. 40.

17 *An Outline of Philosophy*, p. 238.

18 *Ibid.*, p. 242.

19 It would not be certain or demonstrative knowledge. But neither is scientific knowledge certain knowledge.

20 *Religion and Science* (1935), p. 238.

21 The statement 'I think that cruelty is good' or 'I approve of cruelty' would be an ordinary empirical statement, relating to a psychological fact. 'Cruelty is good', however, is a value-judgment.

22 In his *Replies to Criticism* Russell says: 'I do not think that an ethical judgment *merely* expresses a desire; I agree with Kant that it must have an element of universality'. *The Philosophy of Bertrand Russell*, edited by P. A. Schilpp, p. 722.

23 Cf. *The Philosophy of Bertrand Russell*, edited by P. A. Schilpp, p. 724.

24 I am thinking, for example, of Mr. R. M. Hare of Oxford.

25 *Mysticism and Logic*, p. 49 (also *Philosophical Essays*, p. 62).

26 Cf. *Power: A New Social Analysis* (1938), p. 10. This work will be referred to simply as *Power*.

27 *Power*, p. 35.

28 *Ibid.*, p. 274.

29 *The Scientific Outlook* (1931), p. 275.

30 *Power*, p. 283.

31 Russell can be called a socialist, but he has emphasized the dangers of socialism when divorced from effective democracy.

32 If in recent years Russell has paid more attention to campaigning for nuclear disarmament than for a world-government, this is doubtless because the prospect of achieving effective world-government by agreement seems to be somewhat remote, whereas a suicidal world-war could break out at any time.

33 *Authority and the Individual* (1949), p. 105. In this work Russell discusses the problem of combining social cohesion with individual liberty in the light of concrete possibilities.

34 *The Scientific Outlook*, p. 101.

35 *Ibid.*, p. 122.

36 *The Philosophy of Bertrand Russell*, edited by P. A. Schilpp, p. 726.

37 Russell is, of course, as free as anybody else to change his mind. But, this fact apart, we have to remember, in regard to utterances which, abstractly considered, are scarcely compatible, that in a given context and for polemical reasons he sometimes exaggerates one particular aspect of a subject.

38 Cf. *My Philosophical Development*, p. 230.

39 *Our Knowledge of the External World*, p. 214.

40 Cf. *Ibid.*, p. 42.

41 *Human Knowledge*, p. 5.

42 *An Outline of Philosophy*, p. 2.

43 Cf. for example, *My Philosophical Development*, p. 230, where Russell is criticizing linguistic philosophy, which he regards as trying to effect a divorce of philosophy from science.

44 *Contemporary British Philosophy*, First Series, p. 379, and *Logic and Knowledge*, p. 341.

45 *An Outline of Philosophy*, p. 1.

46 *Logic and Knowledge*, p. 281.

47 *Unpopular Essays* (1950), p. 39.

48 *History of Western Philosophy* (1945), p. 10.

49 *Ibid.*

50 *Unpopular Essays*, p. 41.

51 *An Outline of Philosophy*, p. 312.

52 *Ibid.*

53 *Unpopular Essays*, p. 41.

54 *Ibid.*, p. 77.

55 *History of Western Philosophy*, p. 863.

56 'In itself philosophy sets out neither to solve our troubles nor to save our souls', *Wisdom of the West* (1959), p. 6.

57 *Religion and Science*, p. 243.

58 *Unpopular Essays*, p. 41.

59 Cf. *My Philosophical Development*, p. 11.

60 The individuals who ordered the invasion, who planned it, who contributed in any way by fighting, making munitions, acting as doctors, and so on.

61 *An Outline of Philosophy*, p. 1.

62 It is worth noting that inquiry also presupposes a value-judgment, about the value of truth as a goal for the human mind.

63 *The Scientific Outlook*, p. 101.

64 Russell published a book of short stories, *Satan in the Suburbs*, in 1953 and *Nightmares of Eminent Persons* in 1954.

65 *The Philosophy of Bertrand Russell*, edited by P. A. Schilpp, p. 19.

EPILOGUE

1 *Wisdom of the West*, p. 311.

2 The original version of this work appeared in 1921 in Ostwald's *Annalen der Philosophie*. The work was published for the first time as a book, with facing German and English texts, in 1922 (reprint with a few corrections, 1923). An edition with a new translation by D. F. Pears and B. P. McGuiness was published in 1961.

3 A complex proposition is for Wittgenstein a truth-function of elementary propositions. For example, proposition X, let us suppose, is true if propositions *a*, *b* and *c* are true. In such a case it is not necessary to verify X directly in order to know whether it is true or false. But at some point there must be verification, a confrontation of a proposition or of propositions with empirical facts.

4 *Tractatus*, 4.11. Empirical psychology is included among the natural sciences.

5 If one were to say to Wittgenstein that 'the continuum has no actual parts' is a philosophical proposition, he would doubtless reply that it is in fact a tautology or a definition, giving the meaning, or part of it, of the word 'continuum'. If, however, it were understood as asserting that there are in the world actual examples of a continuum, it would be an ordinary empirical statement.

6 The *Tractatus* is, of course, a philosophical work and contains 'philosophical propositions'. But with admirable consistency Wittgenstein does not hesitate to embrace the paradoxical conclusion that the propositions which enable one to understand his theory are themselves nonsensical (*unsinning*, 6.54).

7 *Tractatus*, 4.112.

8 For example, the logical positivists of the Vienna Circle envisaged the philosopher as concerned with the language of science and as trying to construct a common language which would serve to unify the particular sciences, such as physics and psychology.

9 Cf. 4.002–4.0031, 5.473, 5.4733 and 6.53.

10 Such talk is obviously excluded if every proposition is a picture or representation of a possible state of affairs *in* the world. True, Wittgenstein himself speaks about the world as a whole. But he is perfectly ready to admit that to do so is to attempt to say what cannot be said.

11 The Vienna Circle was not a group of 'disciples' of Schlick but rather a group of like-minded persons, some of them philosophers, others scientists or mathematicians, who agreed on a common general programme.

12 These two points, if taken alone, do not constitute logical positivism. Taken alone, they would admit, for example, the possibility of an inductive metaphysics which proposed its theories as provisional hypotheses.

13 A statement is said to possess emotive-evocative significance if it expresses an emotive attitude and is designed, not so much by conscious intention as by its nature, to evoke a similar emotive attitude in others.

14 Cf. *Tractatus*, 5.62–5.641. Cf. also *Notebooks, 1914–1916* (Oxford, 1961), pp. 79–80, where a certain influence by Schopenhauer is evident.

15 Second edition, 1946.

16 We can note in passing that Professor R. B. Braithwaite of Cambridge has made a much-discussed attempt to reconcile his logical positivism with his adherence to Christianity. See, for example, his lecture, *An Empiricist's View of the Nature of Religious Belief*, Cambridge, 1955.

17 These include *The Foundations of Empirical Knowledge* (1940), *Thinking and Meaning* (1947), *Philosophical Essays* (1954), *The Concept of a Person and Other Essays* (1963).

18 This is not always recognized by continental philosophers, some of whom still seem to be under the impression that practically all British philosophers are logical positivists.

19 These are represented by posthumously published writ-

ings. *The Blue and Brown Books* (Oxford, 1958), contains notes dictated to pupils in the period 1933–5. *Philosophical Investigations* (Oxford, 1953) represents Wittgenstein's later ideas.

20 I, s. 124.

21 I, s. 119.

22 Cf. *Philosophical Investigations*, 1, ss. 66–9, 75.

23 Cf. *Philosophical Investigations*, 1, s. 23.

24 *Ibid.*, 1, s. 116.

25 Originally published in the *Proceedings of the Aristotelian Society*, this paper was reprinted in *Logic and Language*, Vol. I (Oxford, 1951), edited by A. G. N. Flew.

26 Cf., for example, *The Language of Morals* (Oxford, 1952) and *Freedom and Reason* (Oxford, 1963), by R. M. Hare.

27 *Philosophical Investigations*, 1, s. 116.

28 See, for instance, the discussion on 'Theology and Falsification' which was reprinted in *New Essays in Philosophical Theology*, edited by A. G. N. Flew and A. MacIntyre (London, 1955).

29 Berkeley has something to say on the matter. Kant refers to symbolic language in a theological context. And Hegel, of course, discusses the 'pictorial' language of religion in its relation to aesthetics on the one hand and philosophy on the other.

30 See, for example, Austin's posthumously published *Philosophical Papers* (Oxford, 1961) and *How to do Things with Words* (Oxford, 1962).

31 In *Sense and Sensibilia* (Oxford, 1962), a posthumous

work representing courses of lectures, Austin tries to dispose of a particular philosophical theory, namely the sense-datum theory.

32 Whether Professor Ryle's attempt is successful or unsuccessful and how far it embodies the author's own theories, are not questions which need detain us here.

33 See, for instance, Professor A. J. Ayer's inaugural lecture at Oxford, which forms the first chapter in his book, *The Concept of a Person.*

34 London, 1959.

35 London, 1959.

36 That is to say, this is the essential factual content of the description. A judgment of value may also, of course, be included or implied.

37 *The Nature of Metaphysics* (edited by D. F. Pears, London, 1957) represents a series of broadcast talks by different philosophers, including Professor Ryle. The general attitude to metaphysics is critical but comparatively sympathetic. A considerably more extensive examination of metaphysics is undertaken by Professor W. H. Walsh of Edinburgh University in *Metaphysics* (London, 1963).

38 *Philosophical Investigations*, 1, s. 109. The fact that some writers have appealed to psycho-analysis as perhaps capable of explaining the recurrence of a particular type of metaphysics, such as monism, shows at any rate that they consider metaphysics to have roots which go deeper than linguistic or logical confusion.

39 This is explicitly stated in the *Tractatus*, 4.111.

APPENDIX

1 Newman does not, of course, exclude the role of grace. But he prescinds from it when he is trying to show that a sufficient ground for belief in God is available to all.

2 It is as well to remember that the constructors of original metaphysical systems have often employed argument to commend views of reality already present to their minds, at least in outline. Yet this fact does not by itself show that a given argument is devoid of force. Analogously, the fact that Newman writes as a Christian believer does not necessarily entail the conclusion that his philosophical reflections are valueless.

3 An Essay in Aid of a Grammar of Assent (3rd edition, 1870), p. 155. This work will be referred to as GA.

4 Ibid.

5 For Bishop Joseph Butler (1692–1752), see Vol. V, Pt. I, of this History, pp. 176–81 and 195–202.

6 Oxford University Sermons (Fifteen sermons preached before the University of Oxford) (3rd edition, 1872), p. 207. This work will be referred to as OUS. Newman obviously means that faith presupposes an exercise of reason.

7 Ibid.

8 We can see here a reflection of the empiricist point of view.

9 OUS, p. 207.

10 Ibid., p. 229.

11 Ibid., p. 230.

12 Ibid., p. 188.

13 Ibid., p. 189.

14 Ibid., p. 230.

15 Ibid., p. 231.

16 Ibid., pp. 212–13.

17 The present writer has no intention of committing himself to the view that we cannot properly be said to know that there is an external world. Of course, if we so define knowledge that only the propositions of logic and mathematics can be said to be known to be true, it follows that we do not know that things exist when we are not perceiving them. But as the word 'know' is used in ordinary language, we can perfectly well be said to know it.

18 It would be misleading to describe The Grammar of Assent as a philosophical work, for in the long run it is concerned with 'the arguments adducible for Christianity' (GA, p. 484). But these arguments are placed in a general logical and epistemological context.

19 GA, pp. 20–1.

20 Ibid., p. 35.

21 So-called doubtful assent is for Newman unconditional assent to the statement that the truth of a given proposition is doubtful.

22 GA, p. 17.

23 Cf. ibid., p. 87.

24 Ibid., p. 99.

25 As for formal demonstrative inference, this, Newman insists, is conditional. That is to say, the truth of the conclusion is asserted on the condition of the premisses being true. And though Newman himself does not deny that there are self-evident principles, he points out that what seems self-evident to one man does not necessarily seem self-evident to another. In any case the possibility of valid reasoning is assumed. If we try

to prove everything and to make no assumptions whatsoever, we shall never get anywhere.

26 GA, p. 102.
27 Ibid., p. 18.
28 Ibid., p. 104.
29 OUS, p. 19.
30 Ibid.
31 GA, pp. 104–5. By Taste Newman means the aesthetic sense, considered as the sense of the beautiful, while by Moral Sense he means in this context a sense of the fittingness or deformity of actions, involving moral approval or disapproval.
32 Ibid., p. 106.
33 Ibid., p. 107.
34 Ibid., p. 109.
35 Ibid.
36 From the 'Proof of Theism', a paper published for the first time in Dr. A. J. Boekraad's *The Argument from Conscience to the Existence of God according to J. H. Newman* (Louvain, 1961), p. 121.
37 GA, p. 101.
38 OUS, p. 18.
39 *Sermons Preached on Various Occasions* (2nd edition, 1858), p. 86.
40 GA, p. 106.
41 Ibid., pp. 60–1.

42 Ibid., p. 61.
43 *Sermons Preached on Various Occasions*, p. 98.
44 GA, p. 61.
45 It should be noted that Newman did not hold that the moral law depends on the arbitrary *fiat* of God. He maintained that in recognizing our obligation to obey the moral law we implicitly recognize God as Father and Judge.
46 GA, p. 420.
47 Ibid., p. 281.
48 Ibid., p. 407.
49 Ibid., p. 352. The illative sense is 'the power of judging about truth and error in concrete matters' (ibid., p. 346).
50 Ibid., p. 337.
51 Ibid.
52 Ibid., p. 338.
53 Ibid.
54 For Kierkegaard see ch. 17 of Vol. VII, Pt. II, of this *History*.

APPENDIX

1 No bibliography has been supplied for Wittgenstein, as his philosophical ideas have been mentioned only in general discussion or incidentally.

INDEX

(The principal references are in heavy type. Asterisked numbers refer to bibliographical information.)

experience (*cont'd*)
  racial E., I: 147, 167
  sense-experience, I: 177, 181,
    225; II: 13, 101, 151–2, 258,
    260
  sentient E., I: 229, 236–7, 244
  stream of, II: 100
  structure of, II: 50
  synthesis of, II: 56
experimentalism, II: 109–38
explanation:
  ultimate E., I: 139
  of universe as a whole, I: 162–3
external world, existence of, I:
    102–6, 114–15; II: 179, 276–7
externality, feeling of, I: 114

facts:
  atomic F., II: 206–7, 208
  existence-facts, II: 207
  general F., II: 207
  molecular F., II: 206
  negative F., II: 207
faith:
  animal F., II: 151
  initial act of F., I: 216, 228, 230,
    242, 246–7
  reasonableness of Christian F.,
    II: 270–80
  religious F., I: 177, 206; II: 56,
    270–88 *passim*
fallibilism, principle of, II: 63–4
falsehood, *see* truth and falsity
falsification, I: 89, 96; II: 62
family, the, I: 200, 220, 313 n. 24
Faraday, Michael (1791–1867),
    I: 128
Farquharson, A. S. L., II: 140
fatalism, I: 101
Fathers of the Church, II: 273
Fawcett, Henry (1833–84), I: 58
Fechner, Gustav Feodor (1801–
    87), II: 102
feeling: I: 37, 43, 106–7, 114–15,
    140, 307 n. 4
  immediate F., I: 229, 236
  impersonal F., II: 235
  social F., I: 51
Ferrier, James Frederick (1808–
    64), I: **183–6**, 196–7, 208, 268
Fichte, Johann Gottlieb (1762–
    1814), I: 178–9, 182, 311 n.
    5; II: 36
fiction-theory of Nietzsche, II: 102,
    219

fideism, I: 215–16
firstness, secondness and thirdness,
    II: 67–8, 76–9, 83–4
Flew, A. G. N., II: 331 n. 25
Flewelling, Ralph Tyler (b. 1871),
    II: 52
force: I: 127–9, 148–9, 163–4,
    257–8
  intrinsic and extrinsic, I: 152
  persistence of, I: 148–9
forces of Nature, II: 117
form:
  grammatical F., II: 196, 257
  logical F., II: 193, 196, 257
Franklin, Benjamin (1706–90),
    II: 13–14
freedom:
  moral F., II: 36
  of the individual, I: 31, 173, 176,
    203–4; II: 53, 186, 328 n. 33;
    J. S. Mill, I: 44, **53–62**; Spen-
    cer, I: 153–8
  of the will, II: 12, 34, 46, 87,
    316 n. 60; J. S. Mill, I: 62–7;
    Green, I: 199–200
  true F., I: 256–7, 260
Frege, Gottlob (1848–1925), II:
    189, 197
French thought, II: 102
function:
  denoting F., II: 193
  propositional F., II: 190, 193,
    207
  syntactical F., II: 190
Fuss, Peter, II: 310 n. 54

Galileo (1564–1642), I: 81
Galton, Sir Francis (1822–1911),
    I: 309 n. 70
games, analogy of, I: 260–1
generalization, I: 69–71, 86–90,
    100, 134, 146, 151, 177, 226–8;
    II: 48, 160, 216
geogeny, I: 151
geometry, I: 76–9; II: 188, 197,
    278
George III, King of England, I: 23
German thought, I: 20, 173–4, 178,
    181, 262–3, 312 n. 33; II: 52,
    273
ghost in the machine, II: 265
Gifford lectures, I: 282; II: 25
God: I: 45, 63, 72, 108–12, 128,
    129, 132–3, 136, 139, 164, 172,
    182, 186, 195–7, 204–5, 207–8,